AMBIGUITY RESOLUTION IN LANGUAGE LEARNING

CSLI Lecture Notes
Number 71

AMBIGUITY RESOLUTION IN LANGUAGE LEARNING

Computational and Cognitive Models

HINRICH SCHÜTZE

CSLI Publications

CENTER FOR THE STUDY OF
LANGUAGE AND INFORMATION
STANFORD, CALIFORNIA

Copyright © 1997
CSLI Publications
Center for the Study of Language and Information
Leland Stanford Junior University
Printed in the United States
00 99 98 97 5 4 3 2 1

Library of Congress Cataloging-in-Publication Data

Schütze, Hinrich.
Ambiguity resolution in language learning : computational and cognitive
models / Hinrich Schütze.
p. cm. — (CSLI lecture notes ; no. 71)
Includes bibliographical references and index.
ISBN 1-57586-075-9 (hbk. : alk. paper).
ISBN 1-57586-074-0 (pbk. : alk. paper).
1. Second language acquisition. 2. Computational linguistics.
3. Psycholinguistics. 4. Ambiguity. 5. Categorization (Linguistics) I. Title.
II. Series.
P118.2.S38 1997
418–dc21 96-29640
CIP

CSLI was founded early in 1983 by researchers from Stanford University, SRI International, and
Xerox PARC to further research and development of integrated theories of language,
information, and computation. CSLI headquarters and CSLI Publications are located on the
campus of Stanford University.

CSLI Publications reports new developments in the study of language, information, and computation. In addition to lecture notes, our publications include monographs, working papers, revised dissertations, and conference proceedings. Our aim is to make new results, ideas, and
approaches available as quickly as possible. Please visit our website at
http://csli-www.stanford.edu/publications/
for comments on this and other titles, as well as for changes and corrections by the author and
publisher.

∞ The acid-free paper used in this book meets the minimum requirements of the American
National Standard for Information Sciences—Permanence of Paper for Printed Library Materials,
ANSI Z39.48-1984.

To my parents, Barbara and Carl Schütze

Contents

List of Figures

List of Tables

Acknowledgements

This book is a revised version of my 1995 Stanford Ph.D. thesis (Schütze, 1995). Numerous people in the linguistics department and at CSLI helped me to acquire the skills and knowledge for doing the research presented here. In particular, I would like to thank Joan Bresnan, Eve Clark, Stanley Peters, John Rickford, Ivan Sag, Peter Sells, Elizabeth Traugott, and Arnold Zwicky.

Martin Kay and Tom Wasow, my co-advisors, Peter Cheeseman, Vaughan Pratt, and David Rumelhart were a wonderful dissertation committee, critical, yet supportive. I am especially grateful to David Rumelhart whose classes introduced me to the "empiricist" way of thinking about language.

Eugene Charniak, Marti Hearst, Michael Inman, Lauri Karttunen, Geoff Nunberg, John Tukey, and Annie Zaenen have also made very helpful comments on presentations and previous drafts at various stages of the research that is described here.

For technical help, I'm grateful to Emma Pease for LaTeX support, Mike Berry for SVDPACK, to the natural language group at the University of Pennsylvania for the Penn Treebank, and to David Stewart and Zbigniew Leyk of ANU for the meschach library.

Gary Cottrell, Chris Manning, and Tom Wasow have had a great influence on the shape of the book. I thank them for their extensive comments and the time they have spent reading previous drafts. In some cases, I have not followed their suggestions, so as always the final product is solely my responsibility.

The revision of the dissertation and part of the computational experiments reported here were done at the Xerox Palo Alto Research Center. I am grateful to PARC and in particular to Jan Pedersen and Kris Halvorsen for their support of my research activities.

1

Introduction

Speaking and writing are among the most creative human activities. Every day we combine words into sentences that we have not said before. Often we utter sentences that have never been said before. How do we do this? How do we generalize from the linguistic behavior we have observed to our own linguistic activity? What is the mechanism that makes this kind of linguistic productivity possible?

These questions have been the central concerns of modern linguistic theory. Traditionally, the answers have been framed by invoking linguistic laws based on operations like substitution, deletion, and quantification that manipulate symbolic representations. For example, the grammatical rule "S → NP VP" states that a sentence (S) consists of a noun phrase (NP) followed by a verb phrase (VP). Alternatives to this approach have always been available in the form of appeals to analogy, but until recently these have been couched in non-formal terms. Only recently have formal non-rule-based approaches such as connectionism and statistical language modeling become more widespread. These alternative approaches incorporate some form of arithmetic operations such as addition, exponentiation, or numerical comparison. Optimality theory (Prince and Smolensky, 1997) can be regarded as part of this movement although its (arguably) non-symbolic mechanism for constraint interaction operates on strictly symbolic representations.

Most linguists presume that the case against non-symbolic approaches to language was made definitively by Chomsky. His argument was that computing the probability of sentences from a corpus of utterances would assign the same low probability to all unattested sentences, grammatical and ungrammatical ones alike, and hence not account for linguistic productivity (Chomsky 1957:16). Yet this argument will seem curious to anyone with some basic knowledge of statistics. For example, after having estimated the mean and the standard deviation of the heights of men from a sample of 30 subjects as being, say, 6 foot 3 inches and 1 foot 6 inches (assuming a normal distribution for heights), nobody would argue that the same equally remote probabilities are assigned to the height 7 feet and the height 200 feet even if both are unattested in the sample of 30. Clearly, given the sample and the model, a man from this population is much more likely to be 7 feet tall than 200 feet tall.

This book presents several quantitative and statistical models that suggest that the familiar objections are groundless. I hope that these concrete examples of a non-symbolic approach to linguistic problems will help extend the range of acceptable formal tools in language research and contribute to defeating the implicit assumption that statistical models are inadequate for representing linguistic generalizations.

No less important, I hope to show that this approach will in fact provide valuable insights into some familiar problems that have dogged the standard symbolic approaches. In the case of gradient linguistic phenomena, non-symbolic approaches have clear advantages both for representation and linguistic explanation. For the question of linguistic innateness, I will show that non-symbolic models need not make questionable assumptions about the innateness of linguistic concepts. Finally, the learning mechanisms that have been proposed in symbolic theories do not deal with ambiguous forms — a serious problem since most frequent forms are ambiguous. In contrast, the non-symbolic learning procedures proposed here can handle ambiguous input. The common thread through all these problems is that the underlying mechanism of linguistic generalization, symbolic or non-symbolic, will be a crucial part of any theory that accounts for them.

The particular linguistic examples discussed in this book will be drawn from three areas: part-of-speech ambiguity, word-sense ambiguity, and subcategorization ambiguity. In order to introduce the relevant data, we first need to define the notion of ambiguity. The following definition of ambiguity will be adopted here: A surface form is *ambiguous* with respect to a linguistic process p if it has several process-specific representations and the outcome of p depends on which of these representations is selected. The selection of a process-specific representation in context is called *disambiguation* or *ambiguity resolution*.

An example of this definition for the case of part of speech is the form "flies" (1).

(1)   Time flies like an arrow.

(2)   a. syntactic-category("flies") = verb
        b. syntactic-category("flies") = noun

(3)   a. [[Time] [flies [like an arrow]]]

    b. [[Time flies] [like [an arrow]]]

There are two possible syntactic representations of "flies" as shown in (2): verb and noun. The outcome of the process of parsing depends on which representation is selected. In processing (1), a parser will find structure (3a) for the verb case and structure (3b) for the noun case.

An example for ambiguity in semantic categorization is the form "suit" in (4).

(4)   The suit is in Los Angeles.

(5)   a. semantic-category("suit") = legal
       b. semantic-category("suit") = sartorial

(6)   a. The legal proceedings are in Los Angeles.
       b. The article of clothing is in Los Angeles.

It has two semantic representations as shown in (5): "lawsuit" and "set of garments" (among others). The outcome of the linguistic process of comprehension depends on which one is selected. Someone hearing (4) will interpret (4) as meaning (6a) if the first representation is selected and as meaning (6b) if the second representation is selected.

In subcategorization acquisition, uncertainty about process-specific representations only occurs during acquisition. For example, verbs specified for manner of speaking do not allow the dative construction (7).[1]

(7)   * I whispered him the news.

If a verb of speaking like "whisper" is used to describe a situation that the child perceives, then the manner of speaking is apparent from the situation. The ambiguity problem in the acquisition of subcategorization is that the child needs to decide whether the verb's representation for the purposes of subcategorization includes the specification of manner (8a) or does not (8b).

(8)   a. manner-feature("whisper") = 1
       b. manner-feature("whisper") = 0

(9)   a. "I whispered him the news," is ungrammatical.
       b. "I whispered him the news," is grammatical.

The affected linguistic process here is generation. If the correct representation of "whisper" is learned, the child will conclude that (9a) holds instead of assuming (9b).

There has been little work on how ambiguity can be acquired and resolved by children or machines, i.e. how the correct generalizations about ambiguous forms can be made. For each of the three topics of the book (syntactic categorization, semantic categorization and verbal

---

[1] Throughout this book, the star will be used to mark ungrammatical strings.

subcategorization), I will describe and evaluate a computational model of how ambiguity and the knowledge necessary for disambiguation can be learned. I know of no previous work on this problem in the acquisition of syntactic categorization. Differences between the Word Space model in this book and a model for learning semantic categorization proposed by Siskind will be analyzed in detail. Steven Pinker's theory of subcategorization acquisition will be discussed and contrasted with the connectionist model to be developed here.

The research strategy adopted here is to concentrate on how the acquisition of ambiguity is possible in principle and to demonstrate that particular types of algorithms and learning architectures (such as unsupervised clustering and neural networks) can succeed at the task. This can only be the first step in a more comprehensive investigation that eventually needs to incorporate and account for data from child language research much more than was done here.

Another aspect of my research strategy is to use text as a model of natural language. Text is different from speech and in particular from the language that is used by parents when they interact with their children. Moreover, the acquisition and resolution of ambiguity is easier when tied in with social interaction because we can exploit additional clues from non-linguistic context, prosody, and our ability to ask questions if a possibility of misunderstanding remains. Despite these potential shortcomings of a text-based study, the problems addressed in this book are general enough to enable us to learn lessons about language independent of the form of its manifestation.

A third general point concerns the origin of ambiguity in language. I will not address this question here and take the abundance of ambiguous forms in natural language for granted. Some researchers see ambiguity as a problematic or accidental property of language (see for example Chierchia and McConnell-Ginet 1991). Historical linguists hypothesize that people create new meanings to enhance the expressivity and informativeness of words (Hopper and Traugott 1993:65). On this view, ambiguity arises from the opposing forces of innovation (which introduces new meanings/uses) and conservatism (which retains old meanings/uses). Zipf sees the *principle of least effort* as the reason for the universality of ambiguity across languages. According to him, ambiguity is a compromise between the speaker's desire to limit the number of words she needs to choose from to express a certain meaning (to minimize the effort in production), and the hearer's desire to limit the number of meanings she needs to choose from to understand a word (to minimize the effort in comprehension) (Zipf, 1949). Acquisition offers an interesting alternative vantage point. The presence of thousands of forms for only subtly different meanings could make language acquisition an unnecessarily long and difficult process. So even if Zipf is wrong to assume that the speaker's effort of access increases with the number of forms in the language, surely the effort of *acquisition* will increase. That the bottleneck of acquisition is the reason for the universality of ambiguity across languages is an intriguing hypothesis, but pursuing it is beyond the scope of the present study.

Taking ambiguity and disambiguation seriously has important consequences for theories of linguistic representation. In symbolic or discrete representation systems, disambiguation can be difficult since criteria like syntactic well-formedness and logical coherence eliminate few of the readings that ambiguity gives rise to. I will argue that gradient representations are more appropriate for resolving ambiguity. They allow us to express notions like "is closer to", "is more similar to" and "is more syntactically well-formed". Both syntactic and semantic disambiguation will make critical use of the notion of proximity.

In subcategorization learning, gradience is important because of what I call the *transition problem.* Most of the knowledge about the dative alternation and other alternations in English is not present at birth. The question is how the child makes the transition from a state without knowledge to adult performance. I will argue that a gradient model explains this transition better than a discrete model in which the acquisition process cannot move forward smoothly.

Finally, ambiguity is also relevant for the question of how much linguistic knowledge is innate. It is often assumed that postulating the innateness of a difficult property of language solves the acquisition problem for it. But in addition to postulating innate categories, one needs to show how they are grounded in perception; for example, how the purportedly innate category of nouns is grounded in the external category of things. Ambiguity makes the grounding problem hard, since it increases the number of possible groundings. Innate knowledge can only help in acquisition if the grounding problem is solved.

In general, there is much pessimism about learning without language-specific innate knowledge. Noam Chomsky writes:

> It seems that there is little hope in accounting for our knowledge in terms of such ideas as analogy, induction, association, reliable procedures, good reasons, and justification in any generally useful sense, or in terms of 'generalized learning mechanisms' (if such exist) (Chomsky 1986:12)

I will show that analogy, association, and induction are quite powerful and can, in concert with general cognitive innate knowledge, but without language-specific innate knowledge, learn important properties of language that are thought to be innate by many.

The book is structured as follows. Chapter 2 introduces Tag Space, a model of the acquisition of part-of-speech categorization and part-of-speech disambiguation. Chapter 3 is about Word Space, a model of the acquisition of semantic categorization and semantic disambiguation. Chapter 4 describes and analyzes a connectionist model of subcategorization acquisition. Chapter 5 summarizes what I have tried to achieve. An appendix treats the mathematical methods used in the book.

2

Distributional Information in the Acquisition of Syntactic Categorization

This chapter investigates the role of distributional information in the acquisition of syntactic categories (or parts of speech) like noun and verb. After a discussion of previous work on distributional analysis and part-of-speech acquisition, I will introduce TAG SPACE, a computational model of part-of-speech acquisition. In contrast to previous approaches, TAG SPACE categorizes occurrences of words in context instead of word types. This property is crucial for addressing the problem of part-of-speech ambiguity.

Another distinctive property of TAG SPACE is its graded categorization. Occurrences of words in context are not discretely categorized, but can rather be assigned to several categories, with various degrees of strength. It will be argued that this representation is advantageous for part-of-speech.

On the basis of experimental evidence about TAG SPACE, it will be argued that distributional information in combination with prosodic and semantic information is sufficient to learn the parts of speech of English, and that syntax-specific innate knowledge is not necessary.

The chapter is structured as follows. The first four sections discuss related work on distributional analysis, gradience in syntactic categorization, and cognitive and computational models of part-of-speech acquisition. Sections 2.5 and 2.7 describe TAG SPACE and its application to the Brown corpus. The last two sections discuss the implications of the model for innateness, ambiguity and gradience and state my conclusions.

2.1 Distributional Analysis

In linguistics, distributional analysis is most commonly associated with the name of Zelig Harris. Harris' brand of structural linguistics was based on distributional analysis. Many problems with his approach are well known, in particular the neglect of semantic aspects of language and the lack of explicitness of his procedures. In this section, I discuss these problems to make clear how TAG SPACE differs from classical distributional analysis.

Syntactic rules manifest themselves in distributional patterns. Many tests for syntactic properties are essentially distributional. But Harris saw distributional analysis as the central concern of linguistics. Any non-distributional data and in particular meaning were not regarded as admissible evidence:

> The main research of descriptive linguistics, and the only relation which will be accepted as relevant in the present survey, is the distribution or arrangement within the flow of speech of some parts or features relatively to others.(1951:5)

In his theory, the analysis of distributional data consists of two steps: "the setting up of elements, and the statement of the distribution of these elements relative to each other." (1951:6) The initial elements are isolated on the basis of identity judgments (e.g. 1951:29): Corresponding segments of repetitions of an identical utterance are called *free variants* of each other. More complicated entities such as phonemes, morphemes or syntactic categories are then built up from the initial elements by searching for groups of elements that do not contrast with each other, because they have identical or disjoint distributions. For example, "a" and "an" can be grouped into one class "indefinite article" since they occur in disjoint environments; "our" and "his" can be grouped into one class "possessive pronoun" since they occur in identical environments.[1]

While distributional and semantic contrasts were equally important for other structural linguists (Bréal, 1899; de Saussure, 1962), Harris only considered purely formal contrasts in his methodology. Apparently he saw semantic evidence as too subjective to deserve scientific attention:

---

[1] Even in these apparently clear cases, there are counterexamples to disjointness and identity:

(1)   a. a historic journey
       b. an historic journey
       c. He lost his cool.
       d. * He lost our cool.

I take this to be an argument for regarding the notion of contrast as graded rather than all-or-none. See below.

There are at present no methods of measuring social situations and of uniquely identifying social situations as composed of constituent parts, in such a way that we can divide the utterance which occurs in (or corresponds to) that social situation into segments which will correspond to the constituent parts of the situation. In general, we cannot at present rely on some natural or scientifically ascertainable subdivision of the meaning range of the local culture, because techniques for such complete cultural analysis into discrete elements do not exist today [. . .] (1951:188f.)

There are also many disparaging remarks about linguists who insist on using criteria of meaning despite these difficulties:

It is hoped that presentation of the methods in procedural form and order may help reduce the impression of sleight-of-hand and complexity which often accompanies the more subtle linguistic analysis. (1951:1)

[. . .] since they [the procedures for arranging the facts] go only by formal distinctions there is no opportunity for uncontrolled interpreting of the data or for forcing of the meaning. (1951:3)

However, Harris did in fact use semantic evidence in the form of identity judgments. Whether two sentences mean "the same" is clearly a semantic decision. Even though judgments of sameness of meaning may be more robust than judgments of meaning per se, the use of identity judgments undermines Harris' claim that his method is more objective than meaning-based methods.

The lack of semantic considerations was Chomsky's main objection to Harris' structuralism. He pointed out that some important syntactic distinctions cannot be described without meaning because they are indistinguishable distributionally. Chomsky's example was (2) (1964:34). It is assumed that it is a syntactic task to specify the mapping from surface form to predicate-argument relations.

Chomsky argued that a distributional analysis fails to differentiate "easy" and "eager" although they exhibit different mappings: "John" is the object of "please" in (2a) and the subject in (2b). This suggests that the distribution of a word is not sufficient for determining its syntactic properties.

(2)   a. John is easy to please.
        b. John is eager to please.

A proponent of distributional analysis could argue that any semantic distinction manifests itself distributionally. Let us consider three candidates for distributional correlates of the difference between "easy" and "eager". First, pleonastic "it" is possible for "easy", but not for "eager", the contrast (3a) vs. (3b). However, (3b) is good if "it" is used referentially in the meaning of a sentence like (3c).

(3)   a. It is easy to please John.
       b. It is eager to please John.
       c. This thing is eager to please John.

Secondly, (4a) is marginally possible as a parallel to (4b), with "himself" being used as an emphatic personal pronoun in (4a) and as a reflexive pronoun in (4b). As a marginal use it will be less frequent, which could help a discovery procedure infer the difference between the two. The problem here is that this argument presupposes knowledge about reflexives and how they relate to the distinction between normal adjectives and tough-movement adjectives. In Harris' approach one of the two syntactic facts (tough-movement or reflexives) has to be learned first to be used in subsequent inferences. The fact that the two uses of "himself" have different functions in the two sentences in (4) should be at least as hard to learn as the difference between "easy" and "eager", so that a failure for the latter leaves little hope that discovery procedures could learn the former without semantics.

(4)   a. John is easy to please himself.
       b. John is eager to please himself.

A third possible distributional criterion for distinguishing the two adjectives would be the pair in (5).

(5)   a. John is easy to please Mary.
       b. John is eager to please Mary.

Again, there is a reading, albeit an implausible one, that make the first sentence acceptable.

(6)   a. John is easy in order to please Mary.

So it seems that (2) is a fairly convincing example of a minimal pair that requires semantics for identifying a crucial syntactic difference.

The problems of ignoring meaning are not limited to small word classes like tough and raising adjectives. Present participles and adjectives pose a similar problem. Both occur in prenominal position as modifiers of a noun and as the complement of *to be*. While there are a few distributional differences like the contrast in (7), we are again faced with the bootstrapping problem: how are we to know that "to look" and a few other environments are to be taken as critical whereas other random correlations in the data are not? The category of present participles is hence another category that a purely distributional analysis is not able to characterize correctly.

(7)   a. He looks good.
       b. * He looks aging.

A second criticism of distributional analysis concerns missed generalizations. Even if a distributional method assigns a correct structure to a sentence, it can still miss important syntactic generalizations. For example, a correct analysis of the sentences in (8) must reflect their recursive structure.

(8)   a. She slept in the hammock that Peter bought in the shop.
       b. She slept in the hammock that Peter bought in the shop that John found in the yellow pages.
       c. She slept in the hammock that Peter bought in the shop that John found in the yellow pages that Mary got from the Post Office.

Distributional analysis can find recursive structures, for example the statement "AN = N" (i.e., N → A N) captures part of the recursive structure of noun phrases (A = adjective, N = noun (1951:265)).

But the problem is that there are several possible recursive analyses some of which, for example (9), are incorrect since they separate the prepositional phrases from the verbs they modify. For example, "the Post Office" is separated from "Mary got". The analysis in (9) makes "the Post Office" a modifier of the first verb, "slept" in (8c).

(9)   a. X → X Y | Y
       b. Y → PREP DET NOUN "that" PROPER-NAME VERB-PAST
       c. S → PRONOUN VERB-PAST X PREP DET NOUN

This example also hints at the third problem of Harris' brand of distributional analysis: lack of explicitness. While care is taken to *justify* every step of discovery with distributional data, the choice of what the next step will be depends entirely on the linguistic knowledge of the researcher. A truly automatic program based on Harris' work would make the wrong choices in many cases and come up with an inadequate description of the syntactic structures that occur in the corpus.

An example of lack of explicitness is the equation "A + ly = D" (1951:263), meaning adjectives with suffix -ly form a class with adverbs. Contrary to Harris' claim, it cannot be derived by procedure 16.2 in the way described by Harris (1951:263). Procedure 16.2 states that two classes are identified if their members occur in mutually substitutable environments. But many adjectives do not have "-ly" adverbs, for instance the adverb "oldly" (derived from "old") does not exist.

This example shows that the researcher chooses the procedures and the part of the data they are applied to. So it is not true that subjectivity is removed in structuralism. In fact, the subjective intervention necessary in structuralism may have worse consequences than the use of meaning criteria since the implications of low-level decisions necessary in applying structural discovery procedures are hard to assess. The approach advocated in this proposal is more explicit than Harris' in that concrete implementations of all proposed computational models are given.

A final problem for Harris is that his definition of contrast and identity make an adequate treatment of gradience difficult. For example, he agonizes over the initial consonant sequences *gl-* and *sl-*. Many words starting with *gl-* have a meaning indicating light and luster:[2]

(10)   glimmer, glint, gleam, glitter, glisten, glass, glaze, gloss

His procedure 12.22 identifies them as possible initial morphemes, but he does not commit himself as to which status the subsequent procedure 12.23 would assign them (1951:178). In the end, he does not assign them a formal grammatical status at all. Instead, he refers the question of how to handle them to future work (1951:194).

This is clearly unsatisfactory, since *gl-* is productive in English. For example, most English speakers would understand a novel word like *gleecing* or *gleeny* as referring to something shiny. Harris cannot deal with this kind of phenomenon because for him distributional contrast is an all-or-none concept: either there is no contrast at all, exactly identical distribution, or two elements are different. The case of *gl-* suggests that a softer notion of contrast would be needed to capture all relevant linguistic generalizations.

A similar point concerns frequency. As was pointed out earlier, a contrast between linguistic objects may hold in the vast majority of environments, but there may be exceptions. For example, an important contrast in English grammar is the distinction between mass and count nouns. However, there is a moderately productive rule that coerces mass nouns into count nouns as in the following sentences.

(11)   a. They produce five different red wines.

        b. How many mineral waters do they carry?

Thus it is impossible to find the distinction between count and mass nouns without frequency information. Harris was opposed to using frequency (e.g. 1951:8). In contrast, the approach taken here will give great importance to both gradience and frequency.

My conclusion is that a structuralist discovery procedure may be

---

[2]The initial consonant sequence "gl" is not a sufficient condition for membership in this cluster. Members with a front vowel and those with nasals or sibilants are more central than others. I will not try to state the conditions for membership precisely.

able to characterize syntax partially. But for many important parts of syntax access to semantic information is necessary for learning syntax. The kind of discovery procedure that was proposed by Harris cannot get at those aspects.

In summary, classical distributional analysis as introduced by Harris is often not stated explicitly enough to make meaningful assertions, lacks a concept of graded contrast, and fails to take semantics into account, which is crucial for discovering important syntactic distinctions. The importance of ambiguity, another problem that is not treated by Harris, will be stressed in the following sections.

2.2 Gradience in Syntactic Categorization

To many, the notion that syntactic categorization might be gradient seems absurd. Bolinger (1961) aptly summarizes the non-continuous view by discussing an example from (Joos, 1950).

> I take as my prime example [for a non-continuous phenomenon] the one given by Joos [...]: *They put their glasses on their noses.* English, he says, categorizes verbs into past versus present, and the tyranny of the categories is such that "the listener will react to exactly one of the categories" in a given dimension, "not ... to more than one, or to none, whether the utterance is ambiguous or not". With the verb *put* in the example, the reader has already made up his mind in favor of past or in favor of present, in spite of the fact that there was nothing to tell him which was intended. (page 13)

Bolinger contends that even the seemingly uncontroversial word "put" can escape the "tyranny of the categories". Usually, the present perfect and the past tense of the reduced question type in (12) can be distinguished in English. But this is not the case for "put" in (13a): "[...] I do not force you to an either-or choice between the two compatible meanings [(13b)] and [(13c)] [...]" (page 17).[3] This example shows that the idea of gradient parts of speech is not as far-fetched as it may seem.

(12) a. See them yet?
     b. Seen them yet?

(13) a. Put them away yet?
     b. Did you put them away yet?
     c. Have you put them away yet?

---

[3] According to Bolinger, no "blend" of the present tense and past tense of "put" is ever possible, but it is not clear, whether one could not find situations in which both parts of speech are invoked.

For Bolinger, the discussion of syntactic categorization is merely a backdrop for his main topic, gradience in phonology. The best-known challenge to syntactic discreteness is probably Ross's work. In his 1972 CLS paper he postulated "instead of a fixed, discrete inventory of syntactic categories, a quasi-continuum, which contains at least the categories shown in [(14)], ordered as shown there." (Ross 1972:316)

(14) verb > present participle > perfect participle > passive participle > adjective > preposition (?) > "adjectival noun" (e.g., "fun", "snap") > noun

According to Ross, verb is the most "volatile" syntactic category, and noun the most "inert." Volatility and inertness manifest themselves in the following syntactic properties:

- **Preposition deletion.** The more adjectival a predicate, the less preposition deletion can apply. (Preposition deletion is obligatory or frequent for most verbs ("* He surprised to me"), rare for adjectives ("opposite me", "near you").)
- **Fact deletion.** The nounier, the harder fact deletion. ("I'm surprised (at the fact) that he is leaving." vs. "my surprise *(at the fact) that he is leaving")[4]
- **Sentential "it".** The nounier, the less acceptable is sentential "it". ("I hate it that he talked." vs. "*my hate of it that he talked")
- **Distribution of "-ing".** The nounier, the fewer category members with "-ing".
- **Raising.** Both subject raising and object raising with verbs, only subject raising with adjectives.
- **Analogical extension of "by"-phrases.** The nounier, the less acceptable are "by"-phrases. ("She is pregnant by Horace." vs. "* her pregnancy by Horace")
- **Preposing of degree adverbs.** The nounier, the more obligatory preposing is. ("He was adored more than appreciated." vs. "? He was desperate more than blue.")
- **Constituent deletion.** The nounier, the fewer constituents need appear in surface structure. ("* He surprised." vs. "(He caused) a surprise.")

The category squish captures the generalization that verbs in English can enter into a great number of syntactic relationships with other phrases whereas the combinatory potential of nouns is more restricted. Other

---

[4]While "my surprise that he is leaving" is awkward, it does not seem to be bad in all dialects. I report here Ross's judgment.

parts of speech occupy an intermediate position on this cline of syntactic "volatility" or "inertness". In other papers, Ross discusses "nounphrasiness" (the degree to which a phrase functions as a noun phrase, Ross 1973b), "nouniness" (the degree to which a word functions as a noun, Ross 1973c), "clausematiness" (the degree to which main clauses and subordinate clauses form separate vs. common syntactic domains, Ross 1973a), and regularity of "there"-constructions (the degree to which they obey general syntactic laws of English, Ross 1974). An attempt to explain category squishes as a case of prototypicality is made in (Ross, 1987).

None of Ross's analyses were particularly rigorous. Reliance on introspection often produces questionable results for discrete judgments. It is even more problematic for gradient phenomena since an introspective good-bad decision is much easier to make than the subtle distinctions that are crucial for demonstrating squishy behavior.

Still, Ross provides a wealth of examples for grammatical phenomena that are hard to accommodate in discrete theories. One can always make the move of splitting categories into finer subcategories so that each subcategory has perfectly discrete properties. But these subdivisions come at the price of missing many important generalizations. For example, if "by"-phrases that modify adjectives and passivized verbs are treated separately, clear commonalities in function are lost. Ross's work, despite its flaws, suggests that a purely discrete theory of grammar is not good enough.

Tabor (1994) stresses the importance of continuity in language change. He investigates three phenomena that are best explained in a continuous model:

- **Frequency linkage.** Related constructions often rise together in frequency. For example, the frequency of periphrastic "do" in affirmative and negative questions rose at the same time and in parallel in the history of English.

- **Q-divergence.** Grammatical change is often preceded by frequency changes (quantitative divergence). For example, before "kind of" acquired its modern adverbial use ("it's kind of windy"), its use in ambiguous contexts like:

  (15) That is a kind of ominous-looking cloud.

  increased significantly.

- **Hybrid structures.** A period of transition between different grammars is marked by hybrid structures that combine elements from old and new grammars. For example, when stranded prepositions became acceptable there was a period with a high number of hybrids like the following:

(16) And eek in what array that they were inne. ("and also in what array they were in")

Tabor shows that each of these three phenomena can be modeled in a continuous model (a connectionist network) whereas they are hard to account for in discrete models. I see as the basic insights of his theory that a) frequency changes are an important factor in language change, b) the transition from one state of the grammar to a qualitatively different one often is a series of quantitative changes, and c) that both properties of language change (sensitivity to frequency and periods of transition) have a natural account only in a continuous model.

Ross's and Tabor's theories and the TAG SPACE model to be introduced below all adopt a spatial metaphor of gradience. Words are located at points on a cline or in a multi-dimensional space. When moving from word A to word B in the space, intermediate locations have successively fewer properties of A and more properties of B.

Probability is a competing metaphor. In a probabilistic model, there are no intermediate spatial locations. Rather, in transforming A to B, the certainty about being at A decreases and the certainty about being at B increases up to the point where there is absolute certainty about categorization of a word or syntactic phenomenon as B.

The two models can obviously be translated into each other (e.g., by defining a similarity measure on probability distributions such as the Kullback-Leibler distance, Kullback 1959). However, there are two important philosophical distinctions between the spatial and probabilistic metaphors. First, in my view there is no uncertainty about a word like "fun" that has adjectival and nominal properties. The reason for its "squishy" status is not that speakers are sloppy or don't have enough information to get it right. Rather, intermediate categories are first-class citizens without the taint of confusion that probabilistic uncertainty carries.

Secondly, probability suggests disjunctiveness: The two categories share the territory of an intermediate instance, but are preserved with all their properties. However, in many cases *novel* properties emerge in intermediate categories, properties which are non-compositional combinations of inherited elements from the parent categories. An example is (16), which is incompatible with the definition of both stranded and pied-piped prepositional relatives since it has two copies of the preposition "in".

Bolinger describes the distinction between probabilistic and spatial perspectives in the metaphor of cakes and kaleidoscopes. He also suggests that the distinction is not really substantive, but rather one of different perspectives on the same problem (see above):

> This suggests a term that may be ambiguous and general at the same time. An imaginative speaker or writer may deliberately choose an ambiguous term in order to plant his audience somewhere in the middle. But such an example is not the best for proving our case, as it may contain a weakness in logic: we cannot be sure whether the combination involves a freedom of the listener to choose one or another, even to hop at will in a series of successive choices, or is homogenized for him in advance. It is the mixture of the kaleidoscope versus the mixture of the cake recipe. With the kaleidoscope we never rest in the middle but only cross it on the way from one alternative to another, and it can be claimed then that the middle is an illusion. (pages 16–17)

This section has presented evidence that gradience, whether cake-like or kaleidoscopic, is an important property of both synchronic and diachronic syntax. My main concerns in the work presented below are learnability of a gradient model and its representation of ambiguity rather than structural syntax or diachronic change. Still, category squishes and frequency-based language change provide important motivation for taking continuity in grammar seriously.

2.3 Cognitive Models of Part-of-Speech Acquisition

This section discusses two cognitive models of the acquisition of syntactic categorization. (Models that focus on computational issues will be discussed in the next section.) Maratsos and Chalkley (1980) hypothesize that children acquire syntactic categories from semantic-distributional patterns. Pinker (1984) introduces a theory of *semantic bootstrapping*. According to him, children initially ground innate syntactic categories in semantic categories (for example, nouns in the category of things) and then develop a more abstract notion of syntactic category. My main criticism of both approaches is that they neglect the problem of part-of-speech ambiguity. In addition, Pinker's approach suffers from a lack of motivation for the indispensability of syntax-specific innate knowledge.

2.3.1 Acquisition by Semantic-Distributional Patterns

Maratsos and Chalkley (1980) propose a theory of acquisition by semantic-distributional patterns (henceforth SD patterns). Two examples of SD patterns are given in (17).

(17)   a. "didn't" + X_n + ... + 'past nonoccurrence of the meaning denoted by X_n'
       b. BE + X_n + "-ing" + 'present occurrence of the meaning denoted by X_n'

X_n denotes a slot that can be filled by words. SD patterns and words form an abstract mental representation in which an SD pattern is linked with all words that have occurred in its variable slot X_n. SD patterns are linked with each other if they share a large number of lexical items. For example, the two patterns in (17) are linked because most verbs occur in both patterns. (page 193)

In Maratsos and Chalkley's theory, this system is used productively by following paths from a word to its known SD patterns and from the known SD patterns to new SD patterns. So if the verb "drive" is used in the progressive (pattern (17b)), then the link between (17a) and (17b) will license its use in the negated past tense (pattern (17a)).

There are several problems with this formulation of the theory. Each of these problems is addressed by adding a special mechanism to the algorithm that builds the network of words and patterns. For example, because of subregularities in past tense formation like "put – put", "cut – cut" and "keep - kept", "dream - dreamt", a link between pattern (17b) and a positive past tense pattern of the form 'X_n + "-ed"', would produce the incorrect generalizations "putted" and "keeped". A special inhibitory mechanism is introduced which blocks "putted" because it has not been perceived in the input. Unfortunately, the authors only make plausible that inhibitory links could prevent the production of "putted". They do not show that the modified theory would still be capable of making desired generalizations. Other special mechanisms introduced to handle similar overgeneralizations are not checked in this way either.

However, the most serious problem with this theory of pattern associations is that part-of-speech ambiguity is completely neglected. For example, the abundance of words with a noun-verb ambiguity would create a link between "I didn't X_n ..." and "the X_n is ...", which would incorrectly generate "the bring is" and "the appear is" from "I didn't bring ..." and "I didn't appear ...". One crucial problem in learning syntactic categories is to *contextualize* occurrences of words. The noun "plant" in "the plant is green" is different from the verb "plant" in "they will plant onions". On the other hand, the patterns "determiner X_n noun" and "adjective X_n noun" are closely linked so that occurrence in one entails acceptability in the other.

Acquisition by SD patterns fails in much the same way as Harris' distributional analysis. Rigid definitions of the concepts of contrast and identity (or SD patterns characterizing contrasting vs. identical syntactic categories) break down for all but the most regular linguistic phenomena and are not appropriate for the pervasive ambiguity present in natural language.

2.3.2 Semantic Bootstrapping

Pinker (1984) criticizes three aspects of Maratsos and Chalkley's theory of SD patterns:

- reliance on negative evidence
- lack of innate knowledge
- inefficient learning algorithm

The first two points are linked since, according to Pinker, either innate knowledge or negative evidence are required for successful acquisition of many linguistic properties including syntactic categories:

> The learnability argument, conceived by Jane Grimshaw (personal communication), is that some of the properties that the child must come to know about grammatical entities are unlearnable in the absence of negative evidence. (which is the situation human children are faced with). (Pinker 1984:48)
>
> [...] most linguistically relevant properties are abstract, pertaining to phrase structure configurations, syntactic categories, grammatical relations, and so on. [...] But these abstract properties are just the ones that the child cannot detect in the input prior to learning, for the reasons I outlined when proposing semantic bootstrapping. (The argument in the previous paragraph owes its force to the fact that the contrapositive (roughly) is true: the properties that the child can detect in the input – such as the serial positions and adjacency and co-occurrence relations among words – are in general linguistically irrelevant.) (1984:49f.)

On the basis of evidence from TAG SPACE, I will argue below that syntactic categories can be learned from easily observable and concrete distributional properties. At least for the case of syntactic categories, it does not seem to be true that "grammatical entities" that are "unlearnable in the absence of negative evidence" are required for successful acquisition.

Pinker's third concern is efficiency. He is worried that the large number of possible correlations between distributional elements could not be handled efficiently:

The second argument concerns properties of elements that *are* detectable from positive evidence. The problem here is the selection of the rows and columns of the contingency table, that is, the properties of elements whose intercorrelations the child will attend to. As I argued in Pinker (1979) , in most distributional learning procedures there are vast numbers of properties that a learner could record, and since the child is looking for correlations among these properties, he or she faces a combinatorial explosion of possibilities. [...] To be sure, the inappropriate properties will correlate with no others and hence will eventually be ignored, leaving only the appropriate grammatical properties, but only after astronomical amounts of memory space, computation, or both.

The experiments presented below will show that distributional part-of-speech learning can be quite successful without astronomical requirements on space and time, showing these reservations about efficiency to be unjustified.

The motivation for semantic bootstrapping is that, even if syntactic categories are innate, part-of-speech acquisition is by no means trivial. Words in parental speech do not come with a marker indicating which symbol in the child's mind they correspond to. In Pinker's theory, children know about semantic properties of certain syntactic categories (for instance the fact that verbs tend to encode actions) and use these as clues in linking words and syntactic structures to innate symbols.

The following conditions for successful linking of an internal symbol are given:

[...] (1) the symbol enters into a set of phenomena that are universally correlated [...]; (2) one of those phenomena must include some notion that is perceptually available to the child in the semantic portion of his or her input [...]; and (3) when parents express that notion in their speech to the child, they must use the symbol in question [...]. If these conditions are true, then the semantic bootstrapping hypothesis can be applied to the problem of how rules incorporating that symbol are first acquired: the child can use the phenomenon that includes the perceptually available notion as the inductive basis for the symbol in question, expecting the rest of the phenomena involving that symbol to follow [...] (1984:45)

Condition (1) guarantees that the symbol in question can be identified in the language to be learned. If the symbol had only idiosyncratic uses in this language, then the child would not know about those uses prior to syntax acquisition. Condition (2) is the heart of semantic bootstrapping: semantic properties are crucial in linking the internal symbol to the outside world. Examples of salient semantic properties are reference to physical objects by nouns and reference to physical actions by verbs (1984:39). Condition (3) ensures that the symbol is actually used with one of its semantic properties in adult-to-child speech.

So there are two sorts of innate knowledge about syntactic categories: knowledge about what type of external category corresponds to the syntactic category; and knowledge about the category's syntactic functions (i.e., grammar-internal knowledge). It is unclear whether the first type of knowledge is necessary. Suppose that an English-speaking child without this type of knowledge makes an error and links physical objects to the internal verb category (innate or otherwise learned). Then almost all utterances about physical objects would be incompatible with their predicted grammatical properties. For example, verbs are specified for tense, but hardly any of the verbs in the input (in reality nouns) would be specified for tense. Overwhelming evidence like this should make it easy for the child to correct her mistake. This suggests that a trial-and-error procedure would be sufficient for linking internal and external categories.

The second type of innate knowledge is about the role syntactic categories play grammar-internally. Even if the parts of speech of a language can be learned without innate knowledge, there are many high-level constraints that can only be stated in terms of syntactic categories like noun and verb. The coordinate structure constraint is an example of a constraint that has been claimed to be part of universal grammar and thus innate (Ross, 1985). But according to Schäufele (1995), there seems to be at least one language that violates it, Vedic. Another example of a possibly innate constraint is the complex noun phrase constraint (CNPC) (1984:48). One needs to make reference to the concept of noun to state it. Consequently, if the CNPC is innate, so is the syntactic category noun. If it can be convincingly shown that there are unlearnable constraints that can only be stated in terms of syntactic categories, then this would be good evidence for the innateness of syntactic categories. However, a similar argument of unlearnability has been made for syntactic categories ("not learnable without negative evidence") and its weakness will be demonstrated here. This suggests that a thorough investigation of constraints like the coordinate structure constraint and the CNPC may reveal that they are also learnable without syntax-specific innate knowledge.

Pinker's third objection to acquisition by SD patterns is a more general version of the argument that children would need negative evidence to learn syntax without innate knowledge.[5] Lightfoot (1991:6) summarizes the negative-evidence argument for innate knowledge as follows:

> In fact, "negative data" (i.e., information that certain data do not exist) are generally not available to children [...] To be sure, children come to know these things and this knowledge is part of the output of the language-acquisition process; but it is not part of the input, not part of the "evidence" for the emerging system, and thus not part of the triggering experience. [...] It is in this sense that the stimulus is too impoverished to fully determine the emergent analysis. In that case children must arrive at (3a) [the correct analysis for a phenomenon discussed by Lightfoot HS] on some other, presumably nonexperiential basis. As an account of this basis, linguists have postulated genotypical information [...].

Consider the example of the null-subject parameter which specifies whether a language allows sentences without overt subjects (like Italian, (18b)) or doesn't (like English, (18a)). I use PHONETIC SUBJECT as a non-terminal for lexical (i.e. non-empty) subjects and ABSTRACT SUBJECT as a non-terminal that expands to either phonetically empty or lexical subjects.

(18) a. PHONETIC SUBJECT + VP
      b. ABSTRACT SUBJECT + VP

In a language like English, the child has to make the inference from (19a) to (19b) to rule out subject-less sentences.

(19) a. Null subjects don't occur.
      b. Null subjects are bad.

This type of inference ("I have not observed X, therefore X is ungrammatical.") would prevent productive use of language, if applied carelessly. In the extreme, only attested sentences would be used, clearly a grotesque proposition. On the other hand, if the null-subject parameter is innate and its default setting is: "Null-subjects are ungrammatical," then acquisition is easy. If there are no subject-less sentences as in English, then the child's grammar will rule out this sentence type. In contrast, one or a few subject-less sentences indicate the admissibility of null subjects. In a sense, the innate default for the null-subject parameter licenses the inference from (19a) to (19b).

The trouble with this argument is that inferences of the type: "I have not observed X, therefore X is ungrammatical," are frequently employed

---

[5] See also Pullum's recent analysis of the Poverty of Stimulus argument, which shows that the evidence given for it is slim and that the study of corpora suggests that children have access to more data than is generally assumed (Pullum, 1996).

for "peripheral" phenomena that nobody would claim to be innate. Reduced conditionals are such a peripheral phenomenon. Examples from the New York Times newswire are given in (20). Conditionals headed by "if" can be used with adjectives in predicative (20a) and attributive function (20b); with adverbs (20c); and with "so" (20d) and "not" (20e).

(20)   a.   ... the plan, if passed, would make court intervention unlikely. (1 June 1990)

b.   ... the ... paperback pairs photographs of celebrities that underscore striking, if unlikely, similarities in appearance. (13 June 1990)

c.   And advocates of change are again calling openly, if delicately, for price liberalization ... (2 June 1990)

d.   ... and, if so, who will serve on the five-member city council. (4 June 1990)

e.   Now it's Marshall who wants to be traded; or, if not, then he says he'll ... leave as a free agent ... (21 June 1990)

None of these uses is possible with another conjunction, "because." The example sentences in (21) are all bad, although completely parallel to those in (20).[6] This idiosyncratic difference between "if" and "because" is clearly specific to English and not part of innate universal grammar.

(21)   a.   * The plan, because passed, will make court intervention unlikely.

b.   * The photographs underscore striking, because unlikely, similarities in appearance.

c.   * Advocates of change are calling cautiously, because delicately, for price liberalization.

d.   * ... and, because so, he will not serve on the five-member city council.

e.   * Marshall doesn't want to be traded; because not, he'll leave as a free agent.

But the inference necessary to rule out the sentences in (21) is precisely of the form: "I have not observed X, therefore X is ungrammatical." For example, since the reduced adverbial sentence "because so" never occurs, children learn that it is not grammatical. Here it is not justified to stipulate an innate parameter that licenses the otherwise blocked inference since the phenomenon is language-specific. If an inference from nonoccurrence to ungrammaticality is possible here, then

---

[6]The example sentences in (20) were found by searching a corpus of the New York Times using the command "grep 'if [a-z]*\,' ". A search for the pattern "because [a-z]*\," did not yield any comparable uses of "because."

why not in the case of the null-subject parameter? The justification of innate knowledge by Pinker and Lightfoot as a necessary remedy against lacking negative evidence applies to "because" as well as the null-subject parameter.

I conclude that children can exploit implicit negative evidence in the form of nonoccurrence of forms and that innate knowledge is not necessary to make up for lacking negative evidence. Chapter 4 will discuss this point in more detail.

In general, it is hard to show that syntax-specific innate knowledge is dispensable since it requires proof of the learnability of all of grammar, which is beyond the scope of this book. I think, however, that the arguments presented in this section seriously undermine the innate-knowledge position. The TAG SPACE model of part-of-speech learning will be further evidence since it learns syntactic categories without syntax-specific innate knowledge.

A final criticism of semantic bootstrapping concerns ambiguity. Like acquisition by SD patterns and distributional analysis, the theory does not fare well with respect to part-of-speech ambiguity. The initial boot-strapping phase would probably not be affected. Since there are many inconsistencies in the initial links between, say, abstract objects and nouns (e.g., nouns describing actions like "the throwing of the ball"), ambiguity would just be an additional source of noise. However, ambiguity would be devastating for the second phase, "structure-dependent distributional learning" (1984:40). For example, the child could infer from distributional evidence that "situation" is a noun in (22) (1984:42).

(22)   the situation justified extreme measures

But the same inference would categorize "plant" as a noun in a sentence like (23a). As a result, the child could produce utterances like (23c) from (23b) (where the article "the" would signify that the speaker is referring to a previously mentioned act of planting). Since nouns can be modified by articles and since "plant" is a noun, there would be no prohibition against modifying "plant" by an article in (23c).

(23)   a. The plant produced fruits.
        b. He didn't plant the tulips.
        c. He didn't the plant the tulips.

The problem of ambiguity is thus not addressed by Pinker (1984).

In summary, both cognitive models discussed here fail to provide a complete account of part-of-speech acquisition because words are treated as unambiguous. In addition, only weak evidence is given for the syntax-specific innate knowledge that is presupposed in semantic bootstrapping.

2.4 Computational Models of Part-of-Speech Acquisition

Part-of-speech tagging has been one of the most active areas of research in computational linguistics in recent years. The simplest taggers are n-gram models (Church, 1989; Charniak et al., 1993), which predict the correct part-of-speech of a word from preceding (or following) words. For example, "kept" is more likely to be a past tense form after "he" and more likely to be a past participle after "has". N-gram taggers require a tagged training text for accurate estimation of transition probabilities between different parts of speech.

Transformation-based tagging as introduced by Brill (1993a),(1993b) also requires a hand-tagged text for training. The model in transformation-based tagging consists of a set of templates for tagging rules such as the ones in (24).

(24) a. change tag X to tag Y after tag Z
b. change tag X to tag Y after word W

Initially, each word is tagged with its most probable tag. The learning mechanism then cycles through all possible rules (i.e., those compatible with the pre-selected rule schemata), tests their effect on the corpus, and chooses the one that improves overall tagging accuracy most. For example, if all occurrences of "to" are tagged as infinitive markers initially, then the rule 'change tag INFINITIVE MARKER to PREPOSITION before "the" ' would improve tagging accuracy. The process of testing all rules and selecting the one with the most beneficial effect continues until no further improvement is possible.

Another rule-based system is history-based grammar (Magerman, 1994), a probabilistic model in which decision trees are trained to make parsing decisions. In the process of parsing, history-based grammar also provides part-of-speech tagging information.

These three models (n-gram models, transformation-based tagging, and history-based grammar) are not strictly models of part-of-speech acquisition since they require a hand-tagged or hand-parsed training text, which presupposes a system of part-of-speech categorization. This property makes them less suitable for investigating the learnability of syntactic categorization.

Hidden Markov Models, another popular tagging method(Jelinek, 1985; Cutting et al., 1991; Kupiec, 1992), can be trained on untagged text, but they still require a pre-categorization of words, i.e. a part-of-speech lexicon that specifies the possible syntactic categories of each word.

Brill and Marcus (1993) have shown that the effort necessary to construct the part-of-speech lexicon can be considerably reduced by combining learning procedures and a partial part-of-speech categorization elicited from an informant. Still, the methods can hardly settle issues of part-of-speech learnability since neither a part-of-speech lexicon nor an informant is available to children when they acquire language.

Some grammar induction techniques can in principle provide part-of-speech tags as a by-product of grammar learning, e.g. the inside-outside algorithm (Charniak, 1993) or certain Bayesian methods (Stolcke, 1994; Chen, 1995). However, due to the difficulty of the problem of grammar induction, most experiments have either tried to learn from tagged text, thus assuming a solution to the tagging problem, (see the examples described in Charniak (1993) and Chen (1995)) or they have imposed artificial restrictions on the size of the vocabulary (less than 20 in Stolcke (1994)).

Apart from tagging, there is a different strand of computational work on syntactic categorization in which syntactic properties of words are inferred from distributional patterns. Kiss (1973) presents a case study of 31 words in a child language corpus. A hierarchical clustering according to shared nearest neighbors produces word classes that correspond well with linguistic intuition.

Elman (1990) trains a connectionist net to predict words, a process that generates internal representations that reflect grammatical category. Again, a hierarchical clustering demonstrates that grammatically similar words are grouped together.

Brill et al. (1990) infer grammatical category from bigram statistics. They also use dendrograms produced by hierarchical clustering to show the success of their method.

Finch and Chater (1992) and Finch (1993) construct vector models in which words are clustered according to the similarity of their close neighbors in a corpus. The technique produces meaningful clusterings for various similarity metrics and several corpora.

Kneser and Ney (1993) present a probabilistic model for entropy maximization which relies on the immediate neighbors of words in a corpus. Words are shown to have intuitive nearest neighbors with respect to a similarity metric defined in the model.

These approaches have in common that they classify *words* instead of individual occurrences. They thus share a shortcoming for which I earlier criticized Maratsos and Chalkley's and Pinker's models. Finch recognizes this problem: (1993:125)

A formal linguistic analysis of a corpus of natural language will not always assign a word the same category for all its occurrences. This

gives rise to *lexical ambiguity,* which this classification procedure [Finch's technique HS] is unable to directly account for. [...]
An analysis of the dendrogram, however, shows that words which are often assigned different categories form a subcategory of their own. This is especially true of words which are sometime[s] nouns, and sometimes verbs. [...]

Finch's defense addresses only part of the problem. It is not sufficient to identify potentially ambiguous words. A syntactic categorization that makes important syntactic distinctions such as the noun-verb distinction only for unambiguous words fails for half of the 40 most frequent words in the Brown corpus (23 of them are ambiguous). If uses of "plant" as a verb or a noun and uses of "to" as an infinitive marker or a preposition are not distinguished, then they can hardly be considered correctly classified.

In previous work (Schütze, 1993), I tried to solve the ambiguity problem by training a neural network to predict the part of speech of a word from its context. However, no information about the word that is to be categorized was used. This scheme fails for minimal pairs like (25a) vs. (25b), where the context is identical and information about the lexical item in question ("rarely" vs. "will") is needed (in combination with context) for correct classification.

(25)   a. The soldiers *rarely* come home.

   b. The soldiers *will* come home.

In the next section, I will introduce TAG SPACE, a model that combines evidence from words and their contexts for syntactic categorization. It will be shown that it is superior to the word-class approaches discussed above.

2.5   TAG SPACE: A Gradient Model of the Acquisition of Syntactic Categorization

This section introduces TAG SPACE, a computational model of the acquisition of syntactic categorization. Its novelty lies in the generally successful acquisition of the parts of speech of English from a natural corpus, in the presence of ambiguity.

I treat syntactic categorization here as part of the knowledge necessary for natural language understanding. One step in making sense of a sentence is to figure out what role each of its words plays in modifying other words or in supplying the predicate and the arguments for the main proposition expressed. The overall architecture of a natural language system that TAG SPACE might be part of is sketched in Figure 1. I will not make any strong claims about the architecture. The

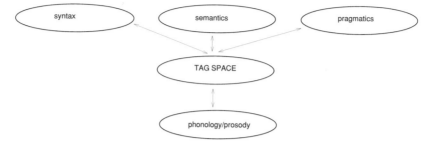

FIGURE 1 The role of TAG SPACE in a complete model of natural language comprehension.

architecture is merely presented to provide motivation and context for the TAG SPACE model.

TAG SPACE receives a tokenized stream from a component dealing with the raw input that a language learner receives. So I assume that a difficult task of language acquisition, the segmentation of a stream of sounds into words, has already been successfully solved.

TAG SPACE next performs a rough syntactic categorization: Each token is assigned a *tag*, a rough description of its local syntactic function (e.g. as a verb or preposition). This step is described in great detail in this section and evaluated in the next.

The tags then are input to the syntax, semantics and pragmatics components which use them to form an initial representation of the sentence. TAG SPACE uses only local context. Since a completely correct syntactic categorization requires the consideration of semantic and non-local syntactic constraints, TAG SPACE makes a number of mistakes. In the architecture proposed in Figure 1, these mistakes would be ironed out in a second step of processing in which the initial hypothesis by the higher-level components would put additional constraints on syntactic categorization. For example, "milk" in "I gave the cat the dog bit milk" would initially be tagged as the object of "bit". Only by looking at the overall syntactic structure of the sentence, it is apparent that it is in fact the object of "gave". This latter "cleaning-up" phase of processing is not part of the computational model presented in this book, but will be discussed in Section 2.8.

Why is there a separate level of tag representation? Many NLP systems, in particular symbolic ones, lack this level. They do not use the type of local context that is captured by tags, going instead directly from words to syntactic structures. The advantage of tags is that they reduce the search space when local context contains helpful information. But they may reduce it too much if local context is misleading, pruning a path that would lead to the correct parse. In this case, an interactive process involving all components is needed to correct the original analysis. So both systems (with and without tag representation) can be justified. There are in fact many computational systems that do make use of a separate level of tag representation (e.g., (Abney, 1991; deMarcken, 1990; Charniak et al., 1994)). The choice of tags here is motivated by the significant amount of information that local context seems to carry for part-of-speech acquisition, a point that will be demonstrated presently.

2.5.1 Vector Spaces and Clustering

The representational medium of TAG SPACE is a multi-dimensional real-valued vector space. Proximity in the space corresponds to proximity in syntactic function. For example, transitive and intransitive verbs are close to each other, whereas verbs and nouns are distant.

	...	the	...	who	...
...					
returns		300		75	
...					
sleep		133		200	
...					

FIGURE 2 Distributional matrix for the construction of (left) syntactic context vectors.

Figures 2 and 3 show a simple example of how to represent words in such a space (the numbers are not from an actual corpus, but were made up for ease of presentation). The distributional matrix in Figure 2 records the number of times that "returns" occurs to the right of "the" (300 times) and to the right of "who" (75 times); i.e., it tells us how often the strings "the returns" and "who returns" occurred in the corpus. According to the matrix, the strings "the sleep" and "who sleep" occurred 133 and 200 times, respectively.

Figure 3 is a geometric interpretation of the matrix. The words "the" and "who" are interpreted as dimensions of a two-dimensional space. The words "returns" and "sleep" are interpreted as points in the space (shown as vectors connecting the origin with the point in question). The word "returns" is located at point (75,300) because it cooccurs 75 times with "who" and 300 times with "the".

We can begin to see how a multidimensional space can capture grammatical properties of words: "returns" is more often used as a noun in the corpus: There are more uses of the noun phrase "the returns" than

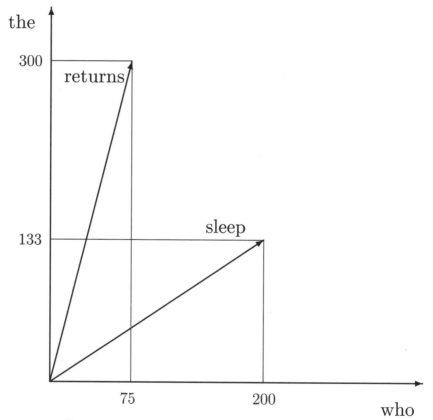

FIGURE 3 Geometric interpretation of syntactic context vectors.

of sentences that contain the string "who returns" (in which "returns" is a verb). The reverse holds for "sleep": it is more often used as a verb. This difference is indicated by the fact that the angle between "returns" and the "the"-axis is smaller than the angle between "returns" and the "who"-axis. A word that is exclusively used as a noun would have a vector that lies on the "the"-axis (no occurrences of the string "who N", many occurrences of "the N"). So the closeness of "returns" to the "the"-axis indicates its dominant use as a noun. Similarly, the closeness of "sleep" to the "who"-axis indicates its frequent use as a verb.

The cosine can be employed to measure similarity between vectors. Cosine assigns a value close to 1.0 if two vectors have similar values on many dimensions, and 0.0 if they are orthogonal, i.e., they have no similar values on any dimension: where the first vector has a non-zero value, the second vector has a zero value and vice versa. It can be shown that the cosine is equivalent to the normalized correlation coefficient:

$$corr(\vec{v}, \vec{w}) = \frac{\sum_{i=1}^{N} v_i w_i}{\sqrt{\sum_{i=1}^{N} v_i^2 \sum_{i=1}^{N} w_i^2}}$$

where N is the dimension of the vector space, and v_i is component i of vector $\vec{v}$.

When we use cosine to compare vectors of the type shown in Figures 2 and 3, we effectively compute a measure of the overlap of left neighbors of words. If the cosine of the vectors of two words is 1.0, then they have perfect overlap of left neighbors: exactly the same left neighbors. If the cosine is 0.0, then they have no neighbors in common.

Part-of-speech similarity between words (and in the next chapter semantic similarity between words) will be defined as the degree of overlap between their vector representations, where the vector representation is constructed from suitable neighbors of the word in a reference corpus. We will have to look at many more dimension words than the two in Figure 3 ("the" and "who"), and we will also use a vector space transformation called Singular Value Decomposition. But the basic idea of TAG SPACE is to use overlap in neighbors as a measure of similarity.

Why a vector space as representational medium rather than another formalism? What is required for our purposes is a measure of similarity between words. The type of vector space we will be using here happens to be a particularly simple way of computing similarities. In addition, it can be visualized (at least in two or three dimensions). Many other methods for similarity computations could have been used, for example, mixture models (Duda and Hart, 1973; Dempster et al., 1977). In a mixture model, one assumes several underlying sources which generate output points, in our case words. For a set of words one can compute a most likely set of sources that would have given rise to this particular set of words. One can then compute similarity as the degree to which words were generated by the same sources.

Most mixture models assume that different features (the left neighbors like "who" and "the" in our case) are weighted differently. It is hard to come up with an automatic method of inferring a good weighting of the features. The advantage of the vector spaces used in this book is that no weighting needs to be inferred. Or rather uniform weighting is imposed, i.e., each feature receives the same weight. So the reason vector spaces as opposed to other mathematical formalisms will be used here is that they are the simplest possible formalism, given the constraints of gradience and data-driven representation.

A multi-dimensional real-valued space is quite different from the attribute-value representations commonly used in unification grammars such as FUG, LFG and HPSG (Kay, 1984, 1986; Kaplan and Bresnan, 1982; Pollard and Sag, 1995). However, the differences are smaller than they appear at first. It has been pointed out by Chomsky that hierarchical category systems (of which attribute-value representations are a generalization) are able to represent degrees of grammaticality and thus gradience:

> [...] it is obvious how [...] a degree of grammaticalness can be assigned to any sequence of formatives when the generative grammar is supplemented by a hierarchy of categories. The degree of grammaticalness is a measure of the remoteness of an utterance from the generated set of perfectly well-formed sentences [...] The more narrowly the mth level categories circumscribe the generated language (i.e., the more detailed the specification of selectional restrictions) the more elaborate will be the stratification of utterances into degrees of grammaticalness. (Chomsky 1961:237)

From this perspective, the real-valued space is the limit of a process of introducing increasingly fine distinctions. An important difference is of course that attribute-value representations are defined for systems in which attributes and their values have a particular semantics. For example, number features will rule out agreement violations, and slash features will link extracted arguments to their predicates. In contrast, TAG SPACE only models similarity of syntactic behavior without a precise specification of syntactic features like number and slash. For this reason, what I present here will be disappointing from the point of view of a thorough linguistic analysis. But recall that the task, learning syntactic categorization from unlabeled input, is much harder than what most other researchers have attempted.

2.5.1.1 Clustering

Just as a vector space is the simplest possible medium for a gradient, data-driven representation, so the simplest possible clustering algorithm will be chosen for dividing words up into part-of-speech classes. The Group Average Agglomerative Clustering (GAAC) algorithm that will be used (described in detail in the appendix) tries to find classes that have a small average distance between members. It is an iterative procedure which starts with all words being separate one-member clusters, and then in each step merging the two clusters such that the average distance between members of the result cluster is minimal.

Some of the vector sets that we will work with are too large for GAAC. In such cases the Buckshot algorithm offers an efficient way to "seed" a clustering using GAAC and then compute it for the full set of vectors. Buckshot selects a sample of vectors, clusters it with GAAC, and then extends it to all vectors by computing the *centroid* of each cluster and assigning vectors to the cluster whose centroid they are closest to. The centroid of a cluster can be thought of as its center of gravity, computed as the (normalized) sum of its members. (Again, the details are in the appendix.)

Clustering can be seen as a special case of the type of mixture model that was mentioned above. Instead of computing for each word-cluster pair the probability that the cluster was responsible for the word, each word is assigned to just one cluster.

There are many other clustering algorithms that share the following properties with Buckshot: cosine as the measure of similarity for vectors (or equivalently for normalized vectors: Euclidean distance), definition of a good, "cohesive" cluster as one with a small distance between members (or, equivalently, with a high correlation between members); and a hard assignment of elements to clusters, i.e. each element is assumed to belong to only one (and at least one) cluster. Although I have not experimented with other algorithms, it is my belief that the results reported here would be qualitatively the same if I had chosen a different clustering algorithm with these properties.

2.5.2 Description of Tag Space

The novelty of the model of syntactic acquisition presented here is that contexts, not word types, are classified syntactically. In spite of this, the first step in bootstrapping is concerned with words since the type of a word is immediately apparent from looking at a text (there is usually just one way of writing it) whereas the type of a context (whether it is the subject or object position of a sentence, the main verb or an infinitive etc.) cannot be as easily observed.

The basic building blocks of the inductions described below are *syntactic context vectors* (to be distinguished from *semantic context vectors* in Chapter 3). Syntactic context vectors are representations of the syntactic behavior of a word with respect to its left or right context. Therefore, we will measure the similarity between two words with respect to their syntactic behavior to, say, their left side by the degree to which they share the same neighbors on the left. If the counts of neighbors are assembled into a vector (with one dimension for each neighbor), the cosine can be employed to measure similarity. It will assign a value close to 1.0 if two words share many neighbors, and 0.0 if they share none. I will call the vector of left neighbors of a word its *left context vector*, and the vector of right neighbors its *right context vector*. The unreduced context vectors in the experiment described here have 250 entries, corresponding to the 250 most frequent words in the Brown corpus.

This basic idea of measuring distributional similarity in terms of shared neighbors must be modified because of the sparseness of the data. Consider two infrequent adjectives that happen to modify different nouns in the corpus. Their right similarity according to the cosine measure would be zero. This is clearly undesirable. But even with high-frequency words, the simple vector model can yield misleading similarity measurements. A case in point is "a" vs. "an". These two articles do not share any right neighbors since the former is only used before consonants and the latter only before vowels. Yet intuitively, they are similar with respect to their right syntactic context despite the lack of common right neighbors.

One solution to these problems is the application of a singular value decomposition (SVD) (Golub and van Loan, 1989). The appendix describes the mathematics of SVD in detail. Roughly, a singular value decomposition can be used to project a set of points in a high-dimensional space to a low-dimensional space. SVD will compute the optimal projection for a set of points and a given dimensionality of the low-dimensional space, where optimal is defined with respect to a least-square measure (the sum of the squares of the differences between the original points and the projected points is minimal, see the appendix for details). In all applications of SVD in this chapter, I chose 50 as the dimension of the low-dimensional space. I used SVDPACK to compute the singular value decompositions described here (Berry, 1992). The corpus used is the Brown corpus as distributed by the Penn Treebank project (Marcus et al., 1993). It has about 1.1 million tokens and 47,025 word types.

The motivation for using the SVD is to address three problems, two of which were just discussed:

- sparseness
- generalization
- compactness

It is obvious how the last point is achieved: by reduction to a low-dimensional space the objects we need to deal with are smaller in size and we gain efficiency.

SVD addresses the problems of sparseness and generalization because a high-dimensional space can represent more information than a low-dimensional space. So some information is lost in the process of dimensionality reduction. For example, most nouns can appear with the determiners "some", "many", "all", "the", and "a". If there is an outlier which appears with "some", "many", "all", "the", and "an", then it will be projected to the region where most nouns are located since the low-dimensional space doesn't have enough degrees of freedom to represent both types of nouns in separate regions. This is an example of how generalization occurs in the application of SVD. Similarly, if there is a noun that occurs only once with the determiner "the", then it will also be projected to the region of nouns that occur with many determiners. This is because the low-dimensional space cannot accommodate all idiosyncrasies for lack of representational capacity. This is an example of how sparseness is addressed.

The first application of SVD is for expository reasons: to show that an SVD-reduced space captures interesting generalizations. SVD was applied to two 47,025-by-250 matrices, L and R. The rows of L are the left context vectors of the 47,025 words in the vocabulary of the Brown corpus. Element l_{ij} of L records how often word j (one of the 250 most frequent words, the one with frequency rank j), occurs to the left of word i (that is, word j is immediately adjacent to word i, on its left side; for example, in "the Post Office", "Post" occurs to the left of "Office"). Element r_{ij} of R records how often word j, occurs to the right of word i.

Both L and R were reduced to 47,025-by-50 matrices using SVD. Table 1 shows the nearest neighbors of two words after the dimensionality reduction. For example, the word whose (reduced) left context vector is most similar to the left context vector of "onto" is "into". The word whose (reduced) right context vector is most similar to "onto" is "reduce". The neighbors are ordered according to proximity in the space.

One can see clear differences between the nearest neighbors in the two spaces. The right-context neighbors of "onto" are prepositions and verbs

word	side	nearest neighbors
onto	left	into toward away off together against beside around down
onto	right	reduce among regarding against towards plus toward using unlike
seemed	left	appeared might would remained had became could must should
seemed	right	seem seems wanted want going meant tried expect likely

TABLE 1 Words with most similar left and right neighbors for "onto" and "seemed".

because both prepositions and verbs govern noun phrases to their right. The left-context neighborhood of "onto" reflects the fact that prepositional phrases are used in the same position as adverbs like "away" and "together", thus making their left context similar. For "seemed", left-context neighbors are words that have similar types of noun phrases in subject position (mainly auxiliaries). The right-context neighbors all take "to"-infinitives as complements. An adjective like "likely" is very similar to "seemed" in this respect although its left context is quite different from that of "seemed". Similarly, the generalization that prepositions and transitive verbs are very similar if not identical in the way they govern noun phrases would be lost if "left" and "right" properties of words were lumped together in one representation. These examples demonstrate the importance of representing generalizations about left and right context separately.

Left and right context vectors are the basis for five different tag induction experiments, which are described in detail below:

- induction based on word type only
- induction based on word type and context
- induction based on word type and context, restricted to "natural" contexts
- induction based on word type and context, using generalized left and right context vectors
- induction based on context vectors of "disambiguated" words

2.5.3 Induction Based on Word Type Only

The two context vectors of a word characterize the distribution of neighboring words to its left and right. The concatenation of left and right context vector can therefore serve as a representation of a word's distributional behavior (Finch and Chater, 1992; Schütze, 1993). Concatenated vectors for all 47,025 words (surface forms) in the Brown corpus were formed. The resulting 47,025-by-500 matrix (47,025 words with two

250-dimensional context vectors each) was then reduced to a 47,025-by-50 matrix using SVD. Finally, the 47,025 50-dimensional reduced vectors from the SVD were clustered into 200 classes, using the fast clustering algorithm Buckshot (Cutting et al., 1992). Buckshot is a group average agglomeration clustering algorithm. Groups are formed so that the average distance between members of a group is as small as possible. Details of the algorithm are given in the appendix.

This classification of word types can be used as a classification of occurrences in context simply by assigning all occurrences to the class of the word type. The classification thus constitutes the baseline performance for distributional part-of-speech tagging. All occurrences of a word are assigned to one class. As pointed out above, such a procedure is problematic for ambiguous words.

2.5.4 Induction Based on Word Type and Context

In order to exploit contextual information in the classification of a token, I simply use context vectors of the two words occurring next to the token.

An occurrence of word w is represented by a concatenation of four context vectors:

- The right context vector of the preceding word.
- The left context vector of w.
- The right context vector of w.
- The left context vector of the following word.

The motivation is that a word's syntactic role depends both on the syntactic properties of its neighbors and on its own potential for entering into syntactic relationships with these neighbors. The only properties of context that we consider are the right-context vector of the preceding word and the left-context vector of the following word because they seem to represent the contextual information most important for the categorization of w. For example, for the disambiguation of "work" in "her work seemed to be important", only the fact that "seemed" expects noun phrases to its left is important, the right context vector of "seemed" does not contribute to disambiguation. That only the immediate neighbors are crucial for categorization is clearly a simplification, but as the results presented below show it seems to work surprisingly well.

Again, an SVD is applied to address the problems of sparseness, generalization and compactness. I randomly selected 20,000 word triplets from the corpus and formed concatenations of four context vectors as described above. The singular value decomposition of the resulting 20,000-by-1,000 matrix defines a mapping from the 1,000-dimensional space of concatenated context vectors to a 50-dimensional reduced space. A tag set was then induced by clustering the reduced vectors of the 20,000 selected occurrences into 200 classes. Each of the 200 tags is defined by the centroid of the corresponding class (the sum of its members).

Distributional tagging of an occurrence of a word w proceeds by retrieving the four relevant context vectors (right context vector of previous word, left context vector of following word, both context vectors of w) concatenating them to one 1000-component vector, mapping this vector to 50 dimensions, computing the correlations with the 200 cluster centroids and, finally, assigning the occurrence to the closest cluster. This procedure was applied to all tokens of the Brown corpus.

We will see below that this method of distributional tagging, although partially successful, fails for many tokens whose neighbors are punctuation marks. The context vectors of punctuation marks contribute little information about syntactic categorization since there are no grammatical dependencies between words and punctuation marks, in contrast to strong dependencies between neighboring words.

For this reason, a second induction on the basis of word type and context was performed, but only for tokens with *natural* contexts. Tokens next to punctuation marks and tokens with rare words as neighbors were not included. Contexts with rare words (less than ten occurrences) were also excluded for similar reasons: If a word only occurs nine or fewer times its left and right context vectors capture little information for syntactic categorization. In the experiment, 20,000 natural contexts were randomly selected, processed by the SVD and clustered into 200 classes. The classification was then applied to all natural contexts of the Brown corpus. By comparing results for all contexts and for natural contexts, we can see how classification accuracy depends on the frequency and type of the surrounding words. The threshold of 10 was chosen arbitrarily here, but we can expect that with larger corpora, the percentage of natural contexts will increase, so that performance for large corpora should be between the figures given for "all contexts" and "natural contexts", although probably closer to "all contexts".

2.5.5 Generalized Context Vectors

The context vectors used so far only capture information about distributional interactions with the 250 most frequent words. Intuitively, it should be possible to gain accuracy in tag induction by using information from more words. One way to do this is to let the right context vector record which *classes of left context vectors* occur to the right of a word. The rationale is that words with similar left context characterize words to their right in a similar way. For example, "seemed" and "would" have similar left contexts, and they characterize the right contexts of "he" and "the firefighter" as potentially containing an inflected verb form. Rather than having separate entries in its right context vector for "seemed", "would", and "likes", a word like "he" can now be characterized by a generalized entry for "inflected verb form occurs frequently to my right".

This proposal was implemented by applying a singular value decomposition to the 47025-by-250 matrix of left context vectors and clustering the resulting context vectors into 250 classes. A *generalized right context vector v* for word w was then formed by counting how often words from these 250 classes occurred to the right of w. Entry v_i counts the number of times that a word from class i occurs to the right of w in the corpus (as opposed to the number of times that the word with frequency rank i occurs to the right of w). Generalized left context vectors were derived by an analogous procedure using word-based right context vectors.

Note that the information about left and right is kept separate in this computation. This differs from previous approaches (Finch and Chater, 1992; Schütze, 1993) in which left and right context vectors of a word are always used in one concatenated vector. There are arguably fewer different types of right syntactic contexts than types of syntactic categories. For example, transitive verbs and prepositions belong to different syntactic categories, but their right contexts are virtually identical in that they require a noun phrase. This generalization could not be exploited if left and right contexts were not treated separately.

Another argument for the two-step derivation is that many words don't have any of the 250 most frequent words as their left or right neighbor. Hence, their context vectors are zero in the word-based scheme. The class-based scheme makes it more likely that meaningful representations are formed for all words in the vocabulary.

The generalized context vectors were input to the tag induction procedure described above for word-based context vectors: 20,000 word triplets were selected from the corpus, encoded as 1,000-dimensional vectors (consisting of four generalized context vectors), decomposed by a singular value decomposition and clustered into 200 classes. The resulting classification was applied to all tokens in the Brown corpus.

2.5.6 Induction for "Disambiguated" Words

In order to assess the impact of part-of-speech ambiguity on the induction procedure, one induction was run on disambiguated words. That is, each word-tag combination was replaced by a new word. For example, "to" occurs with the tags "TO" (infinitive marker) and "IN" (preposition). Each occurrence of "to" with tag "TO" was replaced by the new word "to-TO" and each occurrence of "to" with tag "IN" was replaced by the new word "to-IN". A new disambiguated corpus was created by executing this procedure for all word-tag combinations.

The induction procedure for natural contexts was then run on this disambiguated corpus. 20,000 natural contexts (without rare words and punctuation marks) were randomly selected. Each context was encoded as a 1,000 dimensional vector (consisting of four context vectors, based on disambiguated words). The resulting 20,000-by-1,000 matrix was SVD-decomposed and clustered into 200 classes. Finally, all tokens of the disambiguated corpus were categorized with respect to this classification.

2.6 Evaluation

Categorization tasks are often evaluated by comparing the output of a method with "the truth". In supervised tasks, methods can be trained to produce labels that are directly comparable with the labels used in a test set. But how can we evaluate an unsupervised procedure like clustering? A clustering of elements suggests two kinds of inferences which can be evaluated:

(26) a. **Discrimination.** Two elements assigned to different clusters belong to different categories.

b. **Accuracy.** Two elements assigned to the same cluster belong to the same category.

Here is one way one could evaluate distributional part-of-speech clustering with respect to the Brown tags, assuming there are 30 major tags.

- Cluster all tokens into 30 clusters.
- Measure accuracy as the percentage of token pairs that satisfy Inference 26b.
- Measure discrimination as the percentage of token pairs that satisfy Inference 26a.

Notice that 100% accuracy can be trivially achieved by assigning all tokens to one cluster. 100% discrimination can be achieved by assigning each token to a different cluster. So this evaluation presupposes a reasonable number of clusters.

The problem with this type of evaluation is that it evaluates how well the Brown tag set is reproduced. Although I have not run this evaluation for distributional tagging, both discrimination and accuracy would probably be very low. The reason is that there are many ways to design a set of part-of-speech classes. Why should it be our goal to reproduce one of the many possibilities that was chosen by the collectors of the

Brown corpus? To put it differently, other human-made tag sets would also fare badly if they were evaluated for their ability to reproduce the Brown tag set. So an automatically generated tag set is not necessarily bad just because it does not reproduce the Brown tag set.

For the reasons outlined above, the following evaluation procedure was chosen here:

- Cluster tokens into 200 clusters.
- Label each cluster with the most frequent Brown tag that occurs among its members.
- Evaluate the quality of the clustering using precision and recall.

Precision is the number of correct tokens divided by the sum of correct and incorrect tokens (see Table 3 for an example); that is, precision is the percentage of assignments to a category that were correct. Recall is the number of correct tokens divided by the total number of tokens for a particular category (the total number of tokens of a category is shown in the first column in Table 3 and the other tables); that is, recall is the coverage achieved for a particular category, the percentage of members of that category that were actually assigned to it. The last column of the table gives van Rijsbergen's F measure which computes an aggregate score from precision and recall:[7] (van Rijsbergen, 1979)

$$F = \frac{1}{\alpha \frac{1}{P} + (1 - \alpha) \frac{1}{R}}$$

I chose $\alpha = 0.5$ to give equal weight to precision and recall.

Let me give an example for how to read one of the rows of Table 3, the row marked "ADN". The tag "ADN" (adnominal modifier) occurs 108586 times in the corpus. 34 classes were assigned to this tag. Of all tokens in the 34 classes, 38282 had the correct tag (ADN), and 19528 did not. This means that the precision for the tag "ADN" is:

$$\frac{38282}{38282 + 19528} \approx 0.66$$

(number of correct assignments divided by total number of assignments). Recall for tag "ADN" is:

$$\frac{38282}{108586} \approx 0.35$$

---

[7]Strictly speaking, van Rijsbergen defines the measure E, from which F can be derived as $F = 1 - E$.

(number of correct assignments to a ADN class divided by total number of tokens of tag ADN). The F measure is:

$$F = \frac{1}{0.5\frac{1}{0.66} + (1 - 0.5)\frac{1}{0.35}} \approx 0.46$$

The evaluation procedure just described only evaluates accuracy, not discrimination. (In particular, if n clusters are created, where n is the number of tokens, then accuracy would be 100%. But this argument does not apply here, since only 200 clusters are created.)

I decided to concentrate on accuracy rather than discrimination because in several initial experiments the Brown tags were broken into several smaller categories. In most cases, these smaller categories reflected linguistic distinctions, for example the difference between the base form of a verb used in the present tense ('they run fast') and as an infinitive ('they don't run fast'). In some cases, the distinctions between clusters that contain tokens of the same part of speech reflect purely distributional distinctions that are hard to justify from the point of view of part-of-speech categorization.

tag	description	Penn Treebank tags
ADN	adnominal modifier	ADN* $
CC	conjunction	CC
CD	cardinal	CD
DT	determiner	DT PDT PRP$
IN	preposition	IN
ING	gerunds and present participles	VBG
MD	modal	MD
N	nominal	NNP(S) NN(S)
POS	possessive marker	POS
PRP	pronoun	PRP
RB	adverbial	RB RP RBR RBS
TO	infinitive marker	TO*
VB	infinitive	VB
VBD	inflected verb form	VBD VBZ VBP
VBN	predicative	VBN PRD*
WDT	wh-word	WP($) WRB WDT

TABLE 2 Evaluation tag set. Structural tags derived from parse trees are marked with *.

Ideally, one would want to refine the Brown tag set so that the finer distinctions embodied in distributional clustering can be evaluated. In one case, I was able to incorporate such a distinction by using the parses of the Brown corpus. The tag adjective stands for both adnominal and predicative uses, for example, the uses of "black" in (27).

(27) a. the black cat (adnominal)
b. The cat is black. (predicative)

In a preprocessing step, the Penn Treebank parses of the Brown corpus were used to determine whether a token functions as an adnominal modifier. Adjectives and participles were classified as ADN if immediately dominated by an expansion of a noun, and as PRD, VBN, and VBG if immediately dominated by an expansion of a verb. Nouns and gerunds were classified as N, if they were the head of an NP and as ADN and VBG otherwise. The second tag that was divided up into two smaller categories is TO. Tokens of "to" that head a prepositional phrase were tagged PRP, tokens that head an infinitival phrase were tagged TO (again based on the Penn Treebank parses).

Another finding in preliminary experiments was that distributional tagging does poorly at distinguishing some closely related tags, for example tags of singular and plural nouns and tags of different types of adverbs. For this reason, tags were grouped into metatags as shown in Table 2. In addition, punctuation marks, special symbols, interjections, foreign words and Brown tags with fewer than 100 instances were excluded from the evaluation. For the rest of this chapter, I will use the term "Brown tag" to refer to the tags in Table 2.

As I argued above, the fact that there is some arbitrariness in grouping uses of words into tag classes justifies splitting some tags into smaller categories and grouping other tags into larger categories. As long as there is no compelling argument why one tag set is better than another, linguistically plausible regroupings (such as distinguishing the infinitival marker from the preposition "to" or grouping all adverbs into one group) are legitimate.

However, such a redesign of tag sets would become problematic if two authors each proposed different tag sets and redesigned their evaluation sets to suit their methods. Obviously, an objective evaluation would have to be done against a third neutral set. Or one could look at the parses in the Penn Tree Bank and develop a gradient measure of syntactic similarity between any two syntactic environments. With such a measure, no tag categorization into a fixed number of groups would be necessary, and a fair comparison with any tag induction procedure would be possible.

Despite this caveat I believe that the evaluation procedure adopted here is not problematic. My focus is on comparing different sources of information for tag induction (information on types vs. information on tokens, low-frequency vs. high-frequency items) and on investigating the influence of ambiguity, not on comparability with previous results. Since there have not been any previous numerical evaluations of part-of-speech clustering and since this is the first work on distributional part-of-speech tagging, the results reported here cannot be compared with previous results.

2.7 Experimental Results

d-tag	frequency	# classes	correct	incorrect	precision	recall	F
ADN	108586	34	38282	19528	0.66	0.35	0.46
CC	36808	0	0	0	0.00	0.00	0.00
CD	14674	4	3232	1431	0.69	0.22	0.33
DT	129626	2	125540	31761	0.80	0.97	0.88
IN	142778	3	129421	65134	0.67	0.91	0.77
ING	14753	5	2111	1016	0.68	0.14	0.24
MD	13498	2	13383	13016	0.51	0.99	0.67
N	231434	98	193838	79623	0.71	0.84	0.77
POS	5086	1	4641	1213	0.79	0.91	0.85
PRP	47686	3	43839	21721	0.67	0.92	0.77
RB	54525	7	35364	56291	0.39	0.65	0.48
TO	14497	0	0	0	0.00	0.00	0.00
VB	35342	8	29138	17945	0.62	0.82	0.71
VBD	80058	12	36653	3855	0.90	0.46	0.61
VBN	41146	21	7773	8841	0.47	0.19	0.27
WDT	14093	0	0	0	0.00	0.00	0.00
avg.					0.53	0.52	0.49

TABLE 3 Precision and recall for induction based on word type.

Tables 3 and 4 present results for word type-based induction and induction based on word type and context (i.e., they present results for the experimental setups described in Sections 2.5.3 and 2.5.4). For each Brown tag t, the table lists the frequency of t in the corpus ("frequency"), the number of induced distributional tags $i_0, i_1, \ldots, i_l$, that were assigned to it ("# classes"); the number of times an occurrence of t was correctly labeled as belonging to one of $i_0, i_1, \ldots, i_l$ ("correct"); the number of times that a token of a different Brown tag t' was miscategorized as being an instance of $i_0, i_1, \ldots, i_l$ ("incorrect"); and precision and recall of the categorization of t. Recall that precision is the number of correct tokens divided by the sum of correct and incorrect tokens; and that recall is the number of correct tokens divided by the total number of tokens of t (in the first column). Intuitively, precision is accuracy (what percentage of assignments to a category was correct), and recall is coverage (what percentage of members of a category were covered). The last column shows the F measure.

There are small differences in overall frequency in the tables because some word-based context vectors consist entirely of zeros. There were about a hundred word triplets whose four context vectors did not have non-zero entries and could not be assigned a cluster in the induction from word-based context vectors.

It is clear from the tables that incorporating context improves performance considerably. The F score increases for all Brown tags except CD, with an average improvement of more than 0.20. The tag CD is probably better thought of as describing a word class. There is a wide range of heterogeneous syntactic functions of cardinals in particular contexts: quantificational and adnominal uses, bare NP's ("is one of"), dates and ages ("Jan 1", "gave his age as 25"), and enumerations. In this light, it is not surprising that the word-type method does better on cardinals.

tag	frequency	# classes	correct	incorrect	precision	recall	F
ADN	108532	42	87128	24740	0.78	0.80	0.79
CC	36808	2	28671	1501	0.95	0.78	0.86
CD	14673	1	587	804	0.42	0.04	0.07
DT	129626	6	119534	6166	0.95	0.92	0.94
IN	142778	11	127399	23470	0.84	0.89	0.87
ING	14753	4	3096	4874	0.39	0.21	0.27
MD	13498	2	12983	936	0.93	0.96	0.95
N	231424	68	207828	51496	0.80	0.90	0.85
POS	5086	2	4623	533	0.90	0.91	0.90
PRP	47686	7	44945	12758	0.78	0.94	0.85
RB	54524	16	31184	17371	0.64	0.57	0.61
TO	14497	1	14452	8900	0.62	1.00	0.76
VB	35342	8	29392	6152	0.83	0.83	0.83
VBD	80058	17	64149	8663	0.88	0.80	0.84
VBN	41145	11	25578	11972	0.68	0.62	0.65
WDT	14093	2	1621	1017	0.61	0.12	0.19
avg.					0.75	0.71	0.70

TABLE 4 Precision and recall for induction based on word type and context.

Table 5 shows that performance for generalized context vectors (the experimental setup described in Section 2.5.5) is better than for word-based context vectors (0.72 vs. 0.70). However, the number of Brown tags with better and worse performance is about the same (6 and 7), one cannot conclude with certainty that generalized context vectors induce distributional tags of higher quality. Apparently, the 250 most frequent words capture most of the relevant distributional information so that the additional information from less frequent words available from generalized vectors only has a small effect.

Table 6 looks at results for "natural" contexts, i.e. those not con-

tag	frequency	# classes	correct	incorrect	precision	recall	F
ADN	108586	50	91893	26786	0.77	0.85	0.81
CC	36808	4	34127	6431	0.84	0.93	0.88
CD	14674	3	3327	1530	0.68	0.23	0.34
DT	129626	10	120968	5763	0.95	0.93	0.94
IN	142778	8	123516	22067	0.85	0.87	0.86
ING	14753	2	3798	7159	0.35	0.26	0.30
MD	13498	3	13175	1059	0.93	0.98	0.95
N	231434	70	201890	33204	0.86	0.87	0.87
POS	5086	2	4932	1636	0.75	0.97	0.85
PRP	47686	5	37535	9221	0.80	0.79	0.79
RB	54524	9	29892	18397	0.62	0.55	0.58
TO	14497	1	14486	10722	0.57	1.00	0.73
VB	35342	7	28879	6559	0.81	0.82	0.82
VBD	80058	15	66457	12079	0.85	0.83	0.84
VBN	41145	10	26960	17354	0.61	0.66	0.63
WDT	14093	1	2223	563	0.80	0.16	0.26
avg.					0.75	0.73	0.72

TABLE 5 Precision and recall for induction based on generalized context vectors.

tag	frequency	# classes	correct	incorrect	precision	recall	F
ADN	63771	36	54398	12203	0.82	0.85	0.83
CC	16148	4	15657	1798	0.90	0.97	0.93
CD	7008	1	1857	918	0.67	0.26	0.38
DT	87914	9	82206	2663	0.97	0.94	0.95
IN	100260	10	94714	7023	0.93	0.94	0.94
ING	7268	2	1243	1412	0.47	0.17	0.25
MD	11244	3	10363	476	0.96	0.92	0.94
N	111368	49	100105	14450	0.87	0.90	0.89
POS	3202	1	2912	255	0.92	0.91	0.91
PRP	23946	7	22877	4062	0.85	0.96	0.90
RB	32331	16	21037	9922	0.68	0.65	0.66
TO	11549	1	11068	420	0.96	0.96	0.96
VB	26714	11	24036	4119	0.85	0.90	0.88
VBD	56540	33	51016	8488	0.86	0.90	0.88
VBN	24804	14	18889	7448	0.72	0.76	0.74
WDT	8329	3	3691	670	0.85	0.44	0.58
avg.					0.83	0.78	0.79

TABLE 6 Precision and recall for induction for natural contexts.

taining punctuation marks and rare words. Performance is consistently better than for the evaluation on all contexts, indicating that the low quality of the distributional information about punctuation marks and rare words is a difficulty for successful tag induction.

Even for "natural" contexts, performance varies considerably. It is fairly good for prepositions, determiners, pronouns, conjunctions, the infinitive marker, modals, and the possessive marker. Tag induction fails for cardinals (for the reasons mentioned above) and for "-ing" forms (to be discussed below).

Some of the Brown tags are assigned a high number of clusters (e.g., 47 for N, 37 for ADN). A closer look reveals that many clusters embody finer distinctions. Some examples: Nouns in cluster 0 are heads of larger noun phrases, whereas the nouns in cluster 1 are full-fledged NPs. The members of classes 29 and 111 function as subjects. Class 49 consists of proper nouns. However, a manual inspection reveals that there are many pairs or triples of clusters that should be collapsed into one on linguistic grounds. They were separated on distributional criteria that don't have linguistic correlates.

tag	frequency	# classes	correct	incorrect	precision	recall	F
ADN	53215	37	48043	4850	0.91	0.90	0.91
CC	14398	3	14034	2146	0.87	0.97	0.92
CD	6674	2	1480	1247	0.54	0.22	0.31
DT	81339	12	77384	4778	0.94	0.95	0.95
IN	93955	9	90199	5329	0.94	0.96	0.95
ING	6574	2	1875	2977	0.39	0.29	0.33
MD	10773	2	9790	531	0.95	0.91	0.93
N	102360	47	96376	6881	0.93	0.94	0.94
POS	2949	1	2925	7	1.00	0.99	0.99
PRP	22624	4	19136	3266	0.85	0.85	0.85
RB	29563	24	23321	7433	0.76	0.79	0.77
TO	10355	1	10355	82	0.99	1.00	1.00
VB	24380	9	23733	387	0.98	0.97	0.98
VBD	51499	31	50258	2108	0.96	0.98	0.97
VBN	21832	15	19738	4841	0.80	0.90	0.85
WDT	7805	1	2491	2294	0.52	0.32	0.40
avg.					0.83	0.81	0.81

TABLE 7 Performance for disambiguated words in natural contexts.

Table 7 demonstrates that the acquisition of syntactic categorization would be easier without part-of-speech ambiguity. If disambiguated words are used for part-of-speech induction (i.e., each possible word-tag combination is replaced by a new word as described in Section 2.5.6), then performance of about 90% is achieved for all Brown tags except for four that seem particularly difficult for distributional methods: CD, ING, RB, and WDT.

In the overall model, the tag component computes distributional tags for the words of a sentence, i.e. representations of the words' local syntactic functions. Syntax and semantics then assemble these tags into an initial representation of the complete sentence, taking into consideration global syntactic constraints such as long-distance relationships and agreement. I chose a multidimensional space for representing tags in order to formalize the intuition that local constellations favor and disfavor global constellations *in a graded manner*. For example, the following three examples are given in order of increasing preference for interpreting "to" as an infinitive marker:

(28)   a. to Boston .
       b. to work .
       c. to sing .

This preference in turn influences the initial hypothesis about the structure of the complete sentence. In an environment like (29) which is compatible with both prepositional construction ('to Boston') and infinitival construction ('to sing'), the preference of tag and sentence for, say, the prepositional construction are closely linked: the higher the preference of the tag, the higher the preference of the sentence.

(29)   "I returned _".[8]

If the tag space described here is a good model of the tag component, then proximity in the space must correspond to proximity in grammatical function. For example, the tags in (28) should be close to each other so that syntax and semantics can determine preferences in contexts like (29) which differ quantitatively (according to the distance of, say, "to Boston ." from "to work ."), but not qualitatively.

A good way to test the hypothesis that spatial proximity corresponds to grammatical proximity is to look at neighboring clusters. If the clusters are just randomly arranged in the space with, for example, determiners next to verbs and the infinitive marker next to nouns, then the goal of representing gradedness is clearly not satisfied. On the other hand, if neighboring clusters and the regions between them represent clines like (28) correctly, then the tag space can be claimed to model aspects of the proposed tag component.

Let me first analyze one pair of neighboring clusters in detail, and then present a general analysis of how well spatial proximity models grammatical proximity. In both cases, data from the experiment in

---

[8]The sentence "I returned to sign." is to be read as "I returned in order to sing."

Table 6 are analyzed (natural contexts, words are not artificially disambiguated).

	position	left word		middle word		right word	
cluster 50	0.00	to	0.022	house	0.440	in	0.075
	0.05	to	0.022	house	0.457	in	0.074
	0.10	to	0.022	work	0.454	in	0.073
	0.15	to	0.021	work	0.446	in	0.072
	0.20	to	0.021	work	0.440	in	0.072
	0.25	to	0.021	work	0.437	in	0.073
	0.30	to	0.021	work	0.437	in	0.073
	0.35	to	0.020	work	0.440	in	0.074
	0.40	to	0.020	work	0.446	in	0.076
	0.45	to	0.020	work	0.456	in	0.078
	0.50	to	0.020	work	0.469	in	0.080
	0.55	to	0.020	work	0.485	in	0.083
	0.60	to	0.020	work	0.505	in	0.086
	0.65	to	0.020	work	0.528	in	0.090
	0.70	to	0.019	work	0.554	in	0.093
	0.75	to	0.019	work	0.584	in	0.098
	0.80	to	0.019	work	0.616	in	0.102
	0.85	to	0.019	play	0.649	in	0.107
	0.90	to	0.019	go	0.644	in	0.112
	0.95	to	0.019	go	0.619	in	0.118
cluster 152	1.00	to	0.019	go	0.597	to	0.121

TABLE 8 Word triplets between the centroids of clusters 50 and 152.

2.7.1 A Detailed Analysis of a Cline

If we call the SVD mapping from the 1,000-dimensional space of concatenated context vectors to the reduced 50-dimensional space φ, we can define an inverse function φ^{-1} which takes a 50-dimensional vector and computes the four original context vectors. Table 8 and Figure 4 show part of such an inverse mapping for the centroids of neighboring clusters 50 and 152 and the region between them. Cluster 50 contains words with a noun-verb ambiguity in contexts like (30a) and cluster 152 verbs without such an ambiguity in the same type of context (30b).

(30) a. to house _
       b. to appear _

Table 8 and Figure 4 trace a direct line between the centroids of the two clusters in order to demonstrate the gradience of change when moving between locations in TAG SPACE. Table 8 presents the word triplets that are located at the two cluster centroids and at 19 intermediate points as will be explained in a moment. It is apparent from the table that there is a gradual transition from words with a noun-verb ambiguity whose noun category dominates ("house") to verbs which are rarely used as nouns ("go"). Intermediate points are occupied by "work" and "play", words that have equally salient uses as verbs and nouns.

The word triplets on the cline were computed by applying the inverse function φ^{-1} to the two cluster centroids and 19 intermediate vectors, i.e., the vectors $\vec{w_\alpha}$ for $\alpha = 0.00, 0.05, \ldots, 1.00$.

$$\vec{w_\alpha} = (1 - \alpha)\vec{c}_{50} + \alpha\vec{c}_{152}$$

$$\vec{v_\alpha} = \varphi^{-1}(\vec{w_\alpha})$$

where $\vec{c}_{50}$ is the centroid of cluster 50 and $\vec{c}_{152}$ is the centroid of cluster 152. Each $\vec{v_\alpha}$ consists of four context vectors: the right context vector of the preceding word, the left and right context vectors of the central word and the left context vector of the following word. For each α, Table 8 gives the word whose right context vector is most similar to the first context vector of $\vec{v_\alpha}$, the word whose left and right context vectors are most similar to the second and third context vector of $\vec{v_\alpha}$, and the word whose left context vector is most similar to the fourth context vector of $\vec{v_\alpha}$. The table also lists the distance between each word's vector(s) and the appropriate constituent vector(s) of $\vec{v_\alpha}$.

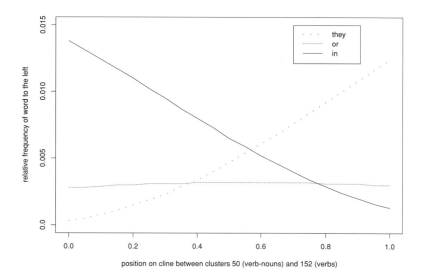

FIGURE 4 The impact of the relative frequencies of three words ("they", "or", and "in") on the categorization of an ambiguous token.

Figure 4 displays the (reconstructed) relative frequencies in the corpus of three words, "they", "or", and "in", in the second context vector of $\vec{v}_\alpha = \varphi^{-1}(\vec{w}_\alpha)$, that is the left context vector of the middle word of the triplet that is represented by $\vec{w}_\alpha$. In other words, for w_l in $\vec{v}_\alpha = v_r w_l w_r x_r$ (the concatenation of four context vectors), Figure 4 shows the relative frequencies of "they", "or", and "in" as recorded in w_l. For example, for $\vec{v}_0 = \varphi^{-1}(\vec{c}_{50})$ we have relative frequencies of 0.0138 for "in", 0.0028 for "or", and 0.0003 for "they". These three numbers correspond to the starting points of the three lines in the figure at 0.0, the position of $\vec{c}_{50}$ on the horizontal axis. In other words, the cluster centroid corresponds to a triplet whose middle word (w) occurs to the right of "in" in 1.38% of all occurrences, to the right of "or" in 0.28% of all occurrences, and to the right of "they" in 0.03% of all occurrences. Consequently, the left context vector of w, w_l, has the entries 0.0138, 0.0028, and 0.0003 for "in", "or", and "they", respectively. The other points on the horizontal axis indicate the relative strengths of "in", "or", and "they" for $0 \leq \alpha \leq 1$.

Figure 4 gives an example of how distributional evidence influences categorization in a graded manner. If a verb like "appear" occurs in many instances of the form "they appear" and in no instances of the form "in appear", then that is good evidence that it is used as a verb in a local context like "to appear ...". (This is the tag at 1.0 in Figure 4, corresponding to the centroid of cluster 152.) If on the other hand a word like "supply" occurs rarely in contexts like "they supply ..." and frequently in contexts like "in supply", then local context cannot determine whether it is used as a verb or a as noun in "to supply [...]". (This is the tag at 0.0 in Figure 4, corresponding to cluster 50.) Information on how often "or" occurs to the left of "appear" or "supply" does not affect the categorization decision because "or" occurs before nouns and verbs with about the same frequency.

The categorization is graded in that increasing evidence for verbhood decreases uncertainty about labeling w in "to w ..." as a verb. The more occurrences of "they w ..." and the less occurrences of "in w ..." are recorded in the corpus, the higher the confidence in categorizing "to w ..." as an infinitive and the closer the resulting tag ends up to cluster 152, the "pure verb" cluster. This example demonstrates that the model successfully formalizes the notion of "category squish". Depending on the available evidence, tags are represented as points on a cline rather than categorized as belonging to discrete categories.

2.7.2   The Structure of Tag Space

This section evaluates how well the internal structure of tag space models similarity of grammatical function. For all tags, the relationship between the tag and its closest neighbor is investigated.

158 tags have tags of the same category as their nearest neighbor. For example, cluster 11 contains mostly uses of "which" as a relative pronoun and its nearest neighbor, cluster 170, relative pronoun uses of "that". Cluster 13 contains prepositions in PP's that modify a noun, its nearest neighbor cluster 42 prepositions in PP's that modify a verb. Cluster 19 contains occurrences of the determiner "an", its nearest neighbor, cluster 56, occurrences of "some", "any", and "many" as quantifiers that modify nouns.

42 tags had nearest neighbors of a different category. A description of these 42 cases follows. The reader not interested in the details of the experiment can skip this section and read the general discussion of the types of errors that were made in section 2.8.

Only 35 pairs of clusters are analyzed in what follows since 7 pairs of clusters were nearest neighbors of each other. The relation "x is nearest neighbor of y" is not symmetric. If x is in a sparsely populated part of Tag Space, and y in a densely populated part, then y can be the nearest neighbor of x, although there are clusters that are closer to y than x.

The 35 tag pairs fall in 6 classes as shown in Table 9:

- unique constructions
- squishes (or clines)
- distributionally similar contexts that can be distinguished on semantic grounds
- distributionally similar contexts that can be distinguished by means of non-local dependencies
- distributionally similar contexts that can be distinguished by different prosody
- rare constructions

Unique constructions. For some tags, the nearest neighbor is of a different category simply because it is unique. The infinitive marker "to" (class 33), first names (class 180), and the use of "that" as a relative pronoun in subject relatives (class 170) are all unique so that the closest tag is only indirectly related (e.g. the use of "to" as a preposition for class 33).

Squishes. Some of the pairs are clines between related syntactic contexts, similar to the cline from cluster 50 to cluster 152 discussed above

type of error	cluster		nearest neighbor	
unique	33	TO	10	IN
construction	180	ADN	79	N
	170	WDT	83	IN
"squish"	56	DT	87	CD
	62	N	50	VB
	85	VBD	136	N
	130	VBD	38	VB
	134	N	195	VBN
	153	DT	2	ADN
only semantically	98	RB	182	ADN
different	99	VBD	184	VBN
	102	RB	99	VBD
	182	ADN	165	RB
non-local	4	RB	83	IN
dependency	26	RB	88	VBD
	35	VBD	190	VBN
	71	VBD	184	VBN
	73	POS	107	VBD
	82	VBN	4	RB
	88	VBD	194	RB
	124	RB	189	VBN
	136	N	167	VBN
	157	VBD	184	VBN
only	57	VBG	139	N
prosodically	139	N	149	VB
different	169	WDT	57	VBG
rare	1	N	34	VBN
construction	18	IN	17	CC
	84	VBD	124	RB
	96	RB	64	ADN
	108	VBD	117	N
	109	RB	117	N
	132	RB	136	N
	172	RB	88	VBD
	175	N	110	VBN

TABLE 9 Clusters whose nearest neighbor is of a different category.

(30). Cluster 56 contains NP-modifying quantifiers like "some" (classified as DT in the Penn Treebank) and cluster 87 NP-modifying cardinals, two closely related classes. The pair of clusters 62 and 50 consists of nouns (cluster 62) and ambiguous noun-verbs (cluster 50) in contexts like "to place in". Similar clines can be observed between 85 and 136 (noun-verbs and nouns), 130 and 38 (inflected and infinitival verbs), 134 and 195 (adnominal and nominal conjunctions, for example "longer *young* and" (mainly adnominal) vs. "this *century* and" (nominal)), and 153 and 2 (determiners like "one" and "both" vs. determiner "this").

Only semantically distinguishable contexts. Cluster 182 contains adjectives like "better", "far" and "more" that can also be used as adverbs. The ambiguity of phrases like "more popular measures" (additional measures vs. measures that are more popular) explains the clines between contexts in which the adverbial reading is preferred (98 and 165) and contexts in which the adnominal reading is preferred (182).

Non-local dependencies. For the largest class of pairs of neighboring clusters with different tags, non-local information plays an important role in categorization. Recall that only the two immediately adjacent words are used as context for categorizing tags. There are two syntactic categories for which local information is often insufficient: adverbs and "-ed" forms.

Adverbs occur in a large variety of different syntactic contexts. It is not clear whether there is in fact a part of speech "adverb" to the same degree that there are nouns and verbs. Schachter (1985) gives a negative definition of adverbs, apparently because he could not find any common positive traits:

> we can say that adverbs function as modifiers of constituents other than nouns. (page 20)

The problem with "-ed" forms is similar. Since past participles in English double as past tense forms, the context vectors of "-ed" forms record both context types, which makes them less characteristic than, say, context vectors of nouns and determiners.

For both adverbs and "-ed" forms, wider syntactic context is needed for reliable categorization. For example, clusters 35 and 190 contain "-ed" forms in the context "-ed to": past tense forms in cluster 35 ("melodies seemed to") and past participles in cluster 190 ("materials needed to"). The syntactic structure of a sentence determines whether the "-ed" form is the main verb or a participle modifying an NP, so non-local context would improve the structure of Tag Space by making past tense forms similar to other past tense forms and past participles similar to other past participles.

For lack of wider syntactic context, the regions of TAG SPACE dealing with adverbs and "-ed" forms do not have a structure that corresponds well with the linguistic facts, and hence the nearest neighbors of adverb and "-ed" clusters are not very intuitive.

Only prosodically distinguishable contexts. One important source of information that is available to the child, but not to the induction procedure discussed here is prosody. Pauses and intonation often indicate the boundaries of syntactic constituents. Three of the clusters in Table 9 would arguably have different neighbors if such boundaries were indicated in the Brown corpus. Cluster 139 contains nouns with a noun phrase as their right neighbor, for example, "of stress one" in "Confucius held that in times of stress one should take short views". The members of clusters 57 and 149 are verbal elements that are similar to nouns: gerunds in the case of cluster 57 ("studying") and verbs that can also function as nouns in cluster 149 ("command", "name"). It would be easy to detect the categorically different nature of 139 on the one hand and 57/149 on the other hand if the prosodic break between the two NP's in contexts like "of stress | one" and the prosodic continuity in contexts like "to command his" were available as input to the categorization procedure. Similarly, cluster 169 contains contexts like "in which the" that (like cluster 139) exhibit a prosodic gap between two NP's that is inaccessible to the purely distributional learning mechanism.

Rare constructions. Finally, the clusters of rare constructions are often categorically (rather than gradually) different from their neighbors because such constructions have only a small influence on the structure of the space. An example for such a rare construction is cluster 34, consisting of past participles of verbs with "of"-complements ("composed of", "reminded of", "spoken of"). Compare a frequent past participle construction like "built on" with "composed of". "built" occurs frequently with prepositions to its right, and "on" occurs frequently with past participles to its left. Consequently, the reduced concatenation vector of, say, "is built on" will be similar to other such past participle + preposition constructions. On the other hand, the right context vector of "composed" records no occurrences of prepositions that are frequently governed by verbs. The left context vector of "of" records few past participles. For this reason, the reduced concatenation vector of, say, is "is composed of" will be dissimilar from "is built on" or "was seen at".

Other rare constructions whose nearest neighbors are "misbehaved" for similar reasons are postposed adverbs like "ago" and "else" (88/172) and adverbs and adjectives in postposed reduced relatives (109/117).

2.8 Discussion

2.8.1 Ambiguity

An important contribution of this chapter is that the problem of part-of-speech ambiguity is addressed. It was not accounted for in previous cognitive and computational models of part-of-speech acquisition. The evaluation of Tag Space demonstrates that learning in the presence of ambiguity is possible. For example, precision and recall for the infinitive marker "to" (which needs to be distinguished from the preposition "to") are 96%. The word "use" is an example of a lexical item with a noun-verb ambiguity. 154 of its 184 verbal uses and 267 of its 275 nominal uses (in the experiment described in Table 6) were classified correctly.

Does Tag Space go too far in that word tokens are tagged according to context only? As mentioned above such an approach would assign "rarely" and "will" to the same part-of-speech class in sentences (25a) and (25b), clearly an incorrect decision. Since Tag Space bases categorization decisions both on context (the two "outer" component vectors of a tag vector) and overall distribution of a word in the corpus (the two "inner" component vectors), "rarely" and "will" are assigned to different classes. However, there are more subtle cases like (31) (suggested by Chris Manning):

(31)   You should help the poor.

Here, a careful analysis is necessary to categorize "poor". In fact, depending on the linguistic theory used, either tagging (i.e., the tag "noun" or the tag "adjective") may be the result of the analysis. I have not done an extensive evaluation of Tag Space for adjectives in syntactic environments such as (31), but I am sure that for many tokens the model does not make the right trade off between context and type. Since each tag vector consists of four component vectors, with two representing context and two representing type, context and type always receive the same weight in the categorization decision. It is not clear that this is correct. It may be necessary to make the weighting dependent on the particular context or the particular type of a token. This question needs to be addressed in future research.

Not all ambiguity was resolved correctly. The two main difficulties for the model are the cases discussed above: words without syntactic bonds with their neighbors and locally ambiguous triples like "(the) van delivered to" where, depending on global context, "delivered" can be a past tense form or a past participle. Additional sources of information (mainly non-local syntactic constraints and semantics) need to be incorporated for completely successful acquisition of ambiguity.

However, the model still provides a better account of ambiguity learning than previous models. This is particularly clear from the experiments on word-based induction and induction from disambiguated contexts. Results of word-based induction (which assumes that words are not ambiguous, see Table 3) are by far worse than those of context-based induction which takes account of ambiguity (Table 4). Similarly, if we manipulate the corpus such that words are unambiguous as assumed by other models, then part-of-speech learning becomes easier (Tables 6 vs. 7).

2.8.2 Gradience

The results of the previous section show that most regions of TAG SPACE model similarity in syntactic function well: Three quarters of the tag groups have the same category as their nearest neighbors. The difference in category between the remaining categories and their neighbors was analyzed in Section 2.7.2. Six types of categories that differed from their neighbors were found: unique constructions, squishes, only semantically distinguishable constructions, constructions characterized by non-local dependencies, only prosodically distinguishable constructions and rare constructions. The first two types do not pose a problem for TAG SPACE. Squishes between categories are what TAG SPACE is intended to represent, so they are a strength rather than a weakness of the model. Unique constructions are by definition different from their nearest neighbors, so that an indirect relation between the unique construction and its nearest neighbor (as for example the use of "to" as an infinitive marker in class 33 and as a preposition in class 10) is not surprising.

The other four types of errors point to limitations of the model. I attribute them to the lack of prosody, non-local syntax, semantics and world knowledge (pragmatics) in the model. These are precisely the components that would interact with TAG SPACE in a complete model of comprehension as sketched in Figure 1. Rare constructions are affected by the absence of all three components in the implementation presented here. I will now discuss the four error types in more detail.

The importance of prosodic information for the acquisition of syntax has been stressed by (Morgan and Newport, 1981). Steedman (1991) argues that prosody helps hearers to select the correct parse among a large number of possible structures. Finch and Chater (1994) draw attention to prosody in the context of part-of-speech induction. The errors discussed under the rubric of only prosodically distinguishable constructions in Table 9 support the view that prosody contributes important information for part-of-speech learning. For example, words like "command" with a verb-noun ambiguity are difficult to categorize correctly when followed by noun phrases, the contrast of "in command a watch" in (32a) vs. "to command a battalion" in (32b). The tagging "preposition noun article noun" is consistent with both strings if taken out of context whereas intonation immediately distinguishes between them.

(32) a. (I gave the officer) in command a watch
      b. (he wants) to command a battalion

Another constraint on part-of-speech categorization that I have neglected is non-local syntactic dependence. I am not only thinking of the classical cases like filler-gap dependencies, but of all constellations where a word does not form a close link with either of its neighbors, so that only wider syntactic context can pin down its syntactic function. Such constellations are fatal in Tag Space since the neighboring words are the only ones used to characterize syntactic context here.

Not surprisingly, parts of speech that tend to bond strongly with a neighboring word (articles with a following noun, the infinitive marker and modals with the following infinitive) are the easiest to induce. Parts of speech that can float relatively freely in the sentence are the most difficult to categorize reliably. Adverbs are the prime example of an element that can exercise a particular function in a large number of positions that are not necessarily close to the phrase that is semantically modified. For example, all three positions of "only" in (33) can express the meaning that you should only ask for John Miller.

(33) a. Only ask for John Miller.
      b. Ask only for John Miller.
      c. Ask for John Miller only.

In a few cases, close syntactic relationships between neighboring words are systematically ambiguous (as opposed to lacking completely, as in the case of "only"). This is why many of the category pairs listed in Table 9 are past participles and past tense forms. The "-ed"-form in strings like 'noun "-ed"-form preposition' can be either the past participle of a reduced relative or the main verb of the sentence in its past tense form.

Both adverbs and "-ed"-forms could be categorized correctly with more context. Except for relatively infrequent inversions, the verb "saw" always occurs to the right of a noun phrase, whereas "only" does not. This generalization eludes the procedure that constructs Tag Space because direct adjacency of noun phrase and "saw" is not required (e.g., in "I only saw John"). Similarly, if a "-ed" form is used in a reduced relative, there must be a different main verb in the sentence, which is not the case for past tense forms. Again, direct adjacency is too limiting a condition for the Tag Space model to pick up on this generalization.

These considerations suggest that incorporating more context than just immediate neighbors would improve performance on parts of speech that are characterized by non-local dependencies.

As for semantic constraints, the adverbial and quantificational readings of a construction like "more popular measures" mentioned in the discussion of Table 9 could be easily distinguished if semantic input was available in the construction of TAG SPACE.

The case of the tags "VBN" and "PRD" (past participles (as in "the *trained* dog") and predicative adjectives (as in "John is *tall.*")) also demonstrates the difficulties of missing semantic information. There are hardly any distributional clues for distinguishing "VBN" and "PRD" since both are mainly used as complements of "to be". Because of phrases like "I had sweet potatoes", forms of "have" cannot serve as a reliable discriminator either. The linguistically inappropriate common tag class for "VBN" and "PRD" was created to show that they are reasonably well distinguished from other parts of speech, even if not from each other. The "semantics" and "pragmatics" components in Figure 1 would be able to distinguish the states described by phrases of the form "*to be* adjective" from the processes described by phrases of the form "*to be* past participle". A complete comprehension model should thus be able to learn the "VBN" vs. "PRD" distinction as well as the "RB" vs. "ADN" distinction discussed above.

A last group of systematic errors is due to rare words and rare constructions. Rare words are difficult because of lack of distributional evidence. For example, "ties" is used as a verb only 2 times (out of 15 occurrences in the corpus). Both occurrences are miscategorized, since its context vectors do not provide enough evidence for the verbal use.

Rare syntactic constructions pose a related problem: There are not enough instances to justify the creation of a separate cluster. For example, verbs taking bare infinitives were classified as adverbs since this is too rare a phenomenon to provide strong distributional evidence ("we do not DARE speak of", "legislation could HELP remove").

As in the case of the other deficiencies of TAG SPACE, it is again plausible that the other components of a complete natural language system would compensate for TAG SPACE's poor performance. The distributional component is most sensitive to frequency. In the extreme case, if a word or a construction occurs for the first time, no distributional evidence is available at all. In contrast, the other components would be much less affected. For example, expectations about the meaning of the sentence based on world knowledge would operate in processing as for any other sentence. If the other components compensate for missing distributional information, then TAG SPACE could characterize rare and frequent items with similar reliability.

There is one additional important source of information for part-of-speech classification that I have omitted in Figure 1: morphology. This is because English morphology is impoverished in comparison to some other languages. An automatic procedure for discovering morphological suffixes would have added another level of complexity to the acquisition model.

One class suffered considerably from the decision to exclude morphology: present participles and gerunds. They are difficult because they exhibit both verbal and nominal properties and occur in a wide variety of different contexts. But they all share one morphological characteristic: the suffix "-ing". The fact that Maratsos and Chalkley (1980) rely heavily on morphology in their model of children's acquisition of part-of-speech also indicates the importance of morphology for part-of-speech acquisition.

I have argued that the cases in which spatial proximity in TAG SPACE does not model grammatical similarity are precisely those for which a more complete model of language comprehension would provide the crucial information (prosodic, non-local syntactic, semantic, or morphological) that would make completely successful acquisition possible. So the deficiencies of the similarity structure are due to its restricted access to relevant information and not due to the basic design of the model. If this is true, then TAG SPACE demonstrates that there is a viable alternative to the traditional concept of parts of speech as discrete and unrelated categories. In TAG SPACE, categories are related to each other by proximity: categories with similar syntactic function are close in the space. In addition, TAG SPACE models clines from one category to another, transitions in which the properties of the first category are gradually weakened and the properties of the other are gradually strengthened. The arguments by Ross and Tabor that were discussed above suggest that such a model of syntactic categorization is preferable to the traditional one.

As I indicated earlier in my discussion of (Chomsky, 1961) the distinction between gradient and discrete models of syntactic categorization is not as clear-cut as what I've just said might suggest. For example, there is the well-known representation of the four basic categories noun, verb, preposition, and adjective in terms of two features, N and V, a noun being $[+ N, - V]$, a verb $[- N, + V]$, an adjective $[+ N, + V]$, and a preposition $[- N, - V]$. Noun and adjective are more similar in such a scheme than noun and verb, so some amount of similarity can be modeled. The finer the categorization the subtler the degrees of difference that are captured. The limit of a process of consecutively finer categorizations is a completely gradient model without categorical distinctions.

There is actually evidence for just such a convergence of the two views. Lexical entries in NLP systems are becoming increasingly more complex to the point of there being a large number of words with unique entries, but only small differences from their "nearest neighbors". A feature lexicon of this kind is not far from the gradient model of syntactic categorization I have defended here.

Finally, there is one advantage of gradient representations that I have not exploited here and will leave for future work: gradient representations facilitate incremental change. Part-of-speech acquisition is a process from ignorance (or near-ignorance if one assumes innate knowledge) to perfect competence. In Chapter 4 I will argue that gradient representations can better model the transition which does not seem to involve any of the abrupt changes that one might expect with discrete representations. Elman's connectionist model addresses this transition problem for learning unambiguous syntactic categories (Elman, 1990). Elman has proposed a general solution for the transition problem in his 1991 paper on the "importance of starting small" (Elman, 1991). He argues that if either the capacity of the learning device or the difficulty of the learning problem are increased gradually, then learning is much easier. For example, in one connectionist simulation the proportion of complex sentences (i.e., sentences with embedded relative clauses) in the training set was gradually increased over time. In another simulation, the memory span of a connectionist model was gradually increased. In both cases, learning was facilitated when compared with a model that was trained with the full training set and the full memory span from the start. The general approach of "starting small" seems a promising avenue to explore in order to address the transition problem in the acquisition of part-of-speech ambiguity.

2.8.3   Innateness

In my discussion of (Pinker, 1984), I showed that the case for syntax-specific innateness is weak. The standard argument of the poverty of the stimulus applies to highly idiosyncratic constructions such as reduced conditionals as well as to the universals most commonly argued to be innate in generative grammar (e.g., null-subject parameter and bounding parameters). Moreover, it is not enough to posit innate categories, one must also demonstrate how they are grounded in language input. There is no convincing argument that linking external and innate internal categories is easier than learning the external categories in the first place. This evidence taken together with the success of the computational model presented here (which has no syntax-specific constraints built in) shows that the arguments for innateness are weak. According to Occam's razor, if both theories of acquisition, the one relying on innate knowledge and the one relying on general cognitive capabilities, are successful in explaining acquisition, then one should give preference to the simpler one, the cognitive theory.

An additional complication for the innateness theory is that part-of-speech systems vary considerably across languages. Even the universality of nouns and verbs has been challenged (Schachter, 1985). Schachter (1985) writes concerning this point:

> It must be acknowledged however, that there is not always a clear basis for deciding whether two distinguishable open classes of words that occur in a language should be identified as different parts of speech or as subclasses of a single part of speech. The reason for this is that the open parts-of-speech classes must be distinguished from one another on the basis of a *cluster of properties,* none of which by itself can be claimed to be a necessary and sufficient condition for assignment to a particular class. And the fact is that languages vary considerably in the extent to which the properties associated with different open word classes form discrete clusters. Typically there is some overlap, some sharing of properties, as well as some differentiation. (Schachter 1985:6)

This is an additional dilemma for the innateness view. If one postulates weak knowledge about syntactic categories ("nouns are objects"), then it is unclear why that knowledge could not be inferred from other cognitive resources. If one postulates strong knowledge about syntactic categories, then that knowledge would actually be an impediment to correct acquisition because it does not capture universal properties. This is because the cluster of properties that categorizes a given part of speech in a particular language can omit any of its (universally) typical properties. A child that is looking for just that property in her native language would be hopelessly confused if she could not find a matching external category.

The only type of innate knowledge I have addressed here directly is innate knowledge about syntactic categories. An in-depth investigation of other types of innate knowledge, for example syntactic constraints such as the CNPC, would require building and analyzing a different set of computational models. However, I think that to the extent that learnability with general cognitive means can be shown for phenomena like syntactic categorization and subcategorization (the latter in Chapter 4), phenomena which are held to be innate by many, the indispensability of other types of syntax-specific innate knowledge will also increasingly come under doubt.

Even if syntax-specific innate knowledge is not necessary, all models discussed here rely on general cognitive capabilities for learning. So there can be no debate that innate knowledge (possibly including language-specific phonetic and phonological capabilities) is indispensable for part-of-speech acquisition.

2.9 Conclusion

I draw three main conclusion from the work presented in this chapter. First, TAG SPACE is a viable alternative to traditional discrete theories of syntactic categorization. Its similarity structure models similarity of syntactic function. Rather than assuming discrete categories with sharp boundaries, the representational medium of a multi-dimensional space can capture smooth clines between categories.

Secondly, the case for syntax-specific innate knowledge in part-of-speech acquisition (as presented for example by Pinker (1984)) was shown to be weak. Instead, I have defended a theory of multiple sources of information for acquisition whose combination is powerful enough to account for successful acquisition in the absence of syntax-specific innate knowledge. Several researchers have stressed the importance of combining multiple sources for acquisition (Braine, 1987; Fisher et al., 1991; Finch and Chater, 1994). However, here it is supported by a thoroughly evaluated computational model, TAG SPACE, which learns without domain-specific knowledge.

Finally, TAG SPACE can deal with ambiguous input. In contrast to previous cognitive and computational models, TAG SPACE provides an account of learning in the presence of ambiguity, one of the most difficult and pervasive phenomena in the study of language.

3

Associational Information in the Acquisition of Semantic Categorization

This chapter presents a computational model of the acquisition of semantic categorization. In particular, I will attempt an account of how *senses* are acquired since semantic categorization can only be considered successful if ambiguity is resolved.

The traditional notion of ambiguity is that words have a fixed number of senses and that only one of the senses is used at any given time. Drawing on research on polysemy, I will defend an alternative view according to which sense individuation is gradient, ranging from coarse distinctions like "outer space" vs. "office space" to fine ones like "exhibition space" vs. "office space". A second well-known phenomenon, which I call co-activation, motivates my claim that several senses of a word can be invoked in one context. I will argue that co-activation is pervasive (and not limited to puns) if fine sense distinctions are taken into account.

These two insights are the basis for a theory of senses as *groups of similar contexts.* A sense is simply a group of contextual uses of a word which are semantically similar with each other and semantically dissimilar to other uses. A closely related theory for semantic similarity of unambiguous words has been put forward by Miller and Charles (1991). The primary means of characterizing contexts will be word associations. This choice was made because this is a source of information that is readily available from the large text corpora that are the basis for the computational experiments. Limitations that result from this constraint will be discussed below.

The concept of a sense as a group of similar contexts of a word will be tested in the computational model WORD SPACE. WORD SPACE consists of a real-valued multi-dimensional space in which each word and each context are represented as a vector. A novel word-sense disambiguation algorithm, context-group disambiguation, is proposed whose performance is evaluated on a large newswire text.

Apart from ambiguity and gradience, innateness is the third common thread in this book. The claim that word senses are innate is not as prominent as similar claims for part-of-speech categorization and subcategorization. Still, there is at least one strong proponent of this view, Jerry Fodor (1975). The assumption also implicitly creeps into some of the previous computational models of semantic acquisition. I will argue that senses do not have to be innate to be acquired.

The chapter is organized as follows. Section 3.1 motivates my view of senses as gradient and capable of coactivation. Sections 3.2 and 3.3 discuss computational models of semantic acquisition and disambiguation. Sections 3.4 and 3.5 describe Word Space, context-group disambiguation, and results of several computational experiments. The last two sections discuss Word Space's implications for the issues that were raised throughout the chapter and state my conclusions.

3.1   On the Nature of Semantic Ambiguity

A common view of semantic categorization is that each word in a sentence is given one semantic category and that further processing proceeds from there. On this view, unambiguous words have only one category. Categorizing them is therefore a simple matter of looking up their semantic category. Ambiguous words have several semantic categories or meanings. In order to assign them a correct semantic category in context, they have to be disambiguated. We find this view expressed in one of the standard textbooks for semantics, (Chierchia and McConnell-Ginet, 1991):

> *Ambiguity* arises when a single word or string of words is associated in the language system with more than one meaning. (page 32)
>
> [A]n ambiguous lexical item can be thought of as several different lexical items that happen to be written and pronounced in the same way. (page 32)
>
> In general, expressions that are ambiguous can be used only with one of their meanings in any given situation. Exceptions are cases of punning and are clearly very special. (page 34)

This view of *senses as symbols* can be summarized as follows:

- **Discreteness.** An ambiguous word has a fixed number of senses, with each sense being clearly delineated from other senses.

- **Exclusiveness.** Only one sense of an ambiguous word is invoked in any given context.

In this section, I will motivate a different view, the view of *senses as context groups*:

- **Gradience.** Different individuations of the meaning of a word are possible. Contexts may invoke different "mixtures" of the senses of a particular individuation, with each sense being activated to various degress ranging from no activation (sense is not invoked) to high activation (sense is primary meaning).
- **Inclusiveness.** Multiple senses of a word can be invoked in a particular context.

Notice that "context-group senses" can be seen as generalizations of "symbolic senses". Instead of one sense individuation there are several, and instead of one sense per context several can be used. Even though I will defend context-group senses below, it is clear that the more restricted notion of symbolic sense is appropriate for many ambiguities. The word "duck" in (1a) is a case in point (from Zwicky and Sadock 1975). (1a) has the two meanings (1b) and (1c). A sense individuation in which the two relevant meanings of "duck" are grouped into one sense is simply not possible. In trying to understand (1a), one can only flip back and forth between the two meanings (1b) and (1c). I will call this type of ambiguity *Necker-Cube* ambiguity in analogy to the two possible mental representations of the Necker Cube which cannot be unified into one.

(1) a. I saw her duck.
     b. I saw her bird.
     c. I saw that she ducked.

The case of Necker-Cube ambiguities raises the question whether the discussion so far has been purely terminological. Have I just introduced the term Necker-cube ambiguity for conventional ambiguity, and extended the notion of conventional ambiguity to shades of meaning that it up to now did not cover?

Based on work by Geeraerts (1993), I will argue below that there is a cline ranging from slight contextual variation (e.g., the dead duck in (2a) vs. the living duck in (2b)) to Necker-Cube ambiguity (the contrast (1b) vs. (1c)). The traditional notion of sense assumes that there is a distinguished point on the cline which separates vagueness (or contextual variation) from ambiguity. If Geeraerts is right, then there is no such point and thus no justification to single out one particular sense individuation as the right one. Further evidence for this position will be given below from an investigation of sense individuation in dictionaries (see Section 3.6.2). The Necker-Cube example is simply meant to point out that stressing the gradience of sense disambiguation does not deny that there are extremes. One extreme of the cline are fine sense individuations which produce contextual variants like (2b) and (2a). Necker-Cube ambiguities are the other extreme of the cline. They introduce sharply different meanings like (1b) and (1c).

(2)   a. The hunter brought a duck home.

       b. The duck was swimming in the pond.

In support of sense co-activation (or inclusiveness), linguistic and psycholinguistic evidence will be given presently that shows the simultaneous use of several senses at the same time. Again, evidence from dictionaries will further strengthen this claim in Section 3.6.2.

3.1.1   The Cline from Vagueness to Ambiguity

Geeraerts (1993) gives evidence that the criteria for distinguishing between vagueness and ambiguity are not consistent, and that this distinction is vague itself. Such evidence for a cline from vagueness to ambiguity supports the gradience of sense individuation and thus the view of senses as context groups. If there is no sharp distinction between vagueness and ambiguity, then we have no reason to give one sense individuation preferred status over another.

Traditionally, three types of tests have been employed to establish ambiguity: linguistic, logical, and definitional criteria. Geeraerts claims that these tests are context-dependent and contradict each other (1993). A lexical item that is ambiguous (i.e. has several core meanings) according to some tests or in some contexts, is vague (i.e. different interpretations are derived from a single core meaning) according to other tests or in other contexts. An exposition of his arguments follows.

The Linguistic Criterion. Geeraerts argues that the linguistic criterion of verb anaphora is context dependent. This classical test was introduced by Lakoff (1970) and Zwicky and Sadock (1975). For example, sentence (3a) cannot refer to a situation where John signs a piece of legislation and Peter signs a bird's bill (for example the bill of a toy bird for a promotion). On the other hand, sentence (3b) is perfectly felicitous if it refers to a situation where John likes his mother's father and Peter likes his father's father. This means that, according to the verb anaphora criterion, "bill" is ambiguous, and "grandpa" is not.

(3)   a. John signed a bill and so did Peter.

       b. John likes his grandpa and so does Peter.

In his review of the criterion, Geeraerts reports Lakoff's judgment that sentence (4a) is infelicitous if John hit the wall unintentionally and Fred did so intentionally. This means that according to the verb-anaphora criterion "to hit" is ambiguous between an intentional and an unintentional reading. But the fact that sentence (4b) (which I just used) is felicitous shows that the verb anaphora test yields vagueness if the distinguishing semantic feature is used to contrast the two readings. It has also been pointed out that an intentional hitting by John and an unintentional hitting by Fred is a felicitous interpretation of (4a) if Fred is imitating John. So the linguistic criterion using verb anaphora is context-dependent.

(4)   a. John hit the wall and so did Fred.

        b. John hit the wall unintentionally and Fred did so intentionally.

The Logical Criterion. The logical criterion is based on the sentence schema (5) (Zwicky and Sadock, 1975).

(5) p and not p.

Ambiguous items can be used felicitously in such a schema because one sense can be invoked in the first mention and another sense in the second mention of the item. No logical contradiction arises. Unambiguous words can not be used felicitously in a sentence like (5) since logical contradiction cannot be avoided in their case.

Geeraerts gives the example of "jade" for a word that seems to be vague: It cannot be used in sentence schema (5) in an unmarked context like (6a). However, it can be contextualized as ambiguous in a context such as (6b).

(6)   a. It is jade and it is not jade.

        b. Well, it is jade if you mean nephrite, but not if you mean jadeite.

Here, a word that is unambiguous in neutral contexts can be made to appear ambiguous according to the logical criterion.

The Definitional Criterion.

(7)   A *bachelor* is an unmarried man thought of as someone who could marry. (Wierzbicka, quoted in Geeraerts 1993)

According to the definitional criterion, a word is unambiguous if there is a single minimally specific definition that covers all uses. Geeraerts attributes this criterion to Aristotle (Posterior Analytics II.xiii (Geeraerts 1993:230)).[1] According to Geeraerts, the definitional criterion is

---

[1] This criterion seems problematic since it would only classify words as unambiguous that can be characterized by strictly necessary conditions. Non-necessary conditions would make a definition non-minimal. One would be forced to conclude that words like "dog" and "bird" are ambiguous according to the definitional criterion: A dog

context-dependent because any definition has to use words that are context-dependent. Consider one of the meanings of "bachelor" (unmarried man). Does "bachelor" have one sense related to this meaning or several senses? At first view, sentence (7) seems like a good definition that covers all correct uses and only correct uses. But the definition contains the problematic word "could". It can refer to the absence of impediments, being entitled to something by law, or a skill.

The last sense is certainly not one that Wierzbicka had in mind in her definition. This suggests that even a seemingly precise definition like (7) is vague. So (7), intuitive though it may be at first sight, hides the polysemy of the words used. Any definition runs into such problems. Geeraerts concludes that the definitional criterion for ambiguity is also context-dependent, just as the linguistic and logical criteria are.

Some of Quine's writings also seem to suggest that the ambiguity-vagueness boundary is fluid. While he uses the logical criterion to distinguish ambiguity from vagueness (Quine 1960:129), his views are compatible with a gradient view of sense individuation to the extent that he equates the meaning of words with classes of stimulations as in the following passage:

> Relative to the initial phase of word learning we may quite reasonably call a word ambiguous (and not merely general) if it has been conditioned to two very unlike classes of stimualtions, each a close-knit class of mutually similar stimulations. [...] There is a real difference genetically between conditioning a word to a continous region of the child's evolving quality space and conditioning it to two widely disconnected regions. (Quine 1960:130f)

Even though Quine does not consider words for which the different "quality spaces" are are so close that the distinction between ambiguity and vagueness becomes blurred, such cases seem a natural consequence of his way of thinking about ambiguity.

In summary, the commonly used criteria for ambiguity and vagueness are context-dependent. They give different results depending on the context in which they are used. Consequently, the traditional notions of ambiguity and sense are not well-defined. Rather, different senses are more or less difficult to conceptualize as a single unified meaning. This evidence supports the view of senses as context groups, according

---

with three legs is still a dog, a non-flying penguin is still a bird, so the conditions "four legs" and "flying" are non-necessary. Geeraerts does not seem to intend such an application of the definitional criterion, but doesn't discuss the problem of non-necessary conditions.

to which different sense individuations are possible for a word, without a single one taking precedence over all others.[2]

3.1.2 Coactivation

I will now defend the second part of the context-group hypothesis about senses: that several senses can be invoked in the same context.

Standard semantic theories take for granted that only one meaning of an ambiguous word or phrase can be used in a given context. I repeat here what Chierchia and McConnell-Ginet write in their textbook:

> In general, expressions that are ambiguous can be used only with one of their meanings in any given situation. (Chierchia and McConnell-Ginet 1991:34)

Of course, there are cases of misunderstanding in which the speaker intends one meaning of an utterance and the hearer either invokes another without being aware of the ambiguity or is aware of the ambiguity, but has insufficient information for a decision. Chierchia and McConell-Ginet are not concerned with such cases of unsuccessful communication. Their claim is that ambiguous expressions can only be *successfully* used with one of their meanings. That is, for successful communication, the speaker must intend one meaning and the hearer must interpret the speaker that way and determine this meaning. In what follows, I hope to show that in many cases, the speaker wants to use several meanings of an utterance and the hearer understands and makes sense of all these meanings.

The first piece of evidence that casts doubt on the one-reading-at-a-time thesis comes from research on priming in psycholinguistics. Swinney (1979) and Tanenhaus et al. (1979) show that in processing ambiguous words both readings are activated initially. The activation of the inappropriate sense dies off after about 200 milliseconds (Tanenhaus et al. 1979:433). Figure 5 shows the time course of processing for the word *pipe* in a context that primes smoking.

These two studies (and several others that have been conducted since) demonstrate initial coactivation of the two readings of an ambiguous word. Here I argue that *persistent* coactivation takes place in many cases. I know of only two studies that have investigated persis-

---

[2]Tuggy (1993) and Cruse (1982) are two other linguists who have argued for a cline from ambiguity to vagueness. Cruse writes:

> [R]eadings which are close together can be co-ordinated without zeugma, but if they are sufficiently far apart, they are incompatible. If this picture is correct, it does not make sense to ask how many senses of "like" there are: there is just a seamless fabric of meaning-potential. (page 79)

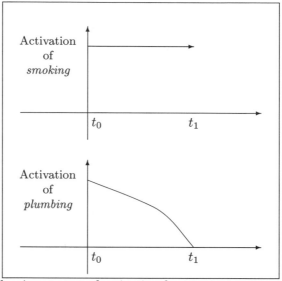

FIGURE 5 The time course of activation for *pipe* in a context that primes *smoking*.

tent coactivation.[3] Seidenberg et al. (1982) compared priming effects of two-way ambiguous words in a) sentences that were compatible with both senses and b) unambiguous sentences. They found no persistent coactivation. However, Hudson and Tanenhaus (1984) point out that Seidenberg et al. measured priming effects after a sentence boundary. So they only showed that in their experiments coactivation did not persist over sentence boundaries.

Unlike Seidenberg et al., Hudson and Tanenhaus (1984) did find coactivation:

> The results in the immediate condition replicate previous research in demonstrating that multiple meanings of ambiguous words are initially accessed. In contrast to previous research with biasing contexts in which ambiguity resolution took place within 200 msec, the 500 msec condition continued to show a multiple access pattern. Thus multiple meanings continue to be available in the absence of biasing context. (page 191)

The only difference in Hudson et al.'s experimental setup was that there was no intervening sentence boundary between the first mention of the ambiguous word and the point 500 msec later at which activation was

---

[3]I am grateful to Gary Cottrell for helping me locate these references.

tested. There is thus clear experimental evidence for persistent coactivation, at least within sentence boundaries.

It is not clear what the degree of ambiguity of the words used in (Hudson and Tanenhaus, 1984) is. The only example given is "pupil", a homonym. Lexical coactivation for homonyms is probably rare because contexts that are compatible with several disparate readings are unlikely to appear in a natural discourse. But the phenomenon is ubiquitous if we take finer semantic distinctions into consideration. McClelland et al. (1989:292) discuss the different, but related uses of *ball* in (8) and conclude:

> It is possible to assert that [...] we are selecting between two alternative meanings — one, let us say, in which the spherical object is smallish, hard and white, and the other in which it is larger, squishier, and probably multicolored. But taken to its extreme, this view seems to lead to a vast explosion of lexical entries, one for each of the possible balls that we can envisage being implicitly described in a sentence. Is there to be a separate lexical entry for every shade of meaning that can be comprehended, for every word in the language?

(8)   a. The slugger hit the ball over the fence.
       b. The baby rolled the ball to her daddy.

An intermediate case between the homonym "pupil" and the meaning shades of "ball" is the noun "interest" with its senses "legal share" and "a feeling that accompanies or causes special attention." This is a case of ambiguity rather than vagueness according to ambiguity tests such as the ones discussed above. (For example, only one of the two senses can be invoked in: "John has an interest in the company, and so does Bill.") But both senses are used at the same time in the sentences in (9). In (9a), the "legal share" sense is primary, but the "attention" sense is also activated: Williams is presumably interested in his investments and pays attention to how profitable they are etc. (9b) conveys that Moore owns his bodily tissue just as he owns other property but the "attention" sense also resonates in interpreting the sentence. (9c) is a third example of a coactivation of both readings. Note that it is hard to translate the sentences in (9) into German, which has no comparable ambiguous word. Neither *Interesse* nor *Beteiligung*, the literal translations of the "attention" and the "legal share" senses of *interest*, capture the semantic richness of the uses of *interest* in (9).

(9)   a. In Texas, Williams, a millionaire businessman with interests in
          oil, cattle and banking, was hurt among voters who considered
          ethics an important issue. (NYTNW, November 1990)

b. [...] the state Court of Appeal [...] ruled that Moore had a valid property interest in his own bodily tissue. (NYTNW, July 1990)

c. "With their vast interests scattered over large areas, U.S. imperialism and its allies will become a huge corpse which can easily be destroyed when its nerve system receives a deadly blow [...]," the newspaper said. (NYTNW, November 1990)

As the psychological evidence cited above suggests, coactivation occurs even for traditional senses like the senses of "pupil". If we take the above arguments for finer sense individuations (the cases of "ball" and "interest") into account, then coactivation is ubiquitous. Coactivation can also be observed for two other types of ambiguity: modification by prepositional phrases and quantifier scope.

3.1.2.1 Coactivation in PP Modification

One source of syntactic ambiguity is that prepositional phrases (PPs) in verb-phrase-final position can modify each of several preceding phrases. For example, although (10a) and (10b) have similar surface forms, the PP in (10a) can only be interpreted as modifying the action expressed by the verb, whereas the PP in (10b) can only be interpreted as modifying the noun phrase "her friend".

(10) a. She saw the accident from her window.

b. She saw her friend from Washington.

In the sentences in (10), it is tempting to equate modification and syntactic attachment: the first PP attaches to the verb, the second to the noun. But a PP can modify a constituent without attaching to it as in the following sentence.

(11) A report appeared about the Italian elections.

I'm concerned here with the question of modification, not attachment.

In their 1991 ACL paper on prepositional phrase attachment Hindle and Rooth remark on the difficulty in determining the constituent which is modified by a PP:

It seems to us that this difficulty in assigning attachment decisions is an important fact that deserves further exploration. If it is difficult to decide what licenses a prepositional phrase a significant proportion of the time, then we need to develop language models that appropriately capture this vagueness. For our present purpose, we decided to force an attachment choice in all cases, in some cases making the choice on the basis of an unanalyzed intuition. (page 233)

Their examples are those in (12):

(12) a. [...] known to *frequent* the same *bars in* one neighborhood.
      b. Inaugural officials reportedly were trying to *arrange* a *reunion*
          for Bush and his old submarine buddies [...]
      c. We have not *signed* a settlement *agreement with* them.

In each case, the prepositional phrase modifies both the noun phrase
and the verb.

Some sentences exhibit a three-fold modification as the following example (pointed out to me by Tony Davis) shows:

(13) He cooked the onions in the pot with the beans.

The PP *with the beans* modifies *pot, onions,* and *cooked.*

Similarly, different attachments of conjuncts can also be coactivated:

(14) The mites live on the surface of the skin of the ear and canal [...]
      (Agarwal and Boggess 1992:15)

Arguably, "on the surface of the canal" and "on the surface of the skin
of the canal" are both activated in interpreting the sentence.

A theory committed to exclusiveness (only one interpretation of an
utterance is used at any given time) could resort to inference in order to
account for the simultaneous invocation of several interpretations. For
example, the primary interpretation of (12a) might be that the bars in
question are located in one neighborhood. Since one needs to be at the
location of a bar that one frequents, the actions described by sentence
(12a) are then inferred to be at the same location too. This position
does not explain which reading is chosen initially and why. It is also at
odds with how effortless the processing of the sentences in (12) – (14)
appears to be: There is no evidence that they involve more inferences
than the interpretation of other sentences do.

3.1.2.2 Scope

Different quantifier scopes can also be coactivated. Consider (15b), a
simplification of (15a).

(15) a. [...] the Labor Department's report, generally considered the
          best single indicator of economic performance and the first com-
          prehensive one published each month, also pointed to height-
          ened inflation. (August)
      b. The Labor Department's report is the first indicator each
          month.

In the following translations of (15b), m ranges over months, i over
indicators, "$\leq$" stands for temporal precedence, "$i \in m$" for "i is published in m". "LDR" abbreviates "the Labor Department's report".

(16) a. $\forall m \, \forall i [i \in m \Rightarrow \text{LDR} \leq i]$

b. $\forall i \, \forall m [i \in m \Rightarrow \text{LDR} \leq i]$

c. $\forall i [[\forall m [i \in m]] \Rightarrow \text{LDR} \leq i]$

Clearly, "each" takes scope over "first" in (15a) (formula (16a)): For any given month it is true that the Labor Department's report is the first comprehensive indicator that is published in that month. I have rewritten (16a) as (16b) to make it easier to compare it with (16c). (16a) excludes the possibility of one-time comprehensive reports being published before LDR. (15a) does not make such a claim. So the translation (16c) with "first" taking scope over "each" is part of the interpretation of (15a). This means that both scopings, (16b) and (16c), are coactivated.

The narrower reading (16c) alone is not adequate since the precedence relation "$\leq$" is not in the scope of "month". If we interpret the precedence relation without reference to a particular month then (16c) is trivially true for indicators that are published each month. For example, each indicator's January publication precedes each indicator's February publication. This shows that both readings contribute necessary meaning for the correct interpretation of (15a).

The phrase (17b) in (17a) is a similar example. X is the group of 80,000 cards referred to in the sentence, c ranges over individual cards, y over years, and "sent_in" holds of card-year pairs $< c, y >$ such that c was sent in y. ι is the description operator defined in (17c).

(17) a. Target, a discount chain with a wide variety of merchandise that has stores in much of the country, used the responses from 80,000 customer-comment cards received each year to design its new store in Apple Valley, Minn., a suburb of St. Paul, to allow for efficient self-service, similar to that provided in a supermarket. (New York Times, Nov. 27 1990)

b. 80,000 cards received each year

c. $\iota x P(x) \doteq P(x) \wedge \forall y \, P(y) \Rightarrow x = y$

d. $\iota X [|X| = 80,000 \wedge \forall c [(\forall y \text{ sent\_in}(c, y)) \Rightarrow c \in X]]$

e. $\forall y [\iota X [|X| = 80,000 \wedge \forall c (\text{sent\_in}(c, y) \Rightarrow c \in X)]]$

f. $\lambda x \, [\text{ Target used } x \text{ for designing the store}]$

The first translation (17d) states that there is a group of cards such that it has 80,000 members and it comprises every card that is received each year. Here cards are conceptualized as generic entities similar to a sum of money that can be payed several times although the actual bills and coins transferred are different on each occasion. Translation (17e) states that for every year, there is a group of 80,000 cards which comprises all cards sent in that year.

Each of the translations (17d) and (17e) covers parts of the proposition expressed by (17a) that are not covered by the other. If (17d) is plugged into lambda expression (17f), then the resulting proposition claims that only cards that were sent every year were used in designing the new store. (17a) makes no such claim: it implies that all cards received over the years were used.

(17e) on its own does not provide a referent that the lambda expression (17f) (part of (17a)) could be applied to. It would not be correct to extend the scope of the universal quantifier over the whole proposition since Target went through the planning process only once, not several years in a row. Only (17d) provides a referent for the main proposition of the sentence. So both readings, (17d) and (17e), have to be invoked to form the full interpretation of (17a).

What the examples (15a) and (17a) share is that the phrase containing the universal quantifier is needed in two places at the same time, in the wide-scope position in order to make the precedence relation interpretable (15a) and in order to guarantee the involvement of individual cards (17a), in the narrow-scope position in order not to exclude indicators that are published less often that once a month (15a) and in order to make a referent accessible to the proposition expressed by the sentence (17a).

I am not claiming that this particular kind of scope coactivation is frequent. But it is interesting because neglecting one of the two interpretations takes away part of the truth-conditional meaning. Both interpretations are necessary to capture the full meaning of the sentences.

3.1.3 Summary

The psycholinguistic evidence presented here shows that there is initial coactivation of all readings of an ambiguous word and that senses are suppressed in disfavoring contexts in subsequent processing. The examples given for lexical, syntactic and scope coactivation suggest that in contexts that are compatible with several readings, these readings are not suppressed and stay activated. Instead, one could hypothesize that, since the different interpretations are semantically related in most cases, only one reading is invoked and others are inferred, possibly using world knowledge.

Nevertheless, I take it that the coactivation thesis (several senses of a word can be simultaneously used) is at least as plausible a notion of ambiguity as exclusiveness (only one sense usable in a context). Taken together with Geeraerts' arguments for a cline from vagueness to ambiguity, this concludes my motivation of senses as context groups. There are strong arguments for both elements of the proposal: gradience (multiple sense individuations of a word, depending on context) and coactivation (multiple senses of a word in a given context).

3.2 Computational Models of Lexical Acquisition

This section discusses three computational models of lexical acquisition and semantic categorization: a neo-behaviorist model, Siskind's model of the acquisition of word-to-meaning mappings, and the Berkeley L0 project.

3.2.1 A Neo-Behaviorist Model

Suppes and his collaborators have developed a neo-behaviorist model of language acquisition for robots (Crangle and Suppes, 1994; Suppes et al., 1992, 1991). It acquires some grammatical knowledge (for example, the fact that only words denoting object categories can appear after "the"), but is focussed mainly on the acquisition of semantic knowledge.

Learning in the neo-beohaviorist model is a series of *trials*. In each trial, the instructor presents the robot with a linguistic expression (for example 18a) and an expression of the robot's internal language (for example 18b). $g is the robot's internal symbol for the action of getting and $s is the symbol for screws.

(18) a. Get the screw.

   b. $g $s

The robot updates its *association memory* on the basis of this input. For the pair in (18), four associations would be updated: "get"-$g, "get"-$s, "screw"-$g, and "screw"-$s. Only two of these updates are correct, but since there are many more expression pairs with an association "screw"-$s than with an association "screw"-$g, the word "screw" will eventually be associated with $s only. Suppes et al. (1991,1992) describe experiments in which a robot learns all associations correctly.

My main criticism of this model is that it cannot handle ambiguity. Suppes et al. acknowledge this problem. They write in the discussion about the association procedure:

> After this association is made, a new grammatical form is generated, and possibly because of the new associations at least one of the old grammatical forms is deleted, for one of the axioms states that a word or internal denoting symbol can have exactly one association, so when a new association is formed for a word any old associations must be deleted. (This strong all-or-none uniqueness assumption is undoubtedly too restrictive for actual language learning by children, but there is some evidence that it holds in the early stages of language learning. It works very well for the kind of systematic language and grammar we are concerned to use in robot discourse, at least at these early stages of development.) (page 240)

Unfortunately, no reference is given for the claim that the all-or-none assumption holds in the early stages of language learning. The subsequent remark suggests that this limitation of the system is motivated by the authors' focus on robot learning rather than human acquisition. The discussion also implies that the authors only consider the less frequent Necker-Cube ambiguity. Ambiguity in the general sense, i.e. uncertainty about what the underlying representation of a surface form is, is a pervasive problem in language acquisition. It does not surface as such in the neo-behaviorist model because of the representational power of the internal language. Since the robot does not have to learn the internal language, much of the difficulty of acquisition has already been solved when learning starts. This point will be taken up in more detail in the next section as the model discussed there assumes that a similar internal language is in place before language acquisition starts.

3.2.2 Siskind's Model of Lexical Acquisition

Like the neo-behaviorists, Siskind also relies on associations which are established by presenting pairs of natural language expressions and internal language expressions (Siskind, 1995, 1994). Hence the first stage of learning a word is to determine the symbols it is associated with. In Siskind's approach, there can be several symbols since the semantics of words are decomposed into primitives. For example, "raise" is represented as "cause(x,go(y,up))". In the second stage of learning a word, the learner determines the correct structural arrangement of the internal symbols. Noise is an additional complication that Siskind takes into account. An initial hypothesis about symbol associations or structural arrangement may turn out to be based on a noisy utterance. Various steps of the learning procedure deal with such cases and revise incorrect hypotheses.

In contrast to the neo-behaviorist model, Siskind addresses the problem of ambiguous input. He introduces the following extension of the learning procedure to cope with ambiguity:

If the current utterance does indeed contain words used in a different sense [than] previously hypothesized, it is likely that an attempt to merge the two senses into one will yield an inconsistency. Selecting the minimal set of senses to split to resolve such an inconsistency will likely correlate with the actual homonymous words encountered. (Siskind, 1994)

Siskind's computational experiments demonstrate that an implementation of this strategy works well. About 98% of all senses are learned correctly (1995). This is an impressive result given that two difficulties the child faces in semantic acquisition are modeled accurately: referential uncertainty and noise. Referential uncertainty occurs when the child is uncertain about what internal language expression to pair up with a natural language expression. Siskind gives the example in (19). A child that hears (19a) and perceives a situation that is truthfully described by (19a), could hypothesize internal language representations corresponding to (19b) or (19c) as well as (19a) since (19b) or (19c) would be equally true of the situation. Referential uncertainty is modeled by pairing 10 different internal language expression with each natural language expression without giving any information which one is the correct translation.

(19) a. John took the ball.
      b. John lifted the ball with his arm.
      c. John wanted the ball.

Siskind also models noise. 20% of all utterances are paired with 10 internal language expressions none of which is correct. Such utterance-meaning-pairs correspond to situations in which the child misconstrues the situation that the natural language expression describes.

Despite the care taken by Siskind to construct a realistic learning model, the model's learning task is much easier than the one faced by the child. Consider again the example (20a) and its translation (20b). How is the child to distinguish causation situations from those that are not? Any situation can be interpreted as being an instance of causation of some kind. Similarly, almost any observable situation can be described by the predicate "TO": There may be an object moving to a particular point, an object pointing somewhere, a person addressing a remark to someone or some similar subsituation. So a large number of primitives could be posited as potentially relevant for each situation, and they could be combined in many ways to give internal language expressions. These considerations suggest that the referential uncertainty in Siskind's model is underestimated by at least one order of magnitude. There are hundreds and thousands of possible internal language descriptions of any situation.

(20) a. John took the ball.
      b. CAUSE (John , GO (ball, TO (John)))

A similar problem is the restricted vocabulary of the experiment: 250 terms. Why is the color of the ball not represented in (20b)? The learning procedure would not be able to learn the sentence: "John took the green ball," because "green" is not representable with the 250 basic terms. If the vocabulary were to be enlarged to encompass all relevant categories, the combinatorial explosion of possible internal language expressions would be truly enormous.

Finally, the learning procedure only acquires abstract knowledge about ambiguity. It could be argued that complete acquisition includes the ability to identify senses in context as well as knowledge about the inventory of possible senses of a word.

In summary, the model of lexical acquisition presented by Siskind is an advance over previous approaches that didn't account for ambiguity, referential uncertainty and noise. However, the problem of referential uncertainty is severely underestimated. The procedure also doesn't provide knowledge on how to understand senses, only on how to acquire an inventory of possible senses. For these two reasons, it is only a partial solution of the task of acquiring semantic categorization.

3.2.3   The L0 Project

The Berkeley L0 Project is to my knowledge the most convincing attempt to model lexical acquisition without implausible assumptions about an internal language. Regier's 1992 dissertation proposes a connectionist model of how *spatial terms* are learned. The input of the model is a pixel array on which visual scenes are displayed. For example, a trajector may be on, under, over, in or next to a landmark. The learning target of the model is a particular preposition that would be appropriate to describe the visual scene. The training regime is to present visual scenes and descriptions of spatial relationships as input and output, and to train the network to choose prepositions that correctly describe the visual input.

A simple unstructured connectionist network with input layer, output layer and hidden layers would probably not be able to learn this task. Such an unstructured network would also be a bad model of human acquisition since a lot of visual processing is enabled by specialized processes and representations in the brain. Regier models several aspects of the brain's specialization for visual processing for which neuroscientists have found evidence: topographic maps of the visual field, orientation-sensitive cells, center-surround receptive fields, neural gating (similar to gates on computer chips), and filling-in (the activation of cells that are surrounded by activated cells).

Regier shows that a connectionist model whose architecture includes such specialized visual processing units is capable of learning a wide range of prepositions in several European and non-European languages. The model thus demonstrates how semantic acquisition is possible without an internal language. Constraints on the general architecture of the perceptual and cognitive system limit the space of possible solutions to the input-to-word mapping. Because the search space is restricted, the connectionist model succeeds at identifying the correct mappings.

The heavy reliance on specialized processing units is justified for visual perception. But it is not plausible for the acquisition of all concepts. For example, chemistry and automobiles are two areas whose concepts are probably acquired without any recourse to specialized innate knowledge. Word Space, the model to be introduced in this chapter, is intended as a model for areas that get only limited help from innate capacities.

3.3 Computational Work on Disambiguation

This section discusses previous computational work on disambiguation. I will argue that most models – with the possible exception of class-based disambiguation – are not adequate as models of how people learn senses and how to discriminate between them. In what follows, I discuss approaches that rely on knowledge representation, machine-readable dictionaries, hand-labeled training sets, and bilingual corpora.

Early work on disambiguation in computational linguistics relied heavily on hand-encoded knowledge. In Kelly and Stone's work, a "disambiguation dictionary" is built

> [...] which would contain for each of a large number of high-frequency ambiguous words of English, a set of carefully constructed rules instructing the machine to examine the current context of the word and, based on what it finds, to make a decision regarding the intended sense.

Cottrell (1989a) models disambiguation as a "constraint relaxation between the lexical entries of the words, the possible syntactic representations, and the possible semantic relations." (1989b:65) For example, syntactic constraints make the use of "marine" as a noun more likely in (21). Semantic constraints suggest that the noun "chairs" refers to pieces of furniture rather than a group of chairpersons. Neither constraint is absolute since "marine" could be an adjective modifying the noun "put" and since a situation in which a marine lifts chairpersons on tables is conceivable. For a given sentence, Cottrell's connectionist model integrates all constraints encoded in the network and finds the most well-formed interpretation.

(21)   The marine put chairs on the table.

McRoy (1992) describes another approach for integrating different sources of information, based on *preferences*. Examples of the types of knowledge used in her system are cluster definitions (a group of senses related to a central concept) and the concept hierarchy of the lexicon.

A source of knowledge that has been often used for disambiguation is dictionaries, either dictionaries created for a special task or machine-readable versions of standard dictionaries.[4] Lesk (1986) disambiguates words according to word overlap of sense definitions in the dictionary with contexts of use. For example, if a context of "cone" contains the word ice-cream, then it will be disambiguated as "a crisp cone-shaped wafer for holding ice cream".

In Hirst's approach ("polaroid words", Hirst 1987), a lexicon organizes nouns in a semantic sort hierarchy and states what sorts verbs subcategorize for. For example, "fire" in (22) has two meanings "dismiss from a position" and "propel from a gun". The object "employee" has the semantic sort "animate". This semantic sort is compatible only with the subcategorization requirements of the sense "dismiss from a position", so the sentence can be disambiguated as meaning that the boss dismissed the employee from her position.

(22)   The boss fired the employee.

A hand-labeled training set is another source of information that can be used for disambiguation. Hearst (1991) records how often features like "is capitalized", "part of speech is noun", "modified by other phrases" etc. occur with each of the senses of a word. This statistical information is then combined in a metric to discriminate senses in unseen text. Leacock et al. (1993) systematically test different statistical methods for combining evidence from the training test: a Bayesian approach, the vector space model, and neural networks. Alshawi and Carter (1994) use another method, least-squares minimization, to combine evidence from different features (or scaling functions).

A fourth source of information that has been used frequently for disambiguation is a bilingual corpus. Brown et al. (1991) show that highly accurate disambiguation of English and French words is possible if their contextually correct translations are known for a training set. Gale et al. (1992b) use a Bayesian model to combine evidence for senses of English words that are identified using an aligned corpus of a second language, French. A similar approach by Dagan and Itai (1994) (see also Dagan et al. 1991) disambiguates using a bilingual dictionary and a parsed corpus in the second language only. No alignment of sentences and not even a corpus in the first language are necessary. For example, Hebrew "lahtom" can mean "to finish" or "to sign" and Hebrew "hoze" can mean "treaty" or "contract". But the English collocations "to finish

---

[4]Krovetz and Croft (1989) present a series of dictionary-based experiments to determine whether disambiguation could aid the performance of an information retrieval system. They are interested in the quantitative analysis of the distribution of ambiguous words and senses rather than in devising and evaluating disambiguation algorithms.

a treaty", "to finish a contract", and "to sign a contract" are rare in a corpus of newswire text whereas "to sign a treaty" is frequent. So the ambiguous Hebrew expression "laḥtom ?al hoẓe" can be disambiguated as "to sign a treaty" by using collocational information from another language, in this case English.

The models discussed so far do not account for the acquisition of the external sources of information they use. They therefore cannot serve as models of how semantic categorization is learned in child language acquisition. There is however one disambiguation algorithm that makes more plausible assumptions about what the child brings to the task of disambiguation: class-based disambiguation.

3.3.1 Class-Based Disambiguation

Class-based disambiguation as introduced by Yarowsky (1992) uses the classes from Roget's thesaurus for disambiguation. Let C range over Roget's categories and w over words. Then the probability that the category of a particular context, for example a sentence, is C can be computed with Bayes' formula as follows:

$$P(C|context) = \Pi_w \text{ in context} \frac{P(w|C)P(C)}{P(w)}$$

$P(w|C)$ is the probability that w is going to be used in a context that has category C. For example, in an automotive context a mention of "car" is much more likely than a mention of "surgery". $P(w)$ and $P(C)$ are the probabilities of word w and category C. It is important to factor in the probability of the word since even a bad indicator of a topic can have a high value for $P(w|C)$ if it is frequent. For example, "school" is frequent and "dimethyl" extremely rare. Consequently, $P(\text{school}|\text{chemistry})$ is larger than $P(\text{dimethyl}|\text{chemistry})$. But "dimethyl" is a much better indicator of the topic of chemistry than "school". On the other hand, the ratio $\frac{P(w|C)P(C)}{P(w)}$ is larger for "dimethyl" than for "school" since "dimethyl" is rare, but a good indicator of chemistry in the few contexts in which it does occur.

The terms $\frac{P(w|C)P(C)}{P(w)}$ are multiplied for all words occurring in a context in order to combine evidence. For example, if a context has as many good indicators as bad indicators for a topic, then the final result $P(C|context)$ will yield about the same value as for a context in which there are only neutral words.

The two "input" probabilities in the equation can be easily computed from a text corpus. $P(w)$ is simply the relative frequency of w in the context. $P(w|C)$ is the relative frequency of the word in all chunks of text that are close to a word belonging to category C. For example, Roget's category 417 lists musical instruments like "banjo", "cello", and "trumpet". All contexts containing one of these words are merged. The relative frequency of word w in this subcorpus is then $P(w|\text{musical-instruments})$.[5]

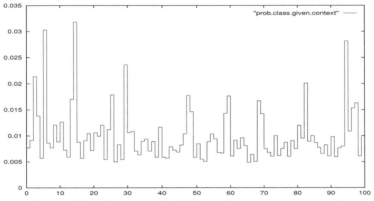

FIGURE 6 Probability for each of 100 Roget's categories given the set of words occurring in a context.

From the values of $P(w)$ and $P(w|C)$, the value of $P(C_i|context)$ can be computed for all categories C_i in Roget's, resulting in a probability distribution like the one in Figure 6. Yarowsky's algorithm then selects the category with the highest probability for the context in question. In Figure 6 this is category 15.

In disambiguation, the algorithm selects only between categories in which the word that is to be disambiguated is listed. For example, the word "interest" occurs in the categories 9, 175, 455, 642, 648, 707, 712, 780, 806, and 922 (these categories are from (Roget, 1946)). For each occurrence, "interest" is assigned the sense whose category has the highest value of $P(C_i|context)$ for the context of the occurrence. Yarowsky shows that this algorithm performs quite well for a sample of test words. On average it is about 90% correct. The implementation for which this result was reported assumed a uniform prior $P(C)$ over categories.

Can we learn something from class-based disambiguation about how human acquisition of senses and the capability to disambiguate comes about? Class-based disambiguation is more adequate to account for the bootstrapping problem than other approaches. It does not presuppose important parts of what is to be learned, like knowledge representation

---

[5]Yarowsky also smoothes the estimates. See his 1992 paper for details.

of relevant senses in an internal language or dictionaries that list the relevant senses. The only knowledge presupposed is the capability to classify situations into broad categories like "danger", "purchase", or "warfare". It seems much more plausible that the acquisition of semantic categorization could start out with such a general categorization capability than with the kind of detailed representations we have seen in the other models.

There are however two other features of Yarowsky's method that make it problematic as a model for how human acquisition proceeds. First, there are actually two types of knowledge that are taken from Roget's. Apart from the categorization that consists of about 1000 categories, Roget's also determines which categories correspond to possible senses of words. This means that a word that does not occur in Roget's cannot be disambiguated by the method.

Secondly, the global categorization into 1000 categories is used for all words. It seems intuitive that many words cannot be fit into the mold of the global categorization. For example, the sense "leader of a musical ensemble" of "conductor" is listed in Roget's under the categories "music" and "director". As a result, a context that is not musical at all, but strongly about directing like (23) would be classified as having the musical sense (there are three indicators of directing, but only one of "material that conducts").

(23)   The director and the manager guided the development of the new lightning conductor.

This problem could be avoided if "conductor" had its individual categories, including one that combines the topics "music" and "director".

Another clear deficiency of the global categorization is that there are intra-domain ambiguities that the algorithm cannot detect. For example, the technical term "distributed processing" in computer science can refer to neural networks and to a network of computers that is organized to solve some common task. Since both senses are in one category (computers), they cannot be distinguished by class-based disambiguation. This suggests that Yarowsky's algorithm should really be viewed as a text categorization algorithm, which can be successfully used for disambiguation. In fact, Hearst has used the method for just this purpose (Hearst, 1994).

The WORD SPACE model introduced below differs from class-based disambiguation in three respects. First, it induces an initial categorization similar to the one captured in Roget's thesaurus without presupposing it. Secondly, an attempt is made to learn which categories correspond to possible senses of a word rather than taking this knowledge from an outside source like Roget's. Finally, WORD SPACE finds an individual semantic categorization for each word, rather than applying a global categorization indiscriminately to all words.

Guthrie et al. (1991) propose a method which bears some resemblance to class-based disambiguation. They use the subject field codes of LDOCE (e.g., economics, automotive, gambling) instead of thesaurus classes for the classification of contexts. For each subject code, a cooccurrence matrix of the words in the sense definitions of that code defines a similarity measure of words with respect to that subject code. I will not describe the details here, but two words are the more similar according to this measure the more often they co-occur with the same words in this subset of sense definitions. The similarity measure defines *neighborhoods* for each sense of a word, the words that are most similar to the sense according to the similarity measure of the sense's subject code. For example, the neighborhood of the sense "to follow a curve or incline" of "bank" contains words like "aircraft" and "road", the neighborhood of the gambling sense words like "money" and "chance".

This information can be exploited for classifying neighborhoods by looking at the overlap between the neighborhoods of a word's senses and the words in the context. Guthrie et al. (1991) choose the sense whose neighborhood has the most overlap with the context. They do not evaluate the algorithm systematically, so it is not clear how its performance compares to Yarowsky's algorithm. Since it is not adaptable to new text sorts, one would expect that it will perform poorly unless the vocabulary of the text matches well with the vocabulary of LDOCE. Since it does not have the adaptability of Yarowsky's model, it seems less helpful in devising a model of human learning of ambiguity.

3.4 WORD SPACE: Sense Acquisition and Disambiguation based on Contextual Semantic Similarity

This section introduces WORD SPACE, a model of sense acquisition and disambiguation. WORD SPACE is a multi-dimensional real-valued space. Proximity in the space models semantic similarity. For example, the vectors of "car" and "automobile" are close in the space, whereas the vectors of "car" and "wine" are distant.

There are three types of entities that are represented as vectors in the space: words, contexts, and senses. Words are represented by word vectors, contexts by context vectors, and senses by sense vectors. Word vectors are derived from word associations, context vectors are derived from word vectors, and sense vectors are derived from the distribution of context vectors for a particular word. Most of this section is devoted to describing the algorithms for performing these derivations. Finally, I will describe a disambiguation algorithm based on these representations, context-group disambiguation.

3.4.1 Psychological Motivation for Context Group Disambiguation

The basic idea of WORD SPACE is an extension of the Strong and Weak Contextual Hypotheses of Miller and Charles (1991).

> *Strong Contextual Hypothesis:* Two words are semantically similar to the extent that their contextual representations are similar. (page 8)
>
> *Weak Contextual Hypothesis:* The similarity of the contextual representations of two words contributes to the semantic similarity of those words. (page 9)

A contextual representation of a word is knowledge of how that word is used. So the two hypotheses state that semantic similarity is (partially) determined by how similar the sets of contexts are that the two words can be used in. The weak form of the hypothesis addresses cases like "department" and "departmental" which are very similar semantically, but behave differently in many contexts because they are syntactically different. In such cases, there are other factors that contribute to determining semantic similarity — e.g. derivational relationships — in addition to substitutability.

The hypothesis that underlies WORD SPACE is an extension of the Strong Contextual Hypothesis to senses:

> *Contextual Hypothesis for Senses:* Two occurrences of an ambiguous word belong to the same sense to the extent that their contextual representations are similar.

So a sense is simply a group of occurrence types with similar contexts. The analogy between the contextual hypotheses for words and senses is that both word types and word occurrences are semantically similar to the extent that their contexts are semantically similar. A group of contextually similar word occurrences is a sense.

A specialized case of the Contextual Hypothesis for Words is that synonyms have identical contextual representations. Since there probably are no true synonyms, a more cautions formulation is that words are near-synonyms if they have nearly identical contextual representations. Analogously, according to the Contextual Hypothesis for Senses, two occurrences belong to the same sense if they have nearly identical or at least very similar contexts.

Miller and Charles determine the similarity of contexts by the "Method of Sorting" (1991:15). Subjects are given a set of sentences that contain one of two words that are to be compared (e.g., "car" and "automobile"). The two words are replaced by "–" in all sentences. Subjects are then asked to sort contexts into two groups according to which of the two words they think can appear in a context. Contextual similarity is then computed from the number of shared contexts of the two words.

Since this book is concerned with acquisition (as opposed to subjects' intuitions after acquisition) and since the only large-scale knowledge sources that I have access to in machine-readable form are corpora, an alternative to the Method of Sorting has to be found. There are two types of information that can be easily extracted from corpora, distributional information (which was used for TAG SPACE) and associational information. Every instance of cooccurrence between two words in a sentence (or larger context) contributes associational information. For the purposes of semantic similarity, associational information is much more helpful than distributional information. As we saw in the last chapter, distributional information partially characterizes syntactic categories, but it does a poor job at semantic categorization since many relations between close neighbors are between function words and content words. (Of course, function words are crucial for understanding the meaning of a sentence, but it is not clear whether they contribute much to the initial acquisition of semantic categorization.) Therefore, I will only use associational information for characterizing contextual similarity here. The exclusion of other sources of knowledge (for example, predicate-argument relations and world knowledge) limits the model's success in many cases. I will return to this point in Section 3.6.

Contexts consist of words, so one needs a representation of words in order to represent contexts and compute a measure of contextual similarity from that. Consequently, there are three steps in WORD SPACE that get us from associational information to senses:

- Induction of word vectors from associational information
- Computation of context vectors from word vectors
- Induction of sense vectors from context vectors

These steps are described in the following sections.

3.4.2 Derivation of Word Representations

A vector for word w is derived from the close neighbors of w in the corpus. Close neighbors are all words that co-occur with w in a sentence or a larger context. In the simplest case, the vector has an entry for each word that occurs in the corpus. The entry for word v in the vector for w records the number of times that word v occurs close to w in the corpus.

This vector representation captures the typical topic or subject matter of a word. For example, the vector of "astronaut" will have high counts for "spacecraft", "moon", and "NASA", indicating that the word "astronaut" is about the topic "outer space and its exploration". By looking at the amount of overlap between two vectors, one can roughly determine how closely they are related semantically (only roughly, since sense distinctions are not taken into account yet). This is because related meanings are often expressed by similar sets of words. Semantically related words will therefore co-occur with similar neighbors and their vectors will have a lot of overlap.

This similarity can be measured by the cosine between two vectors. The value of the cosine is higher the more overlap there is between the neighbors of the two words whose vectors are compared. If two words occur with exactly the same neighbors (perfect overlap), then the value of the cosine is 1.0. In contrast, if there is no overlap at all, then the value of the cosine is 0.0. The cosine can therefore be used as a rough measure of semantic relatedness between words (a rough measure which does not yet take sense distinctions into account).

There is a technical difficulty in the proposal just made, having to do with the size of the vectors. Since the vocabulary of languages typically has tens of thousands of words (and even a couple of thousand words in early childhood), computations on the word vectors just described would be inefficient. Sense disambiguation is almost instant, so a more compact representation has to be found.

My strategy to achieve more compactness is to apply a singular value decomposition (SVD), in a way similar to its application in TAG SPACE.

The starting point of the computation is to collect an m-by-n term matrix C, such that element c_{ij} records the number of times that words i and j cooccur in a window of size k. For the experiments conducted for this book, k was set to ∞, that is, any two tokens in the same document were regarded as cooccurring with each other. Association data were extracted from 17 months of the New York Times News Service (NYTNS), June 1989 through October 1990.

The values $m = 20000$ and $n = 1000$ were chosen for the constants

m and n, that is, matrix C has 20,000 rows and 1000 columns, corresponding to the 20,000 and 1,000 most frequent words, respectively.[6] This matrix was then decomposed using SVD and reduced to 100 dimensions. As a result, each word is represented as a 100-dimensional vector.

3.4.2.1 Sample Synonyms

The net effect of this computation is to produce for each unique term a dense 100-dimensional vector that characterizes its cooccurrence neighborhoods. Table 10 shows some of the associations found in the experiment. The Table lists for each word in the left column its nine nearest neighbors in the vector space. Each row displays a word and its nine

accident	repair faulty personnel accidents exhaust equipped MISHAPS injuries sites
advocates	passage PROPONENTS argument address favoring compromise congress favors urge
litigation	LAWSUITS audit lawsuit file auditors auditor suit sued proceedings
tax	taxes income;tax new;tax income;taxes taxpayers incentives LEVIES taxpayer corporate;taxes
treatment	drugs syndrome administered administer study administering PROCEDURE undergo aids

TABLE 10 Five terms and their nearest neighbors.

nearest neighbors. For example, "repair" is the nearest neighbor of "accident". Word pairs used as terms are displayed as couples separated by semicolon. (All pairs of adjacent words that occurred at least five times in the training text were added as terms to the vocabulary.) Words in upper case are hand-selected synonyms as might be found in a manually constructed thesaurus. They are particularly interesting because they are unlikely to cooccur with their mates and hence illustrate that the distributional analysis effectively uses second-order cooccurrence (sharing neighbors in the corpus) rather than simple first-order cooccurrence (occurring next to each other) to find synonyms.[7]

---

[6] A list of about 100 stop words was excluded, i.e. function words like "the" and "who" that do not contribute interesting associational information.

[7] The opinion that synonyms don't occur with each other is widespread in corpus linguistics, but I do not know of any systematic study of this question. The following data about the pair astronaut-cosmonaut is compatible with the view that synonyms don't occur with each other: Five months of the New York Times newswire had 7 occurrences of "cosmonaut", 70 occurrences of "astronaut", but no sentence in which both occurred.

3.4.3 Derivation of Context Representations

The word vectors just derived solve part of the semantic categorization problem as for example shown in Table 10. If two words have similar semantics then they will be located close to each other in Word Space. However, a unitary representation for words is inappropriate for ambiguity. For example, both senses of the word "suit" ("lawsuit" and "garment") are conflated in its word vector.

We need to go back to the individual contexts of use in order to acquire information about sense distinctions. I will use *context vectors* to represent contexts.[8] A context vector is the centroid (or sum) of the vectors of the words occurring in the context:

$$(24) \quad \vec{c} = \sum_i \vec{v}(w_i)$$

where $\vec{c}$ is the context vector, the words w_i are the words occurring in the context and $\vec{v}(w_i)$ is the word vector of word w_i. The centroid "averages" the direction of a set of vectors. For example, the centroid of two vectors is the vector that runs half way between them. The intuition underlying the computation of context vectors is that word vectors have several components, corresponding to different topics like "agriculture", "education", or "automobiles". If many of the words in a context have a strong component for one of the topics, say "automobiles", then the average of all vectors, the context vector, will also have a strong component for the topic. On the other hand, if only one or two words represent a particular topic, then the context vector will be weak on this component. So the context vector represents the strength of different topical or semantic components in a context.

To compute the context vector, a word vector is weighted according to its discriminating potential. A rough measure of how well word w_i discriminates between different topics is the log inverse document frequency used in information retrieval: (Robertson and Sparck Jones, 1976; Salton and Buckley, 1990)

$$(25) \quad a_i = \log_2\left(\frac{N}{n_i}\right)$$

where N is the total number of documents and n_i is the number of documents that w_i occurs in. For example, even if the words "China" and "obtain" have about the same absolute frequency, "obtain" will occur in many more documents than "China" because documents containing "China" will often be about China and therefore mention the word several times. In contrast, there's no such strong tendency for "obtain". Consequently, the occurrences of "obtain" are spread over many docu-

---

[8]See Wilks et al. (1990), Deerwester et al. (1990), and Gallant (1991) for context vectors that are derived from information other than word cooccurrences (dictionaries, word-in-document occurrences and hand-encoded semantic features).

ments (high document frequency), whereas the occurrences of "China" are concentrated in few documents (low document frequency). This difference corresponds with the intuition that "China" is a good document discriminator and "obtain" a bad document discriminator.

Document frequency would correspond to the total number of situations w_i is used in in a more realistic learning situation. If a word is used once per situation of use, n_i would be the number of situations it is used in, otherwise n_i would be lower.

This weighting corresponds to the information content a word contributes. For all but the most frequent words, a_i is approximately equal to the entropy of the probability distribution $P(S$ is a situation in which word w occurs). That is, a_i is the number of yes/no questions that one would have to ask in the optimal strategy to gather as much information as is conveyed by w_i. The more questions are necessary, the more information knowledge about the use of w_i contributes, and the higher the weight of the word's vector in the computation of the context vector. (See Wong and Yao (1992) for a discussion of the relation between inverse document weighting and information theory.)

With weighting, the equation for computing a context vector becomes:

(26) $\quad \vec{c} = \sum_i a_i \vec{v}(w_i)$

where a_i is the weight defined in (25).

3.4.4 Derivation of Sense Representations

Sense representations are computed as groups of similar contexts, in accordance with the Contextual Hypothesis for Senses. All contexts of a word like "suit" are collected from the corpus. For each context, a context vector is computed. This set of context vectors (each corresponding to an occurrence in the corpus) is then clustered into a predetermined number of coherent clusters or context groups (using the Buckshot algorithm, see appendix). The number of context groups depends on the intended grain of the sense individuation. A small number of context groups is chosen for a fine-grained individuation and a larger number for a coarse-grained individuation.

The representation of a sense is simply the centroid of its cluster. It marks the portion of the multi-dimensional space which is occupied by the cluster. This representation is used in the disambiguation algorithm described below.

Note that in the case of Necker-Cube ambiguity, the context groups will correspond to the major senses of a word. For example, the contexts of the "garment" sense of "suit" are more similar to each other than to contexts of the "lawsuit" sense. The two senses will thus each get their own group. We will see however that in some cases this prediction is not borne out since only associational information is used in Word Space. Associational information does not characterize contexts sufficiently in many cases.

3.4.5   The Disambiguation Algorithm

The disambiguation algorithm, which I call *context-group disambiguation,* is based on the word, context, and sense representations described above. It can be stated as follows. For an occurrence t of word v:

Disambiguation without Coactivation
- Collect all words w_i that occur in t's context.
- For each w_i, retrieve its word vector $\vec{u}_i$.
- Compute the context vector $\vec{c}$ of t's context as the weighted sum of all word vectors $\vec{u}_i$.
- Retrieve all sense vectors $\vec{s}_j$ of v.
- Assign t to the sense j whose sense vector $\vec{s}_j$ is closest to $\vec{c}$.

This algorithm selects the context group whose sense vector is closest to the context vector of the occurrence of the word that is to be disambiguated. Context vectors and sense vectors capture semantic characteristics of the corresponding context and sense, respectively. Consequently, the sense vector that is closest to the context vector has the best semantic match with the context. Therefore, context-group disambiguation categorizes the occurrence as belonging to that sense.

The algorithm described above assigns only one sense per occurrence. It can be generalized for coactivation as follows. For an occurrence t of word v:

Disambiguation with Coactivation
- Collect all words w_i that occur in t's context.
- For each w_i, retrieve its word vector $\vec{u}_i$.
- Compute the context vector $\vec{c}$ of t's context as the weighted sum of all word vectors $\vec{u}_i$.
- Retrieve all sense vectors $\vec{s}_j$ of v.
- Assign t to the n senses $j_1, \ldots, j_n$ whose sense vectors $\vec{s}_{j_k}$ are closest to $\vec{c}$.

This simple generalization is capable of modeling coactivation phenomena. For example, if a context vector is located between two sense vectors, then the context is assigned to both senses for $n = 2$.

In summary, Word Space represents three types of entities: words, contexts, and senses. Word representations are derived from associational information, context representations are derived from word representations by computing a centroid, and sense representations are derived from context representations by clustering contexts into semantically coherent groups. Context-group disambiguation assigns an occurrence of an ambiguous word to the sense whose sense vector is closest to the context vector of the occurrence or, in the coactivated case, to the n senses whose sense vectors are closest to the context vector.

3.5 Experimental Results

In order to test context-group disambiguation, it was applied to the disambiguation of ten artificial ambiguous words and ten natural ambiguous words that appear with reasonable frequency in the New York Times corpus. Table 11 glosses the major senses of the twenty words.

Artificial ambiguous words or *pseudowords* are a convenient means of testing disambiguation algorithms (Gale et al., 1992c; Schütze, 1992). It is time-consuming to hand-label a large number of instances of an ambiguous word for evaluating the performance of a disambiguation algorithm. Pseudowords circumvent this need: Two or more words, e.g., "banana" and "door" are conflated into a new type ("banana-door"). All occurrences of either word in the corpus are then replaced by the new type. It is easy to evaluate disambiguation performance for pseudowords since one only needs to go back to the original text to decide whether a correct decision was made.

The pseudowords shown in Table 11 were created as follows. All word pairs were extracted from the corpus, i.e. all pairs of words that occurred adjacent to each other in the corpus in a particular order. All numbers were discarded since numbers do not seem to involve sense ambiguity. Pseudowords were then created by randomly drawing two pairs from those that had a frequency between 500 and 1000 in the corpus. Pseudowords were generated from pairs rather than simple words because pairs are less likely than words to be ambiguous themselves. Pair-based pseudowords are therefore good examples of ambiguous words with two clearly distinct senses.

The column "pos" in Table 11 shows the parts of speech of the senses of the ambiguous word. Some senses can be realized as verbs or nouns (e.g., sense 2 of "plant").

Table 12 indicates how often the ambiguous word occurred in training and test set, how many instances were instances of rare senses, and the baseline performance that is achieved by assigning all occurrences to the most frequent sense. In the evaluation given here, only the two most frequent senses are taken into account. As can be seen from Table 12,

word	sense	pos	definition
pseudoword 0	1	N	wide range
	2	N	consulting firm
pseudoword 1	1	N	heart disease
	2	N	reserve board
pseudoword 2	1	N	urban development
	2	N	cease fire
pseudoword 3	1	N	drug administration
	2	N	fernando valley
pseudoword 4	1	N	economic development
	2	N	right field
pseudoword 5	1	N	national park
	2	N	judiciary committee
pseudoword 6	1	N	japanese companies
	2	N	city hall
pseudoword 7	1	N	drug dealers
	2	N	paine webber
pseudoword 8	1	N	league baseball
	2	N	square feet
pseudoword 9	1	N	pete rose
	2	N	nuclear power
capital	1	N	stock of goods
	2	N	seat of government
interest	1	NV	a feeling of special attention
	2	N	a charge for borrowed money
motion	1	N	movement
	2	N	a proposal for action
plant	1	N	a factory
	2	NV	living being
ruling	1	NV	an authoritative decision
	2	V	to exert control, or influence
space	1	N	area, volume
	2	N	outer space
suit	1	N	an action or process in a court
	2	N	a set of garments
tank	1	N	a combat vehicle
	2	N	a receptacle for liquids
train	1	N	a line of railroad cars
	2	V	to teach
vessel	1	N	a ship or plane
	2	N	a blood vessel

TABLE 11 Senses of artificial and natural ambiguous words.

word	training	test	rare senses	baseline
wide–range consulting–firm	1422	149	0%	62
heart–disease reserve–board	1197	115	0%	54
urban–development cease–fire	1582	101	0%	50
drug–administration fernando–valley	1465	122	0%	52
economic–development right–field	1030	88	0%	68
national–park judiciary–committee	1279	122	0%	70
japanese–companies city–hall	1569	208	0%	58
drug–dealers paine–webber	1183	104	0%	55
league–baseball square–feet	1097	143	0%	66
pete–rose nuclear–power	1245	103	0%	52
capital/s	13015	200	2%	64
interest/s	21374	200	4%	58
motion/s	2705	200	0%	55
plant/s	12833	200	0%	54
ruling	5482	200	3.5%	60
space	9136	200	0%	56
suit/s	7467	200	12.5%	57
tank/s	3909	200	4.5%	90
train/s	4271	200	1.5%	74
vessel/s	1618	144	13.9%	69

TABLE 12 Number of occurrences of test words in training and test set, percent rare senses in test set, and baseline performance (all occurrences assigned to most frequent sense).

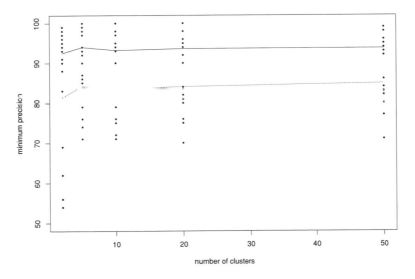

FIGURE 7 Minimum precision of context-group disambiguation for different numbers of clusters.

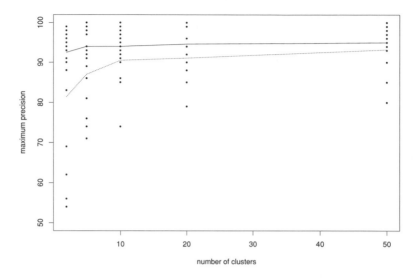

FIGURE 8 Maximum precision of context-group disambiguation for different numbers of clusters.

rare senses make up at most 13.9% of the instances of a word and much less for most words. Note that rare senses were not discarded in training.

Training and test set were taken from the New York Times News Service. The training set consisted of all months from the period June 1989 through October 1990. The test set was taken from November 1990 and May 1989. The test set was truncated after the first 200 occurrences of the word if there were more than 200 occurrences (hence a constant number of 200 occurrences for nine of the ten natural ambiguous words).

Five experiments were conducted to determine the effect of window size, number of dimensions, number of clusters, and degree of supervision on disambiguation performance. In each of the following figures, the solid line indicates average performance for pseudowords and the dotted line average performance for natural words. Performance for each word and value is also plotted individually as a dot.

Figures 7 and 8 show how disambiguation performance depends on the number of clusters used. Ideally, contexts in the test set should be disambiguated according to the sense of the closest cluster in the training set. For this procedure, the senses of the clusters in the training set need to be known. Unfortunately, labeling all instances in the training set would take several weeks. For this reason, two experiments were

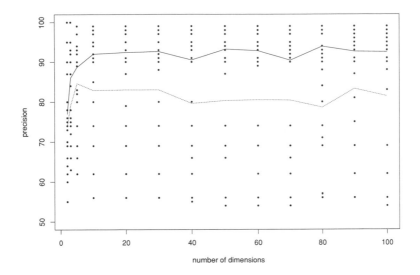

FIGURE 9 Precision of context-group disambiguation for different dimensionalities.

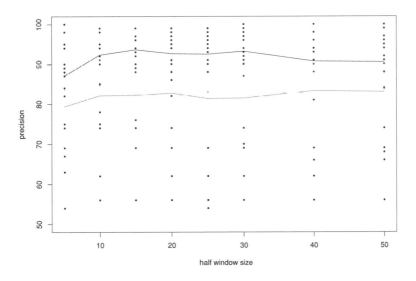

FIGURE 10 Precision of context-group disambiguation for different window sizes.

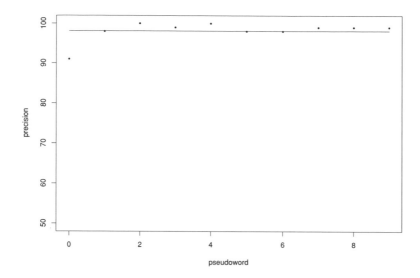

<small>FIGURE 11</small> Precision of supervised disambiguation.

conducted that approximate the performance of an algorithm that would label instances according to the closest cluster in the training set:

- **Lower bound algorithm.** Clusters were assigned to senses based on a rough categorization of instances in the training set. For the rough categorization, instances in the training set were clustered into n clusters ($n = 2, 5, 10, 20, 50$) and clusters were labeled by inspecting a few of their members. All members of a cluster were then assigned the label of their cluster. This procedure gives a lower bound since the rough categorization of the training set contains many errors. Performance for different cardinalities is shown in Figure 7.

- **Upper bound algorithm.** Clusters in the test set were assigned according to majority membership of the cluster in the test set. This algorithm gives an upper bound since the best possible performance for a given set of clusters is achieved if every cluster in the test set is assigned to the category that most of its instances belong to. Performance for different cardinalities is shown in Figure 8.

The two figures suggest that performance increases from 2 to 10 clusters, but that a larger number of clusters does not result in further improvement. However, note that this conclusion only holds for an evaluation on two major senses. If fine sense distinctions are important, a larger number of clusters may well be beneficial (as in the example "living space" vs. "office space" given below).

Figure 9 shows how performance for two clusters and dimensionality of the representation space interact (i.e., the number of dimensions of word, context, and sense vectors). Clearly, the spaces with two and three dimensions are inferior to higher-dimensional spaces. Surprisingly, the figure does not show convincingly that using more than 10 dimensions is beneficial for performance. Further work is necessary to determine whether this result holds true only for structures with two clusters, or whether structures with many clusters can benefit from higher-dimensional spaces.

Figure 10 demonstrates that computing the context vector of an occurrence based on windows of size 30 or more is better than computing them for size 10 windows and possibly slightly better than for size 20 windows. (All windows are centered on the ambiguous word.) Words at a distance of more than 15 from the ambiguous word do not seem to contribute helpful information for context-group disambiguation.

A final experiment was conducted to compare context-group disambiguation with a supervised algorithm. The supervised algorithm used was Linear Discriminant Analysis (LDA) on context vectors. LDA computes a one-dimensional projection of the cloud of context vectors of an ambiguous word so that the instances of the two senses are separated as well as possible. Since such a supervised algorithm requires a labeled training set, it could only be applied to the pseudowords. Figure 11 shows performance for the ten pseudowords as well as average performance. The figure confirms that supervised disambiguation is a much easier task than unsupervised disambiguation: average performance is more than 98% and the error rate for all pseudowords but one is 2% or lower.

Figures 7 – 11 only present the distribution of precision numbers and their averages. The reader can consult Table 13 for results for individual words.

3.5.1 Analysis of Results

It is also helpful to analyze individual classification decisions as opposed to the averages over all instances presented so far. The two following case analyses give examples for typical correct and incorrect classification decisions ("suit") and for finer grained distinctions that are discovered with cluster structures of more than two clusters ("space").

window size	50	50	50	30	50
number of dim's	100	100	5	100	100
number of clusters	10	10	2	2	2
supervised?	no	no	no	no	yes
min / max	min	max	–	–	–
wide–range consulting–firm	72	74	62	74	91
heart–disease reserve–board	97	97	97	99	98
urban–development cease–fire	95	99	99	99	100
drug–administration fernando–valley	98	98	74	96	99
economic–development right–field	100	100	99	99	100
national–park judiciary–committee	95	95	92	97	98
japanese–companies city–hall	94	94	92	92	98
drug–dealers paine–webber	93	94	93	94	99
league–baseball square–feet	93	93	82	89	99
pete–rose nuclear–power	95	96	97	97	99
capital/s	90	90	93	93	–
interest/s	79	91	92	92	–
motion/s	72	86	89	88	–
plant/s	94	94	80	76	–
ruling	76	92	90	88	–
space	71	85	66	56	–
suit/s	94	95	94	96	–
tank/s	90	93	90	90	–
train/s	75	85	83	74	–
vessel/s	94	94	69	69	–

TABLE 13 Some of the results from Figures 7 – 11 on a word-by-word basis.

The following two contexts of "suit" were correctly classified as belonging to the senses "garment" and "lawsuit" respectively:

Gene, long haired and laid back, preferring jeans and blazer to a suit, went to film school ...
The suit was filed in federal court ...

On the other hand, the following context was misclassified as being an instance of the sense "lawsuit":

Sharpton said, "I have been on the attorney general's case, and I will be on his assistants like a suit jacket throughout the arraignment and the trial."

The analysis of these three instances is obvious. In all three cases, there were relatively reliable indicators for one of the two senses (words like "jeans", "filed", and "attorney"), but in the third case these indicators were misleading. This analysis suggests that the algorithm will do the better the more the sense distinctions correspond to distinctions in topic. There's a clear difference between the topics "law" and "clothes". Therefore, the algorithm does well for "suit".

A much harder case is "space". Both the "outer space" meaning and the "limited extent" meanings are fragmented over many different topics. Here are some of the classes that were found in clustering the context vectors:

- NASA space program: the shuttle, satellites, space capsules (class 1)
- space and scientific research (class 3)
- space and weapons, Star Wars (class 8)
- space in art (exhibition space, stage space) (class 4)
- line space (as in "or use the space below to write me") (class 6)
- office and living space (class 7)

The fact that classes 4, 6, and 7 are instances of a more general sense was not recognized. However, this example supports the claim that the distinction between senses is really a cline. While the difference between "office space" and "exhibition space" definitely is not a case of Necker-Cube ambiguity, it may well be that different concepts are associated with the two interpretations since the way they are experienced is quite different.

Finally, the case of the ambiguous word "interest" demonstrates that context-group disambiguation works well even if only one of the senses is clearly topically distinguished. The "interest rate" sense has as many good indicators as the two senses of "suit". However, the general sense of "interest" is not topically well distinguished. Still, disambiguation is very reliable.

3.6 Discussion

This section discusses Word Space and its relevance for the notions of sense and ambiguity. The discussion is divided into three blocks, corresponding to three disciplines that have contributed work on ambiguity: computer science, lexicography, and linguistics. Finally, I will briefly discuss Word Space's implications for Fodor's hypothesis about the innateness of semantic categorization.

3.6.1 Ambiguity in Natural Language Processing

It is commonly known in the field of Natural Language Processing that even simple sentences have a large number of possible readings. Apart from syntactic and scope ambiguities, lexical ambiguity is the main culprit for the proliferation of readings. Lexical ambiguity includes not only what I have called Necker-Cube ambiguity, but also finer distinctions that are necessary, so that the reasoning component of an NLP system can make correct inferences. For example, in the CYC project (Lenat and Guha, 1989) the proper name *Fred* is represented by several different symbols: for the person Fred, Fred's body, Fred's mind, Fred as a child, Fred as an adult, Fred on vacation in France. The large number of representations is necessary, because a single symbol "Fred" would license unwanted inferences. For instance, Fred's being 32 years old would license the inference that he was 32 years old 20 years ago if the representations for Fred as a child and Fred as an adult are not kept distinct.

Usually, most of the proposed readings are not correct. The standard assumption is that only one is intended. Even if, as I have argued, several readings can be coactivated, the problem of excluding a large number of incorrect ones remains. One strategy is to assign this task to the inference component. For example, the PP "on the 20th" modifies to "rehearse" in (27), because Christmas is on the 25th, Christmas masses are on the same day, and therefore not on the 20th. Here the inference component can rule out the bad reading that the mass took place on the 20th.

(27)   They rehearsed the Christmas mass on the 20th.

Putting the burden of disambiguation on the inference component is problematic because most readings cannot be distinguished by what is logically possible or impossible. Even the implausible reading that the mass took place on the 20th can be contextualized for (27). And even an apparently contradictory reading can be the right one to select if it is used metaphorically, sarcastically or as an outright lie.

If logical possibility or impossibility is not the right criterion, then disambiguation must be based on preferences, probabilities, degrees of appropriateness, or some other non-discrete measure that can be used to rank readings. It is not clear how purely symbolic representations for lexical items and syntactic structures could give rise to such a ranking. This is one of the key motivating factors for WORD SPACE: vector representations of words, senses and contexts in the multi-dimensional space can capture degrees of appropriateness. For example, the closer a context vector is to a particular sense vector, the stronger the evidence that this sense is the correct one (or one of the correct ones). Graded information is passed from words to contexts to senses. The various possible readings can be ranked and the correct one selected. In a purely discrete system, such a ranking is hard to achieve.

Of the computational models in the literature that I have discussed, only two adopt discrete representations. The neobehaviorist model is concerned with semantic categorization in the absence of ambiguity, so it does not address ambiguity. Siskind only models the acquisition of ambiguity, but not disambiguation itself. I suspect that for disambiguation, a non-discrete component would have to be added to his model.

All other models solve the disambiguation problem by some method of ranking that involves a real-valued measure. The fact that most computational models of disambiguation adopt non-discrete methods indicates that gradience may also be crucial in explaining the acquisition of syntax and semantics by children.

A possible objection to the relevance of computational work for acquisition is that none of the models discussed, including mine, achieves human performance. Most models have a performance of about 90% on average. This is far better than the baseline of always picking the most frequent sense of an ambiguous word, which results in correctness of 70% (according to Gale et al. 1992a). But human performance is better still: between 96% and 99% (Gale et al., 1992a).

I attribute the difference in performance to the limited amount of information that most computational models discussed use. In particular, the associational information used in WORD SPACE often does not characterize contexts sufficiently for correct disambiguation. The above-mentioned threat by Sharpton to be like a suit jacket on the attorney general's assistants is a case in point. Most of the associations here are with legal terms. But a more fine-grained analysis would detect that "suit jacket" is the unit critical for disambiguation here.

In general, WORD SPACE only disambiguates well if sense distinctions are mirrored by topical distinctions. The distinction between suit as garment and suit as lawsuit corresponds almost perfectly to the distinction between the topics "clothes" and "law". There are many cases of ambiguity where topical distinctions are not as helpful, and Word Space would not achieve a performance of 90% for them.

Although many of the models discussed achieve 90% performance, they do so with quite different means. Most use sources of information that are not available to the child like training sets or bilingual corpora. This makes them less plausible as models of the acquisition of ambiguity. It is more plausible that the child has access to the global categorization used in class-based disambiguation. However, the second ingredient for the disambiguation procedure in class-based disambiguation, knowledge about the classes in which senses for a particular word occur, is again implausible as something that is known a priori.

Word Space uses none of the outside sources of information that any of the other methods rely on. Only language input, in the form of text corpora, is available during learning. Of course, I do not claim that children learn based on such surface information only. I simply excluded clearly implausible input like bilingual corpora. Unfortunately, semantic representations for the content of large corpora are not available, so they could not be included in the model, although non-associational semantic information is clearly very important for children in acquisition.

Despite these limitations, Word Space performs quite well, which is surprising given that it starts out with so much less than other algorithms. This success demonstrates that Word Space is viable as a model of sense acquisition and disambiguation.

3.6.2 Ambiguity and Gradience in Lexicography

Two distinctive properties of disambiguation in Word Space are non-unique sense individuation and coactivation. The distribution of context vectors for a particular word can be carved up coarsely or finely, depending on the granularity of the distinctions between senses. Multiple senses can be coactivated at the same time, by invoking several senses that share semantic characteristics with the context in question instead of invoking only the one that shares most semantic characteristics.

My main evidence for non-unique sense individuation was Geeraerts' argument for the context-sensitivity of ambiguity tests. According to these tests, two different interpretations of a word w can be two senses in one context (making w ambiguous), but just different shades of the same meaning in another context (making w unambiguous). This suggests that the decision whether or not to draw a line between two interpretations of a word (leading to ambiguity or vagueness) depends on a variable threshold of semantic distinctness, rather than an absolute criterion. This variability supports the thesis of non-uniqueness of sense individuation.

My main evidence for coactivation came from psycholinguistic experiments that demonstrate initial coactivation of all readings of an ambiguous word. The activation of senses against which the context of use is biased falls off after a couple of hundred milliseconds. I gave examples from lexical, syntactic and semantic ambiguity which are best explained by postulating that coactivation persists if the context of use favors several readings. This evidence supports the thesis of coactivation.

Perhaps the oldest discipline that deals systematically with ambiguity is lexicography. In a recent study of dictionaries, Adam Kilgarriff (1993) also comes to the conclusion that senses can be contextually coactivated and variably individuated:

> Sometimes two senses of a word are mutually exclusive, but more often they are not, and for some usages, both senses contribute different elements to the meaning. (page 381)
> Often, the senses as identified in the dictionary identify points on a continuum of possibilities for how the word is used and dictionary senses might equally have been written which divided up the space differently. (page 381)

He finds potentially coactivated contexts for 60 out of 69 ambiguous words he investigates (page 378). It is possible that some of the coactivated senses are ruled out by the overall context (in the study only 15 words of the context were available on average). However, Kilgarriff writes:

> [I]n some cases, it seemed very unlikely that any amount of context would have disambiguated. I hope the examples below and in the appendix will convince the reader of the validity of this claim [...]

Here are some of the examples: (The contexts are cited as given by Kilgarriff. Unfortunately, many are truncated.)

- **image.**
  - ○ **Sense 1.** a picture formed in the mind
  - ○ **Sense 2.** the general opinion about a person, organization, etc., that has been formed or intentionally created in people's minds
  - ○ **Coactivated context.** the Hollywood "senator" had a noble looking image – as public relations prose sometimes puts
- **color.**
  - ○ **Sense 1.** red, blue, green, black, brown, yellow, white, etc.

- ○ **Sense 2.** (plural) a special sign, cap, BADGE etc., worn as a sign of one's club, school, team, etc.
- ○ **Coactivated context.** "Wicki's blacks and greys are not only the colours of the lost and the forgotten, but they are
- **competition.**
  - ○ **Sense 1.** the act of competing; the struggle between several people or groups to win something or gain an advantage; RIVALRY
  - ○ **Sense 2.** the (other) competitors
  - ○ **Coactivated context.** houses. For better or for worse this would bring competition to the licensed trade. He said: "that

The words "critical" and "distinction" are examples of continua that are not properly accounted for by a fixed sense individuation:

"Critical" [...] participate[s] in a common pattern relating a "neutral" sense of the word to a "far end of the scale" sense. (page 386)

One could slice this continuum into smaller parts instead of choosing the two extremes as focal points as was done in LDOCE:

- **critical.**
  - ○ **Neutral end of scale.** providing a careful judgment of the good and bad qualities of something ("Her new book received critical acclaim.")
  - ○ **Far end of the scale.** of or being a moment of great danger, difficulty, or uncertainty, when a sudden change to a better or worse condition is likely; of or being a CRISIS ("The next two weeks will be critical.")
- **distinction.**
  - ○ **Neutral end of scale.** the fact of being different; clear difference
  - ○ **Far end of the scale.** the quality of being unusually good; excellence

The following two usages seem between the two ends of the scale:

(28) a. few nervous children are diffident about facing a critical audience of their own fellows. To overcome

  b. separate bream species. It can not even claim the distinction of being a bream "variety" or "

The difficulties of choosing one sense individuation rather than another are widely known in lexicography. For example, Morton quotes Philip Gove, the editor of Webster's Third, as saying (Morton, 1994):

Rather grotesquely, after centuries of lexicography and language study of one sort or another, it appears that no one has answered the question of how we may know with sharp clarity and definitive exactness when a word has one meaning alone ... and when it has two or more quite discrete meanings.

Similarly, Atkins (1993) agrees with Lyons (1969) that "the choice of one polysemous entry or two or more homonymous entries"

is, the last resort, indeterminate and arbitrary ... it rests upon the lexicographer's judgment ... the arbitrariness of the distinction between homonymy and multiple meaning is reflected in the discrepancies in classification between different dictionaries. (page 39)

Lexicographers are arguably the ones who have spent most time and research on the concept of sense. The fact that their sense definitions give rise to coactivation and continuity supports my claim that senses can be flexibly individuated and simultaneously used.

3.6.3 Ambiguity and Gradience in Linguistics

3.6.3.1 The Semantics-Pragmatics Distinction

A critic of gradient sense individuation could object that of all sense individuations that I claim to be possible only the coarsest one truly delimits senses from each other whereas finer distinctions are really between different contextualizations of one sense rather than different senses. In other words, only Necker-Cube ambiguity is real ambiguity, whereas finer individuations capture meaning nuances rather than ambiguity. In linguistics, this is the line between semantics and pragmatics, meaning and use. Semantics is the theory of core meaning, pragmatics the theory of how to use it in context, for example how to adapt a core meaning contextually.

The semantics-pragmatics distinction has been critically examined in cognitive linguistics, notably by Langacker (1988) in *Cognitive Grammar*. One of his central claims is that the semantics-pragmatics distinction, the distinction between linguistic and world knowledge, is fuzzy rather than a sharp boundary.

In his discussion of the meaning-use (or meaning-reference) distinction, Langacker (1988) criticizes what he calls the rule-list fallacy: restricting the admissible entities of linguistic theories to being either completely general rules or completely idiosyncratic, individually stored items. Instead he advocates a view of linguistic knowledge that permits entities of any intermediate regularity and productivity. For instance, the paradigm of past tense formation in (29) is moderately productive.

It was extended to "quit" and "fit", but it is not as productive as the "-ed" past tense.

(29) a. put – put – put
       b. cut – cut – cut

(30)   The cat is on the mat.

The rule-list fallacy is also relevant for the semantics-pragmatics distinction. Consider the use of sentence (30) at an exhibition match for a wrestler who has pinned down a tiger on a mat (Langacker 1987:158). There isn't anything conventional about this use, it can only be understood by using rule-like entities such as "All tigers are cats." Langacker writes about (30):

> Suppose now that tiger-wrestling becomes a fad, and that sports commentators hit upon [(30)] as a cliché to describe the moment of defeat for the tiger. In this case [(30)] quickly becomes a conventional unit of English whose semantic pole refers specifically to a tiger-wrestling event. (1987:158)

Any intermediate degree of conventionalization can be realized in our linguistic system. If the interpretation of a linguistic unit is "constant in a series of usage events" (1987:158) then more and more "chunking" will occur that can lead to storage as an idiosyncratic unit in its last stage. A sharp division between what is inferred and what is retrieved, between the pragmatic extension and the core semantics, seems implausible in light of examples such as (30).

Example (30) demonstrates an important point in Cognitive Grammar: that frequency and saliency of the interpretation of a linguistic unit lead to different degrees of conventionalization. A particular interpretation of a linguistic unit can move on a cline from innovation to complete conventionalization. For an innovation, the full meaning is produced by filling out the core meaning with inference rules and other world knowledge. For a completely conventionalized interpretation, the full meaning is retrieved from semantic memory. If Langacker is right and interpretations of linguistic units can occupy points anywhere on this cline, then there is no basis for a sharp semantic-pragmatics distinction. This argument further justifies multiple sense individuations in WORD SPACE, a feature of the model that presupposes that there is no such sharp distinction.

3.6.3.2 Prototypicality

A special case of gradience in semantic categorization is prototypicality (see for example Lakoff 1987). Geeraerts characterizes prototypicality as follows: (1989:592–593)

- Prototypical categories exhibit a family-resemblance structure, or more generally, their semantic structure takes the form of a radial set of clustered and overlapping meanings [...]
- Prototypical categories exhibit degrees of category membership; not every member is equally representative for a category [...]
- Prototypical categories are blurred at the edges [...]

In order to test the ability of WORD SPACE to represent prototypicality, I performed a case study for the word "interest". I chose a fine sense individuation for "interest", i.e., a set of context vectors of "interest" was classified finely (into 15 clusters). All contexts of "interest" in 25,000 articles in five months of the New York Times News Service were clustered using Buckshot. The fifteen clusters found corresponded to subsenses of "interest" that subdivided the supersenses PERCENT and CONCERN. The sentences in (31), (32), and (33) are the first contexts in the corpus that were assigned with high confidence (cosine of 0.80 or higher) to three of the clusters: cluster 14 "national interest" (31), cluster 5 "group interests, lobbying" (32), and cluster 8 "individual interests" (33). (The word "interest" is printed in bold face in each sentence.) The fact that the first three high-confidence instances correspond so well to the prototype of the cluster shows that the clusters are intuitive with respect to a faithful rendering of prototypicality effects although they also contain some exceptional contexts which were not characterized well by associational information.

(31) a. "The big producers of OPEC, including Iraq, Iran and Saudi Arabia, have an *interest* in stable oil prices [...]" (NYTNW, June 1990)

   b. Abu Hisam [...] also had extensive discussions with East German secret police on military technical training, [...] and intelligence on American and Israeli *interests* in Western Europe [...] (NYTNW, July 1990)

   c. A prime goal of the London summit was to send a clear signal to the Kremlin that NATO no longer constitutes a threat to vital Soviet security *interests* [...] (NYTNW, July 1990)

(32) a. [...] the most explosive issue is likely to be the right to represent Southern Baptist *interests* in Washington. Moderates favor leaving the lobbying to the Baptist Joint Committee on Public Affairs [...] (NYTNW, June 1990)

   b. [...] the alcoholic beverage industry has started a radio advertising campaign against the measure. Alcohol and wine *interests* also support a much smaller tax hike proposal [...] (NYTNW, June 1990)

   c. Common Cause [...] said Thursday that savings and loan *interests* contributed more than $11 million to members of Congress during the 1980s [...] (NYTNW, June 1990)

(33) a. "Evita," which opened in New York in 1979, may finally make it as a film. Madonna has long been *interested* in the title role [...] (NYTNW, June 1990)

   b. Despite his father's success as a pro, Domingo said it was his older brothers who sparked his *interest* in playing college baseball. (NYTNW, June 1990)

   c. Alan Alda's new film starts out well enough, then takes an abrupt turn and becomes a different, and far less *interesting*, movie. (NYTNW, June 1990)

Figure 12 shows principal components 2 and 3 of the matrix of correlation coefficients of the 537 contexts in the three clusters. (Some of the contexts were identical since articles and parts of articles are often repeated in the News Service. For this reason Figure 12 actually shows fewer than 537 elements.) Words in clusters 8, 5, and 14 are plotted using the letters "i" 'individual', "g" 'group', and "n" 'national', respectively. The scattergram shows that the subsenses exemplify the first property of prototypicality: the context space of "interest" exhibits a family resemblance structure, a radial set of clustered and overlapping meanings. The clusters are overlapping in the sense that the points between the cluster centers have assignments greater than zero for several clusters, so in a sense they belong to several clusters at the same time. Only the letter corresponding to the primary cluster is plotted here.

The second characteristic of prototypicality, the gradience of membership, is modeled in that the distance of a context from the center corresponds to the degree of membership in the cluster. For instance, context 150, my (32a), is part of the dense lump in the center of the "g" cluster. Similarly, context 2144, my (31c), is in the center of cluster "n". These two contexts are prototypical examples of the use of "interest" in the senses "group interest" and "national interest", therefore the classification program assigned them with a high probability to their respective clusters. Consider on the other hand contexts 5902 and 7965 in the corpus, (34a) and (34b) below. Here, the assignment is less certain and the contexts consequently show up at the fringes of their clusters. The reason is that (34a) can be interpreted as expressing a national interest (or what the head of the Democratic Front for the Liberation of Palestine thinks is in the interest of the Palestinian people), but it

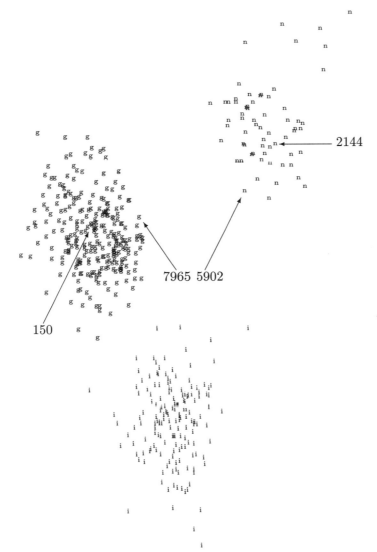

FIGURE 12 Prototypicality in the context space of "interest".

is phrased as an individual interest: *"he* was interested . . . ". Similarly, (34b) describes Senator Pete Wilson's lobbying in personal conversations with President Bush, but it is lobbying for the state of California, so the interests involved are state interests and therefore close in meaning to national interests. Both (34a) and (34b) are slightly atypical uses of their respective subsenses of "interest". Therefore they appear at the fringes of their clusters.

(34) a. A moment later, he [Hawatmeh, the head of the Democratic Front for the Liberation of Palestine HS] insisted that he was interested in attacking only Israeli military targets. (September)

b. The Republican candidate for governor said he has nonetheless effectively represented the state's interests in personal conversations with President Bush [. . .] (October)

Finally, the third property of prototypicality, that categories are fuzzy and blurred at the edges, is apparent from the scattergram. In fact, fuzziness and membership gradience are closely related: it is the fuzzy fringe that contains contexts that have been assigned with low confidence, contexts such as (34a) and (34b). On the other hand, since the degree of membership is gradient there can be no clean delineation of a subsense, resulting in the blurry appearance of the clusters in Figure 12.

The borders of the clusters contain many uses that do not fit in very well, and there are also some clearly incorrect assignments. But the above examples show that the space comes close to a faithful account of prototypicality. The disambiguation results suggest that the clues imposed by different words as to what subsense of "interest" is activated in a given context are successfully integrated.

This case study underscores the importance of gradience in WORD SPACE'S representational medium. The real-valued multi-dimensional vector space can represent the characteristic properties of prototypicality: family resemblance among different subsenses, centrality, and membership gradience.

3.6.3.3 Labov's Study of Gradience in Categorization

An empirical study of prototypicality (although this term was not used by him) is Labov's investigation of the word "cup" (Labov, 1972). Labov designed a set of drawings of cups and cup-like objects which were varied according to several dimensions, for example width-to-depth ratio and presence of a handle. These drawings were presented to subjects in contexts in which the function of the cup was to hold food, tea, or flowers or the function remained unspecified. Subjects were asked to name the object on the drawing.

Labov found that both width-to-depth ratio and function strongly influenced categorization. For example, objects were categorized as vases only in the flower context, with few exceptions. But even in the flower context, categorization as a cup dominated for high width-to-depth ratio. Labov summarized his findings in the following definition:

The term cup is regularly used to denote round containers with a ratio of width to depth $1 + r$ where $r \leq r_b$, and

$$r_b = \alpha_1 + \alpha_2 + \ldots + \alpha_\nu$$

and α_i is a positive quantity when the feature i is present and 0 otherwise.
Cup is used variably to denote such containers with ratios of width to depth of $1+r$ where $r_b \leq r \leq r_t$ with a probability of $r_t - r/r_t - r_b$. The quantity $1 + r_b$ expresses the distance from the modal value of width to height. (pages 366-7)

The features are: with one handle, made of opaque vitreous material, used for consumption of food, used for consumption of liquid food, used for consumption of hot liquid food, with a saucer, tapering, and circular in cross-section.

The value r_b is the boundary between categorical and variable categorization of objects as cups. Objects whose width to depth ratio is below the threshold are always called cups whereas objects with a ratio between r_b and another value r_t have a certain probability of being called a cup. This probability decreases linearly from 1.0 at r_b to 0.0 at r_t.

Labov chooses this model because many of the experiments he describes yield a close to linear relationship between width-to-depth ratio and probability of being categorized as a cup – linear between the two values that he calls r_b and r_t in the definition just given. The value for r_b varies from function to function (food vs. tea vs. flowers etc.) For example, the context food favors the label "bowl" more than the context tea does.

The exact form of this definition is unlikely to be correct. For example, the features do not seem to be independent of each other. Seeing the object on a saucer is a very strong clue, which will diminish the effect of weak clues like material and shape in cross-section. But in the absence of any strong clues, the latter can have a strong effect on categorization. The model also neglects the influence of context on categorization (something I try to capture with the flexible context vectors in WORD SPACE). A guest in a house where flowers are displayed in cups will probably change her categorization behavior. Labov concedes that other models (for example, a hyperbolic formulation) would also be compatible with the data he presents.

Despite these possible shortcomings, Labov's experiment clearly demonstrates gradience in semantic categorization. Subjects do not flip categorically from the label "cup" to the label "vase" when the width-to-depth ratio exceeds a certain value. Instead, there is a smooth transition in the preference of one label over another. Labov's findings are therefore further evidence for the importance of gradience in semantic categorization as they are formalized in the Word Space model. Labov makes a similar point in the concluding remarks of his article with reference to Aristotle:

> A secular approach to further research in semantic description will necessarily carry us outside of the schools, beyond the limitations of scholastic intuitions, and beyond the categorical view which survives intact in the doctrines of the schoolmen. (page 369)

3.6.4 Innateness

Full innateness of semantic categorization is rarely claimed, but at least one philosopher, Jerry Fodor, has defended this position (Fodor, 1975):

> To put it tendentiously, one can learn what the semantic properties of a term are only if one already knows a language which contains a term having the same semantic properties. (page 80)
>
> It follows immediately that not all the languages one knows are languages one has learned, and that at least one of the languages which one knows without learning is as powerful as any language that one can ever learn. (page 82)

Innatism is more implicit in the two acquisition models that rely on an internal language. In the neobehaviorist model, a word can only be linked with an element of the internal language, i.e., an internal symbol with the right meaning must be present from the start. In Siskind's model, only a small inventory of semantic primitives is presupposed, which in itself is not problematic. However, since only a few of the large number of combinations of these primitives are tested as possible correlates of a word in the input, strong innate constraints on what kind of combinations are possible would have to be added in order to make the model fully workable.

Word Space shows that semantic categorization can be acquired quite successfully without strong innate knowledge. This undermines Fodor's claim that one can only learn meanings of terms that have exact innate analogues. Moreover, an innate semantic category is only of benefit if inducing the outside category and linking it to the corresponding innate category is more easily accomplished than learning the allegedly innate category from scratch. As in the case of syntactic categories, no evidence is given that the complexity of acquisition is actually lower, if all semantic categories are innate.

The most implausible aspect of Fodor's position is that all possible concepts that a child will ever acquire during her life time are present at birth, including the most complicated technical terms. It is hard to conceive of a plausible explanation as to how all possible concepts could have become hard-wired in the course of evolution.

A more plausible set of assumptions about innate mechanisms is made by Regier in the L0 project (Regier, 1992). Most features of his learning system are justified by results from psychological or neuroscientific research. However, it is also true that spatial cognition, the topic of Regier's thesis, is arguably one of the domains that is pre-structured most by innate knowledge. It is therefore not clear how well the success of L0 would generalize to other domains. WORD SPACE is more general in that it relies only on the criterion of contextual similarity for forming semantic categories. Defining contextual similarity in terms of associational information is not sufficient (for discussion see, for example, Resnik 1993) and a better model would have to impose constraints from other areas of cognition (e.g., spatial and visual cognition) on the measurement of similarity. Still, WORD SPACE demonstrates the viability of a model of the acquisition of semantic categorization without an innate internal language that is as powerful or almost as powerful as the language that is to be learned.

3.7 Conclusion

In this chapter, I have introduced WORD SPACE, a model of the acquisition of semantic categorization and lexical disambiguation. WORD SPACE acquires semantic categorization based on contextual similarity without dependence on an internal symbolic language or other innate knowledge. WORD SPACE is based on a notion of sense which is novel in two respects: a) the uses of a word can be grouped into senses in several ways, depending on context; b) the senses of a word can be used simultaneously, i.e. they are not mutually exclusive. A wide array of evidence was given to justify both coactivation and non-unique sense individuation, including the non-discreteness of the semantics-pragmatics distinction, prototypicality in linguistic categorization, and a lexicographic study. I hope that the perspective on semantics I have taken here, which takes ambiguity as a central property of language rather than a design flaw, will prove fruitful for developing both better NLP applications and more adequate theories of language.

4

Semantic Information in the Acquisition of Subcategorization: A Connectionist Account

One of the most complex parts of English grammar is the subcategorization of verbs, i.e. the syntactic means by which verbs express their arguments. This chapter presents an account of how the ability to select the correct subcategorization frame is acquired. I will first discuss the theory of subcategorization acquisition proposed by Steven Pinker in "Learnability and Cognition" (Pinker, 1989) (henceforth LC): Lexical Rule Theory (LRT). Then an alternative account will be developed, based on a connectionist model of the acquisition of the dative alternation.

Of the three models presented in this book, the connectionist model of subcategorization most clearly demonstrates the benefits of statistical learning algorithms for acquisition. It will be argued that LRT is needlessly complicated and does not account for overregularization and other phenomena attested in subcategorization learning. I will argue that, once statistical learning is taken seriously as an alternative to symbolic rule-based learning, the connectionist model emerges as a more adequate account of subcategorization selection.

Several readers of drafts of this book have suggested that subcategorization selection is a relatively minor subpart of acquisition. For example, acquiring a complete semantic representation of words, including the morphosemantic features that we will assume to have been learned in a previous phase in this chapter, is a much harder problem. Subcategorization selection was chosen as a case study of how a better account of linguistic generalization is possible in a non-rule-based formalism. My hope is that such a concrete example can serve as inspiration for solving other learning problems in a non-nativist framework.

How do the problems of ambiguity, gradedness and nativism manifest themselves in subcategorization? Ambiguity in subcategorization learning is different from part-of-speech and sense ambiguity. Recall the basic definition of ambiguity: different underlying representations of a surface form that cause different behavior of a linguistic process. In the case of part of speech and word sense, ambiguity is a property of the adult language. The word "suit" has two senses, and the word "flies" two parts of speech in adult competence. In the case of subcategorization, ambiguity only occurs during acquisition. An example are verbs specified for manner of speaking which do not allow the dative construction:

(1)   * I whispered him the news.

Sentences like (1) violate some people's sense of well-formedness in a more subtle way than outright ungrammatical structures do. Still, there is virtually universal agreement that (1) is not correct English.

The question I will address in this chapter is how the child arrives at a representation of verbs like "whisper" that guarantees correct subcategorization. If a verb of speaking is used to describe a situation that the child perceives, then the manner of speaking is apparent from the situation. The ambiguity problem in the acquisition of subcategorization is that the child needs to decide whether the verb's underlying representation for the purposes of subcategorization includes the specification of manner or doesn't. Only in the latter case would the dative construction be legal (we will see later that verbs specified for manner disallow the dative alternation). So the process influenced by different possible underlying representations of a verb like "whisper" is the production of subcategorization frames. At the end of acquisition, the speaker has settled on one of the representations as the correct one, and all ambiguity has been resolved.

One problem in modeling the acquisition process is what I call the *Transition Problem:* How does the child progress from the initial state without knowledge about subcategorization to the final state of perfect knowledge. I will argue that a gradient connectionist model explains the transition better than discrete models like the one proposed by Pinker in LC.

The connectionist model and Lexical Rule Theory also differ in their use of innate knowledge. LRT relies on linking rules and certain constraints on linguistic representations. The connectionist model and its representations reflect only general cognitive constraints, e.g., the ability to recognize the focus of attention or to categorize two actions as simultaneous or temporally disjoint. I will argue that subcategorization acquisition without syntax-specific prior knowledge is possible despite claims to the contrary by Pinker and others.

4.1 Baker's paradox

(2)   a. She gave the student a book.
      b. She gave a book to the student.
      c. * She donated the church a book.
      d. She donated a book to the church.
      e. ... because He envied him the tree of life ... (Brown Corpus)
      f. * He envied the tree of life to him.

Verbs differ in how they express their arguments or subcategorize for them. Consider the different grammatical means employed by verbs that have both a theme and a benefactive or malefactive role. The verb "give" uses either the dative construction (2a) (also called the ditransitive construction) or a prepositional construction with "to" (2b). The alternation between these two constructions is called the *dative alternation*. With "donate", only a "to"-PP can encode the beneficiary (2c),(2d). For some verbs that take an argument that is being adversely affected, for example "envy", the dative construction is obligatory[1] (2e), (2f).

These data are summarized in Table 14.

verb	grammatical constructions	
	dative	"to"-PP
"give"	yes	yes
"donate"	no	yes
"envy"	yes	no

TABLE 14 Encoding of benefactive and malefactive arguments in English.

The variety of subcategorization schemes raises a puzzling question: How can the correct subcategorization of verbs be learned given the variation between the different possibilities in Table 14? Certain assumptions about this problem lead to a paradox that was first described by Baker (Baker, 1979). In the formulation of Gropen et al. (1989), it arises from three premises:

---

[1] There is also a small number of verbs that can express the beneficiary or maleficiary as the direct object and the theme as a prepositional phrase, e.g. "envy" in (3).

(3)   I envy you for your youth.

Since there seem to be no systematic alternations for this type of argument I will not cover it here.

a. A verb's subcategorization is unpredictable from intrinsic properties of the verb.

b. There is no negative evidence in subcategorization learning.

c. Subcategorization is productive (i.e., children will use subcategorization frames that they have not heard).

There is some evidence for each of the premises. In many cases, subcategorization seems idiosyncratic to the point of being unpredictable with many pairs of semantically highly similar verbs that have different subcategorization behavior (a). The existence of negative evidence in natural language input to children has been generally denied (b). And both children and adults produce novel subcategorization frames like "He was communicated that his performance was unsatisfactory." and sometimes outright errors, a point we will come back to later (c).

The three premises taken together give rise to a paradox. If subcategorization is unpredictable (premise a), then it must be learned for each verb individually. With no negative evidence available (premise b), the child would have to limit herself to repeating subcategorization frames perceived in parental speech. But this contradicts premise c), productivity (i.e. the child will use verbs with unattested subcategorization frames). Hence, the three premises result in a paradox, since children apparently do succeed in acquiring subcategorization correctly.

Baker (1979:547ff.) resolved the paradox by giving up productivity. He proposed restrictions on possible rules that excluded rules like the dative alternation. If children could not form a rule capturing the dative alternation, they would be forced to learn each verb's subcategorization frames separately. Under the assumption that subcategorization is not productive, lack of negative evidence and arbitrariness would not be a problem in this theory.

However, there clearly is productivity in subcategorization as first pointed out by Wasow in a reply to another paper by Baker (about a similar paradox in morphology). Speakers of English will use a new verb like "satellite" with the dative construction even if they have not encountered this use in other people's speech:

(4)   Wasow says he will satellite me his answer next week. (Wasow 1981:325)

Therefore, the reason for the paradox must (at least partially) lie in the other two assumptions, absence of negative evidence and unpredictability. At least one of them has to be weakened or abandoned. Since the absence of negative evidence has been one of the fundamental tenets of generative grammar, most researchers have tried to show some degree of predictability in subcategorization. In particular, the most complete and worked out account of subcategorization acquisition so far, Steven Pinker's "Learnability and Cognition," falls into that category. His account will be discussed in Section 4.2. My own proposal adopts weakened versions of the three premises, thereby avoiding the paradox. It is the subject of section 4.3.

4.1.1 Early work on Semantic Regularity

It may not be immediately clear why Baker was so pessimistic about predicting subcategorization from inherent properties such as meaning. There seems to be quite a lot of systematicity in the subcategorization of verbs. The first major study of semantic regularity in subcategorization, albeit not from the point of view of acquisition, was Georgia Green's "Semantics and Syntactic Regularity" (Green, 1974). For example, she noticed that verbs of "future not having" such as "charge", "fine", and "deny", only allow the dative construction to express an adversely affected participant, not a prepositional construction. The absence of alternation in this class thus has a semantic correlate.

Given that there are such semantic correlates, why doesn't semantic predictability offer an obvious account of how subcategorization is learned? The reason is that the correlations are weak for some semantic features and that there are many exceptions. So while semantic regularity can help the language learner to find patterns in verbs' subcategorization behavior, it is too partial to be a complete solution to the paradox. This partiality of regularity led Richard Oehrle, who was responsible for the second early study of the dative construction after Georgia Green's, to argue against a semantic account (Oehrle, 1975, 1976). He writes about the limited regularity of semantic and morphological factors in Green's theory.

> It would be an illusion to think that even in combination they [semantic and morphological constraints HS] adequately specify it, however. Many cases remain which we have nothing to say about. For example, why does the verb "lower" undergo the dative alternation whereas the verbs "raise" and "lift" do not? [...] The theory outlined above does not treat such cases correctly, but this is a defect common to all theories of the dative alternation of which I am aware. (Oehrle 1976:138)

Because of objections like this one to an account solely based on semantic regularity, there was little work on exploring the importance of meaning for subcategorization in the decade after Green's and Oehrle's dissertations. It is symptomatic of the antisemantic bias of theoretical linguistics in this time that Baker saw no need to justify his unpredictability assumption.[2] But with the resurgence of lexical approaches to grammar in the early and mid-eighties, it became clear that intrinsic properties of lexical items could not be ignored anymore. Steven Pinker's 1989 book on argument structure in fact made the semantic-based approach the dominant view in theoretical linguistics. However, the problem of exploiting partial regularity while not being misled by it, the problem that made Oehrle and Baker discount semantic regularity as an important factor, still remains. We will return to it in our critique of Pinker's theory.

4.2 The Lexical Rule Account of the Acquisition of Subcategorization

This section describes the account of subcategorization learning proposed by Pinker (1989) and Gropen et al. (1989). The theory defines two representational levels, lexicosemantic structure and argument structure and a mapping between those two levels. The mapping mechanism consists of discrete and partially innate linking rules. The crucial departure from Baker is that the application of linking rules is semantically (and also morphologically) conditioned by the meaning that is encoded in lexicosemantic structure. Pinker retains Baker's two other premises, that no negative evidence is available in acquisition and that subcategorization is productive.

The proposal set forth in LC can be best explained with an example. The sketch in Figure 13 is not an attempt at formalization (notice the missing variables that would bind the right entities in the event structures and the predicate argument structures). Rather it is intended to capture the gist of LRT. But first a definition of some linguistic terms that we will need, simplified for our purposes:

(6)   a. The *external* or *first* argument of a verb is its subject. Example: "Mary" in "*Mary* gave John the book."

       b. The *direct internal* or *second* argument of a verb of transfer is the thing that is transferred. Example: "money" in "Mary gave *money*." and "Mary gave John *money*".

       c. The *second internal*, *indirect* or *third* argument of a verb of transfer is the recipient if expressed as an object. Example: "John" in "Mary gave *John* money".

---

[2]This doesn't mean that everybody agreed that semantics were irrelevant for subcategorization. In fact, Wasow writes in the above mentioned reply to Baker: "How are such subcategorizations to be learned? ... It seems to me that this is another case in which meanings might be useful. It has frequently been suggested ... that at least some of the cooccurrence restrictions in question were actually semantic restrictions."

(5) a. EVENT

$$\text{EVENT} \left[\begin{array}{l} \text{ACT (giving)} \\ \text{THING}_1 \text{ (Mary)} \\ \text{THING}_2\text{:Y (John)} \end{array} \middle| \begin{array}{l} \\ \text{(RESULT-)} \\ \text{STATE} \end{array} \left[\begin{array}{l} \text{HAVE (holding)} \\ \text{THING}_2\text{:Y (John)} \\ \text{THING}_3 \text{ (the book)} \end{array} \right] \right]$$

b.

$$\text{EVENT} \left[\begin{array}{l} \text{ACT (giving)} \\ \text{THING}_1 \text{ (Mary)} \\ \text{THING}_2\text{:Z (the book)} \end{array} \middle| \text{EVENT} \left[\begin{array}{l} \text{GO} \\ \text{THING}_2\text{:Z (the book)} \\ \text{PATH} \left[\begin{array}{c} \text{to} \\ \text{PLACE} \end{array} \middle[\begin{array}{l} \text{at} \\ \text{THING}_3 \text{ (John)} \end{array} \right] \right] \end{array} \right] \right]$$

c. $\text{EVENT} \left| \dfrac{\text{ACT}}{\text{THING}_1} \right.$ ⇒ *external (= first) argument*

d. $\text{EVENT} \left| \dfrac{\text{ACT}}{\text{THING}_2} \right.$ ⇒ *direct internal (= second) argument*

e. $\text{EVENT} \left| \begin{array}{l} \text{ACT} \\ \hline \text{STATE} \left| \dfrac{\text{HAVE}}{\text{THING}_3} \right. \end{array} \right.$

⇒ *second internal (= third) argument*

f. give(Mary,John;book)

g. Mary gave John the book.

h. give(Mary;book), to(John)

i. Mary gave the book to John.

FIGURE 13 The dative alternation in Lexical Rule Theory: An example.

d. The recipient can also be expressed as a *prepositional phrase* headed by "to": "Mary gave money *to John*."

Now we can look at the example of LRT in Figure 13 in detail. (5a) and (5b) give two alternative lexicosemantic structures for the event of Mary giving John a book. (5a) focuses on the resulting state (John holding the book) whereas (5b) focuses on the event of transfer (the book moving over to John). Lexicosemantic structures are translated into argument structures by means of linking rules such as the ones in (5c) – (5e). Each linking rule specifies a minimal feature structure. The rule is only applied to lexicosemantic structures compatible with this minimal feature structure. A linking rule also has a designated entity which determines the object in lexicosemantic structure that will be linked to an argument (underlined). In our example, the linking rules produce (5f) from (5a) using the three rules (5c), (5d), and (5e); and (5h) from (5b) using (5c) and (5d) (in addition, in (5h), "to(John)" is produced by a rule that transforms a particular PATH-PLACE-THING structure with an argument into the predicate "to" with the same argument; this rule is not shown in the figure). (5f) and (5h) correspond to sentences (5g) and (5i), respectively. Note that no second internal argument can be produced from (5b) since the path specification for this argument requires "STATE" as the second part of the path, not "EVENT" as in (5b).

(7)   a. He taught me English.

b. He taught English to me.

A key feature of LRT is that the alternation between prepositional and dative construction is reduced to two different underlying lexicosemantic structures. Contrasting pairs like (7) are evidence for pragmatic differences between the two constructions, i.e. differences in implication, focus etc. Only (7a) implies that the teaching was successful. If (7a)'s underlying semantics is analogous to (5a), i.e. if it focuses on the result of teaching, then the implication of success is to be expected. On the other hand, the lexicosemantic representation of (7b), corresponding to (5b), focuses on the process of knowledge being transferred, and is neutral with respect to the outcome of the teaching. For other verbs, it is much harder to find convincing evidence for pragmatic differences between dative and prepositional construction. We will not be concerned with this question since it is not crucial for the part of the theory that deals with acquisition. However, it is indispensable for the lexical rule account that there be different lexicosemantic representations for different subcategorization frames. In cases where we don't find pragmatic nuances, we can stipulate that the difference between the two representations is purely formal.

To make the well-formedness of a particular argument structure dependent on the existence of a corresponding lexicosemantic structure is of course not a solution to the problem of how children learn which argument structures can be used with which verbs. It just moves the problem from the level of argument structure to the level of lexicosemantic structure. The critical component of the theory for solving the learning paradox is thus the system of constraints that generates certain lexicosemantic structures and rules out others. It is here that semantic conditions are used. Semantic criteria define so-called broad-range and narrow-range conflation classes. Two narrow-range classes are verbs of instantaneous imparting of force ("throw") and verbs of continuous imparting of force ("push"). Only the former class allows the dative construction:

(8)   a. Mary threw John the ball.

        b. * Mary pushed John the cart.

Before we embark on an investigation of broad-range and narrow-range classes, it is important to stress that lexicosemantic structure is only meant to represent certain basic information about the semantics and pragmatics of an utterance. For example, the sentences (9a) and (9b) would be represented exactly the same way as (5g) and (5i), i.e. their lexicosemantic representations are (5a) and (5b), respectively.

(9)   a. Mary handed John the book.

        b. Mary handed the book to John.

Pinker (1989) defines an inventory of primitives for lexicosemantic representation, consisting of atoms like "EVENT", "ACT", and "PATH". The primitives are combined in hierarchical structures such as those in (5) with a few additional structural relations like coreference (e.g. the coreference of the two "THING$_2$" in (5b)). Pinker motivates this restriction of the power of the representational formalism by showing that idiosyncratic information is often not relevant for subcategorization. For example, "hand" and "give", two verbs that only differ in the idiosyncratic specification of the manner of transfer (general or by means of a hand), have identical subcategorization behavior. It is obvious that one needs some classification of semantic information according to how relevant it is for subcategorization. The fact that a verb describes a kind of transfer (abstract or concrete) makes it a strong candidate for allowing the dative construction. On the other hand, the use of a hand in the transfer seems less relevant for grammatical behavior. The art is to find a classification of semantic information that makes the right predictions, and one that is learnable. Broad-range and narrow-range conflation classes are intended to be precisely such a classification.

4.2.1   Broad-Range and Narrow-Range Classes

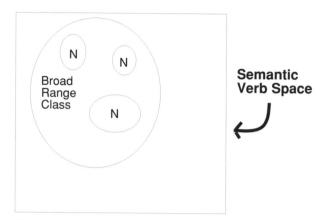

FIGURE 14   Narrow-range classes ("N") and broad-range classes in LRT.

The proposal put forth in (Pinker, 1989) can be schematized as shown in Figure 14. The square symbolizes the semantic space of all verbs. For any particular construction (e.g. the dative construction or the prepositional "V NP to NP" construction), verbs are governed by broad-range and narrow-range conflation classes. The large circle ("Broad Range Class") is the broad-range class of verbs that is semantically compatible with the construction in question. For example, the broad range class of verbs compatible with the dative construction contains all verbs that are about some form of transfer. A verb outside of the broad-range circle yields a completely ungrammatical sentence if used with the frame since the most basic semantic appropriateness conditions are not satisfied. In contrast, every verb within the region of the broad-range class can be understood when used with the construction, even if such a use is not grammatically well-formed. For example, "donate" is semantically compatible with the dative construction, but a sentence such as (10) is ill-formed though interpretable.

(10)   She donated the church a book

Narrow-range classes serve the purpose of differentiating those interpretable uses of a construction that are grammatically well-formed (members of a narrow class) from those that are grammatically ill-formed (not members of a narrow class). Narrow-range classes are rendered as small circles marked "N" within the broad-range class circle in Figure 14.

In the case of the dative construction, verbs like "give", "throw", and "envy" are in narrow-range classes that license fully grammatical use of double objects. Narrow-range classes also constitute the part of the theory that accounts for productivity. If a new verb is created that falls semantically into one of the narrow-range classes, then it will fully participate in the construction.

4.2.2 Acquisition of Conflation Classes

Two different learning mechanisms are used in LRT for broad-range classes and narrow-range classes. Broad-range classes are acquired by reverse inference from syntactic argument structures using innate linking rules. While this account is in principle successful at explaining acquisition, it may rely too heavily on innate knowledge as will be discussed. Narrow-range classes are acquired by inducing a classification on lexico-semantic representations of verbs. I will raise two problems with this proposal: the Transition Problem (the impossibility of gradual change of the representations in Lexical Rule Theory), and the Ambiguity Problem (the acquisition of the correct underlying representation of a verb if several are compatible with the situation of use).

4.2.2.1 Broad-Range Classes

The definition of a broad-range class specifies the semantic grid that must be minimally part of the semantic definition of a verb in the class. For example, the broad-range class of verbs allowing the dative construction is defined by an event of an agent acting on the recipient with the result of a theme being transferred from the actor to the recipient (5a). In LRT, broad-range classes are learned by reverse application of linking rules (1989:265). Suppose that the child has the means of analyzing (11a) as the predicate argument structure (11b).

(11)   a. Mary gave John the book.

      b. give(Mary,John,book)

      c. EVENT $|$ $\begin{array}{c}\text{ACT}\\\text{THING}_1\end{array}$ $\Rightarrow$ *external (= first) argument*

      d. EVENT $|$ $\begin{array}{c}\text{ACT}\\\text{THING}_2\end{array}$ $\Rightarrow$ *direct internal (= second) argument*

      e. EVENT $\left|\ \begin{array}{c}\text{ACT}\\\text{STATE}\end{array}\right|\ \begin{array}{c}\text{HAVE}\\\text{THING}_3\end{array}$

      $\Rightarrow$ *second internal (= third) argument*

Then she could infer much of the structure of the broad-range class definition in (5a) by reverse application of the linking rules (11c) – (11e) (repeated from 5). Since there is a second internal argument in (11b) ("book"), part of the class definition must be a structure containing the left side of linking rule (11e). Since there is a first internal argument ("John"), the class definition must also have a substructure corresponding to the left side of (11d) etc. A large part of the definition of a broad-range class can by inferred by this procedure. Pieces of information not induceable from argument structures could then be added by abstracting over verbs actually existing in the language. Checking against attested lexical forms would also let the language learner choose between alternative broad-class definitions in cases where more than one linking rule with identical right hand side can produce a given argument structure (Pinker 1989:266).

My main objection to this proposal for learning broad-range classes is that it crucially relies on the innateness of linking rules. No direct evidence for this hypothesis is given in LC. Innate linking rules are often justified by citing the near-universality of certain kinds of linking. For example, most languages link the agent of an event to the subject of the clause. However, there are many languages that link patients to subjects. Even if only five percent of the world's languages are of this type (Pinker 1989:251), it is not clear how representative the sample of existing languages is for possible human languages. It also needs to be stressed that terms like "agent" and "subject" are abstract concepts whose definition varies from language to language. A researcher looking for a particular kind of linking rule may find it by defining "agent" and "subject" appropriately, although other definitions would support a different system of linking rules. In general, the inference from typological frequency to genetic innateness is highly problematic. With the same justification one could say that straight hair must be universally innate since numerically it is more common than curly hair.

In summary, no convincing account of broad-range class learning is given in LC because it relies on the central hypothesis that linking rules are innate, a hypothesis that is not supported by strong evidence.

4.2.2.2 Narrow-Range Classes

Whereas broad-range classes capture the semantic core of a particular construction (for example, transfer for dative), narrow-range classes specify finer grained semantic regularities to discriminate groups of verbs that allow the full paradigm of argument structures (e.g., dative and prepositional construction) from groups that have deficient paradigms (e.g., only dative or only prepositional construction). Narrow-range classes (or motivated classes) are introduced in LC as follows ("narrow classes licensing a lexical rule" (1989:109)):

A motivated class is a family of items whose membership conditions are too varied and unusual to be deduced a priori from universal principles or constraints, but whose members hang together according to a rationale that can be discovered post hoc – so the family is not an unstructured list, either. The full motivation for a subclass may come from the psychology of the first speakers creative enough or liberal enough to extend a linguistic process to a new item, as such speakers are unlikely to make such extensions at random. Thereafter the subclass might be learned by simply memorizing its definition, by grasping its motivation all at once with the aid of a stroke of insight recapitulating that of the original coiners, or by depending on some intermediate degree of appreciation of the rationale to learn its components efficiently, depending on the speaker and the subclass involved. (1989:109)

This characterization leaves many questions unanswered. How can a definition be memorized if it isn't available to the language learner in the first place? Is it possible to rely on a "stroke of insight" to recover the motivation of the original coiners of a narrow class if their motivation was rooted in the linguistic structure of their time, e.g. in the fact that their was a morphological dative that alternated freely with certain prepositional constructions? Given the fact that subcategorization judgments seem moderately stable, why would one expect that an "intermediate degree of appreciation of the rationale" of a narrow class is consistent across speakers? In LC, some of these questions are addressed in the "Strong Hypothesis for Narrow-Range Rule Formation":

The Strong Hypothesis. "Upon noticing that a pair of individual verbs are morphologically and semantically related in a way captured by a nonaffixing broad-range rule, the learner would create a rule whose semantic operations mapped the narrow conflation class specification for one onto the narrow conflation class specification of the other. In other words, the generalization that the learner would make would be: if verb X alternates, other verbs with the same grammatically relevant semantic structure alternate, too." (1989:274)

The seed for the formation of a narrow-range rule is hence the comparison of (the semantics of) individual verbs. Unfortunately, the simplest scheme for comparison would not model acquisition correctly (1989:278): transfer of subcategorization frames does not only occur in the case of identical semantic representations, i.e. in cases where new and old verb's semantics differ only in grammatically irrelevant idiosyncrasies. For example, "bounce" specifies the manner of motion, so its lexicosemantic grid is different from the verb "move" (no specification of motion). In

LRT, the similarity of "bounce" to "move" is the basis for producing (12b) from (12a), in analogy to the derivation of (12d) from (12c).

(12) a. The ball bounced.
      b. I bounced the ball.
      c. The ball moved.
      d. I moved the ball.

The notion of identity in the strong hypothesis therefore needs to be replaced by similarity of lexicosemantic grids. In this modified scheme, the learner would strip a new verb of all idiosyncratic semantic features and compare it with existing verbs (similarly stripped of idiosyncrasies) in the broad-range class. She would then determine subcategorization for the verb according to closest match among existing verbs with similar semantics. There is some speculation about varying importance of features for determining similarity in the discussion of narrow-range classes in LC (p. 279). "Manner" should not prevent "move" and "bounce" from being in a common class. On the other hand, the single feature "imparting of force" (continuous vs. instantaneous) needs to keep apart the differently behaving verbs "throw" and "pull". The number of distinguishing features could also be important for similarity judgments (p. 279). Apart from these considerations, no attempt at defining the notion of similarity of grammatically relevant semantic structure is made. Since narrow class formation is founded on the concept of semantic similarity, the LC account must be considered incomplete. The crucial part for solving Baker's paradox, the acquisition of narrow-range classes, is thus missing from Lexical Rule Theory.

4.2.3   The Transition Problem

At the heart of the difficulty with similarity is a more fundamental problem, a problem shared by other exclusively symbolic approaches. A learner masters subcategorization when she has acquired the definitions of narrow-range classes or, equivalently, the rules that determine class membership. In contrast to broad-range classes, these definitions are learned without innate help, so there is no information about them at the outset of learning. For each of the classes, there must therefore be a point where the learner creates its definition and undergoes a transition from a rule-less state to a rule-governed state. Presumably, the transition from non-rule to rule would correspond to the realization by the learner that a large cluster of verbs with similar lexico-semantic grids is really one of the narrow-range rules in the language. Instead of looking up the closest neighbor of a new verb, subcategorization behavior would then be determined by the rule. However, the decision whether a group of verbs is a "large cluster of verbs with similar lexico-semantic grids" seems to be quantitative in nature. There is always noise in the input, either in the form of incorrect subcategorization frames (Gropen et al., 1989:251), or in the form of exceptions.

For example, "present" and "donate" belong to the "giving" class semantically, but using them in the ditransitive construction results in marginal and completely incorrect sentences, respectively:

(13)　a. * They donated the trust fund a large sum of money.
　　　b. ? They presented her a bouquet.
　　　c. He gave her a present.

So one cannot demand that a transition from non-rule to rule can only occur if there isn't a single exception or it would never occur. If quantitative factors play an important role in the transition from non-rule to rule, it is hard to see how a purely symbolic learning procedure could succeed in acquiring verb subcategorization correctly. I will call this difficulty for a symbolic account the *Transition Problem*.

The transition problem is a serious challenge for a view of language as a symbolic system of rules and representations. Only on the assumption that strong innate knowledge reduces learning to choosing among a small number of alternatives is an obvious symbolic solution to the transition problem possible. Section 4.3 presents a connectionist model that gradually evolves from ignorance to perfect knowledge of subcategorization and therefore avoids the problem of abrupt transitions. It will be argued that with weak innate knowledge, learning in the presence of errors and ambiguity must rely on quantitative information to successfully acquire subcategorization.

4.2.4　The Ambiguity Problem

There is a basic unclarity in Lexical Rule Theory as to whether lexicosemantic representations describe the abstract meaning of a verb or a particular situation of use. Sometimes lexicosemantic representation seems to be a description of the semantics of the verb, its core meaning abstracted over all situations of use. Consider verbs whose dativizability depends on the absence of specification of manner. Of course, in most situations in which a verb is used, manner is specified indirectly, since it can be inferred from other words or from background knowledge as in (14a) where an adverbial phrase specifies the manner of speaking. In order for LRT to work, manner is not an admissible part of the lexicosemantic representation of "tell" in (14a). Otherwise "tell" would not dativize, in analogy to "shout" in (14b) (which cannot undergo the dative alternation because it inherently specifies manner). Hence the intended object of representation must be the abstract meaning of the verb in this case.

(14) a. He told me his story in a loud voice.
     b. * He shouted me his story.

(14a) is a case where the representation of the situation would rule out the dative construction although it is possible. Similarly, there are cases where the representation of the situation would predict the possibility of a dative, although such a possibility does not exist.

(15) a. I moved the ball to him by throwing it.
     b. * I moved him the ball by throwing it.
     c. I threw him the ball.

For example, the core meanings of (15a) and (15c) are the same. But only "throw" allows the dative construction whereas it is out for "move" (15b). Again, the intended object of representation must be the verb proper.

(16) throw, toss, flip, slap, kick, poke, fling, blast

But in many cases lexicosemantic descriptions seem to be intended as descriptions of the *situation* in which the verb is used. For example, Pinker writes about the verbs in (16) (classified by him as dativizable):

> [A]mong the verbs that can result in a change of possession but do not necessarily do so, some subclasses can be reinterpreted by a narrow lexical rule to denote changes of possession, by means of which they inherit the double-object argument structure, and other[s] cannot. (Pinker 1989:110)

Here, it is not the core meaning of the verb that decides dativizability. Instead, the transfer component of the dative construction is added to the basic meaning of "kick" in a sentence like (17a). Since argument structures are generated from the underlying lexicosemantic representation in Lexical Rule Theory, this means that the underlying representation here is about the situation, not about the verb (which lacks the transfer component of meaning).

(17) a. Lafleur kicks him the puck; he shoots, he scores! (1989:110)
     b. Lafleur kicks the puck to him; he shoots, he scores!
     c. I saw him kicking an empty coke can down the road.

It is not only the core meaning of the dative, i.e., transfer, that is imposed on the verbs in (16) in ditransitive uses. Instantaneity is another semantic element that is added to the basic verb meaning. For example, (17b) is in principle vague as to how many strikes of the stick it took Lafleur to get the puck to his teammate (although in the context of ice hockey, one expects there to have been only one strike). (17c) is another example that shows that "kick" is vague as to the number of strikes applied. But (17a) implies that there was one instantaneous action that got the puck to Lafleur's teammate. If (17b) is intended to refer to a situation where several strikes were applied, then it can't be transformed into (17a). Again, this argues for taking the lexicosemantic description of the underlying situation as the basis for generating argument structure. Only on this assumption can the generation of (17a) in a non-instantaneous meaning be prevented.

Transfer and instantaneity are *semantic* factors that pertain to the situation of use rather than to the verb's core meaning. There also seem to be *pragmatic* factors that facilitate dativizability. For example, "deny" and "refuse" are generally regarded as verbs that allow the prepositional construction with "to" only marginally, or not at all (Levin 1993, p. 47, her (119); Pinker 1989, p. 111; Hornby 1974, p. 721; Benson et al. 1993, p. 70, p. 202). However, when there is special focus on the beneficiary, e.g. it is stressed contrastively or it is a heavy NP, then the "V NP to NP" construction is possible as has been observed by Green (1974:174) and Wierzbicka (1986:161).

(18) a. The council denied them its seal of approval.
      b. ? The council denied its seal of approval to them.
      c. The National Council [. . .]
         denied its seal of approval to 11 of 50 programs examined. (NYTNW 08/28/90)
      d. They refused her a license.
      e. ? They refused a license to her.
      f. In 1982 it rejected the Playboy publisher Hugh Hefner as "unfit" to hold a casino license [. . .]
         It also refused a license to the hotelier Barron Hilton in 1984 [. . .] (NYTNW 08/26/90)

For example, (18b) and (18e) are much worse than (18c) and (18f) because an NP without focus is marginal with "deny" and "refuse" whereas a focussed NP is acceptable.

Some authors have made similar claims for "allow". Boguraev and Briscoe (1989) characterize the prepositional construction as marginal with "allow". According to Wierzbicka (1986), "deny" and "allow" share the property of licensing "V NP to NP" only if there is focus on the second NP. ((Benson et al. 1993:8) write that "deny" and "allow" are "usually" not used with preposition.)

(19) a. The furlough program allowed them up to three months of annual leave.

    b. ? The program allowed up to three months of annual leave to them.

    c. [...] the state's prison furlough program
    [...] allowed leave to a convicted killer
    (NYTNW 06/01/90)

To illustrate, the sentence (19c), which stresses the NP governed by "to", is much better than the unfocussed NP in (19b).

Apart from focus, a prohibition against using a pronoun as a theme in the ditransitive construction is another pragmatic factor influencing subcategorization. The following examples are for the pronoun "it".

(20) a. ? John denied his children love, just as his parents had denied him it.

    b. John denied his children love, just as his parents had denied it to him.

    c. ? Mary protested, when the commission gave Peter a license, but refused her it.

    d. Mary protested, when the commission gave Peter a license, but refused it to her.

    e. ? The previous administration had denied them leave, but the new director allowed them it.

    f. The previous administration had denied them leave, but the new director allowed it to them.

In each case, the propositional construction is much more acceptable since (American?) English avoids using a pronoun as the theme of the ditransitive construction.

Verbs like "deny", "refuse", and "allow" are evidence that pragmatic factors are important in determining the acceptability of the dative alternation. Since pragmatic factors cannot be part of the core semantics of a verb, a theory that aims to correctly delimit the set of argument structures that can be generated must describe the situation of use in the underlying lexicosemantic representation, rather than the verb's core semantics.

What does this evidence mean for the object of lexicosemantic representation, should it be individual situations or verbs' core meanings? The answer is a little of both. In the case of "tell", the contextual specification of manner should not be represented in order to correctly predict that "tell" differs from verbs like "shout".

In the case of "deny", the contextual specification of focus needs to be included in order to correctly predict that the prepositional construction is possible.

If this criticism is right, then Lexical Rule Theory is confronted with a fundamental problem, which I will call the *Ambiguity Problem*. As with word sense and part of speech, the same lexical item can correspond to different underlying representations, depending on how much of the context needs to be added to the basic verb meaning. For example, only "deny" with focussed beneficiary allows the prepositional construction, "deny" with unfocussed beneficiary does not. So the pragmatic factor "focus" is crucial for learning the correct subcategorization for "deny". In contrast, "give" places no such restriction on its argument structure: both focussed and unfocussed beneficiary can be expressed using "to"-PPs. This situation puts the learner in a dilemma. How is she to know that in (19c) focus is the crucial pragmatic factor that licenses the prepositional construction, whereas focus is irrelevant for licensing the argument structure of (21)?

(21)   She gave it to a convicted killer.

Pinker attempts to solve this problem by designing a restricted representational language and stipulating that whatever can be represented in this language is part of the representation that predicts argument structure. This attempt fails because a) there are bits of information whose representation would result in incorrect argument structures (the case of "manner" in (14a)) and b) there are bits of information crucial for subcategorization behavior that cannot be represented like heaviness of NPs (the case of "deny").

Subcategorization on the one hand and part of speech and word sense on the other are similar because the learner has to choose between different underlying representations. But there are also differences. Most importantly, disambiguation of underlying representations of lexicosemantic structure never affects comprehension. If a child chooses the wrong sense of a word, then she will misunderstand the sentence. This is not possible for subcategorization, since the different possible representations of the verb only carve out different parts of the total representation of the sentence. For example, if focus is not included in the verb's representation, then it will be represented as a contextual feature if it was recognized at all. (If it was not recognized, then different explanations for why a particular subcategorization was chosen cannot correct the error, since we are assuming that the child hasn't learned yet that a particular argument structure can signal focus.)

So comprehension is not affected by ambiguity in subcategorization. An incorrect hypothesis about underlying representations of argument structures only does harm to the child's production. For example, if the child chooses the wrong representation for (19c), one that doesn't contain focus, then she may wrongly conclude that "deny" allows the ditransitive construction without restriction.

My conclusion is that both the core semantics and the situation of use have to be available in a representation that correctly generates argument structure and that learning how to combine the two is one of the key elements of acquiring subcategorization. Section 4.3 will introduce a connectionist model that learns to combine verb-specific and context-specific information and thereby solves the Ambiguity Problem.

4.2.5 Summary

In summary, Lexical Rule Theory suffers from three key problems.

- It relies on the problematic assumption of innateness for broad class learning.
- The discrete nature of its representations and processes runs into the Transition Problem: It is not clear how the child would progress from the initial rule-less state to a rule-governed state.
- The proposed learning model does not address the Ambiguity Problem. It fails for verbs that allow certain subcategorization frames for only some of their semantic-pragmatic variants (e.g., prepositional frame only with focussed argument).

4.3 A Connectionist Account of Subcategorization Acquisition

This section describes the connectionist model of subcategorization (4.3.1) and presents experimental results (4.3.2).

Before getting started, though, let me motivate the choice of a connectionist network for modeling subcategorization learning. Of course, the reason for choosing it is not that neural networks are faithful models of how neural tissue functions in the brain. Rather, there are three abstract characteristics of children's learning of subcategorization that can be well modeled using neural networks:

- supervision
- locality
- representational power

First subcategorization learning is supervised. Unlike many hidden properties of natural language (e.g., syntactic structure), subcategorization frames can be easily observed and distinguished.[3] The task of pre-

---

[3]For frames like "V NP to NP", it can be hard to decide whether the phrase "to NP" is actually subcategorized for or whether it is an adjunct of the verb. In what follows, nothing will hinge on the argument-adjunct distinction. The model to be

dicting possible subcategorization for a verb is therefore a supervised learning task. Connectionist networks are excellent models for supervised learning.

Secondly, subcategorization learning is local, i.e. learning takes place one subcategorization frame in the input at a time, rather than by collecting all frames that occur over a long period (a week or a month) and then processing all these frames together. Connectionist networks can be trained pattern by pattern, which is a strictly local learning regime. Many learning algorithms, for example decision trees (cf. Ling 1994), are trained globally: a large number of training instances is processed together. This training regime most likely is not a good model of child language acquisition.

Finally, the task of learning subcategorization is quite complex. The child needs to learn which semantic features are good indicators of certain frames, when context plays a role, which verbs are exceptions etc. Neural networks are capable of representing functions of high complexity (Rumelhart et al., 1995). Therefore, a connectionist model is well suited to capture the complexities of subcategorization.

4.3.1 Description of the Model

This section describes a connectionist model for a *subcategorization selector*, a device that determines preferences for subcategorization frames given a verb, its morphosemantic characterization, and a specification of context. In a more comprehensive model of natural language generation, the subcategorization selector would be linked to a generator. The generator would choose subcategorization frames on the basis of the selector's preferences, avoiding frames that the generator has ruled out for a particular verb and context. It would use other criteria for making a subcategorization choice if the selector gives equal preference to several different frames, criteria like context coherence or prosody.

The subcategorization selector is a simple device that maps a specification of a particular context of use, a verb, and its morphosemantic profile into a set of preferences for subcategorization frames. This section describes the architecture of the selector, the regime used to train its internal representations from input data, and the representation of the input data.

---

developed here is a general model of the acquisition of the expression of "verbal roles", regardless of whether they are arguments or adjuncts.

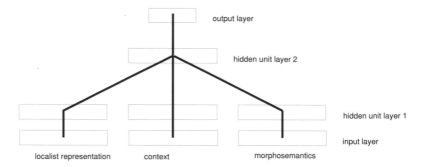

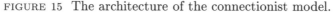

FIGURE 15 The architecture of the connectionist model.

4.3.1.1 Network architecture

Figure 15 shows the architecture of the model. There are three input blocks: a block of localist[4] units (one for each of 179 verbs, see below), one block for contextual features, and one block for morphosemantic features. Each input block is fully connected with a block of 10 hidden units in hidden unit layer 1, i.e., every unit in the input block is connected to every unit in the corresponding hidden layer block. Each of the blocks in hidden layer 1 is fully connected with the block in hidden layer 2 (also consisting of 10 hidden units).

Finally, there are two output units one for the dative construction and one for the prepositional construction with "to". The block in hidden layer 2 is fully connected with the two units in the output layer.

The blocks in hidden layer 1 are responsible for forming generalizations specific to one mode of input. For example, a hidden unit for localist representations may capture the generalization that two or three verbs share an idiosyncratic behavior such as allowing the ditransitive although they are latinate. Or a hidden unit for morphosemantics may capture the generalization that specified manner prohibits the ditransitive in conjunction with the feature "verb of speaking", but not in conjunction with the feature "ballistic motion" (the contrast "* whispered him a secret" vs. "!threw him the ball"). The second hidden unit layer is for generalizations that involve different input modes, for example a combination of contextual and morphosemantic features.

In order to investigate whether the outcome of the experiments de-

---

[4]Localist representations contrast with distributed representations. In localist representations, there is a one-to-one mapping between entities to be represented and input units. In the present case, each verb has a dedicated input unit, and each input unit (in the localist block) represents only one verb. In distributed representations, a group of input units represents an entity as a pattern of activation, and each entity makes use of all input units.

pends on the size of the hidden-unit blocks, three experiments with 20, 30, and 40 units per hidden-unit block are run in addition to the main one with 10-unit blocks.

4.3.1.2 Training regime

The net is trained using the backpropagation algorithm (Rumelhart et al., 1986). Training proceeds by presenting one of the verbs, propagating activation forward through the network to the selection units, computing the error between the selected frames and the actual occurring frame, and backpropagating the error. An example for input and output will be discussed below (Tables 17 and 18). For a given verb, localist and morphosemantic features are the same for each occurrence. In contrast, contextual features are not fixed. For example, the beneficiary of a verb can be focused or unfocused. Therefore, the pattern for a given verb can specify the feature focus to be plus or minus.

The network was trained in 1500 iterations, where each iteration consisted in presenting all verb patterns 25 times to the network.

The rationale for the training regime is that each occurrence of a verb with a subcategorization frame is a learning experience for the child. If her current grammar specifies the incorrect frame, for instance the ditransitive for "donate," then each occurrence of "donate" with the prepositional frame will push the grammar towards the correct subcategorization specification.

This regime models an important aspect of the child's learning situation in that no explicit negative information is available during training. At no point is the network told: "This frame is not possible for this verb." Only positive information is available from each training instance.

A second variety of negative information is what I will call *global negative information*. If information from perceptual input is collected, then negative evidence can easily be derived from memory. For example, if all instances of "donate" are stored, then one can determine by memory look-up that "donate" allows only the prepositional construction. (Such an inference would only be possible for frequent verbs, but still be correct in many cases.) It is not clear whether this form of learning is available to the child. In order to strengthen the argument that no syntax-specific innate knowledge is required for subcategorization learning, training will be done without any global negative information. The parameters of the subcategorization network will be changed on the basis of strictly local information only. This setup guarantees that neither local nor global negative information is used during training.

Finally, the robustness of natural learning is also modeled. For this purpose, the target of a learning instance is degraded with probability .01. A random number generator for the interval [0.0,1.0] is activated for each pattern. If its output is in the interval [0.00,0.01], then the target pattern is flipped: if it specifies the prepositional frame before, it will now contain the ditransitive frame and vice versa. This feature of the training regime models the fact that people sometimes use incorrect subcategorization frames. Therefore, a successful model of subcategorization learning needs to account for learning in the presence of error.

4.3.1.3 Input representation

There are three types of input nodes: localist, contextual, and morphosemantic nodes.

There is exactly one localist input node for each verb. A verb's localist input node is on if the verb is presented and off otherwise. Localist representations are necessary for exception verbs. If a particular verb has subcategorization properties different from verbs with identical or similar morphosemantic features, then the identity of the verb must be known to select the correct subcategorization frame.

class	label	example
9.4	Verbs of putting with a specified direction	lower
11.1	"send" verbs	send
11.2	"slide" verbs	slide
11.3	bring and take	bring
11.4	"carry" verbs	carry
13.1	"give" verbs	give
13.2	"contribute" verbs	contribute
13.3	Verbs of future having	bequeath
13.4.1	Verbs of fulfilling	furnish
17.1	Verbs of throwing	throw
37.1	Verbs of transfer of a message	preach
37.3	Verbs of manner of speaking	babble
37.4	Verbs of instrument of communication	email
37.7	Verbs of communication of propositions	announce
119	Verbs of future not having	begrudge

TABLE 15 Verb classes covered in the model. The table gives class number and class label from Levin (1993).

There are 179 verbs in the model, essentially the verbs of change of possession covered by Pinker (1989) and Boguraev and Briscoe (1989). Some rare verbs like "heft", "mulct" or "to sweep (someone a curtsy)" were omitted. For notational convenience, I will refer to verb groups by the class numbers and labels that Levin uses in her investigation of English verb classes and alternations Levin (1993) (see Table 15).

Two properties of context are modeled in the simulation: focus and instantaneity. The input node for focus is on if the beneficiary of the verb is focussed, and off otherwise. For example, the beneficiary (Mary) is focussed in (22a) and unfocussed in (22b).

(22) a. Who did he give the book? He gave it to Mary.
      b. What did he give Mary? He gave her the book.

The second contextual feature in the simulation is instantaneity. The input node for instantaneity is on if the action in the described context is instantaneous, and off otherwise. For example, the action described in (23a) is instantaneous (one instance of kicking), the action described in (23b) is non-instantaneous (several instances of kicking).

(23) a. Standing in a corner, she kicked the ball to John.
      b. She was kicking a can while walking down the hall.

The third type of input unit represents morphosemantic properties of verbs. Table 16 lists the features and gives examples of verbs that have a positive or negative value for the feature or are unspecified with respect to it. The features represent distinctions between verb classes with different subcategorization behavior, proposed by Green (1974) and Levin (1993). Many of the features are correlated. For example, all "manner of speaking" verbs are also specified for the more general feature "manner". Such correlations occur because the features were selected as a plausible representation of the information available to the language learner, rather than for maximal parsimony.

The features also correspond to parts of Pinker's lexicosemantic representations, but are sometimes defined differently. For example, the feature "latinate" is defined in terms of multisyllabicity and stress, not historical origin, since it is not clear to what extent native speakers know the etymological facts (tacitly or consciously). A short description of each feature follows.

latinate A verb is categorized as latinate if it is polysyllabic and stressed on the last syllable, if it has a latinate prefix like "de-" or "trans-", or the latinate suffix "-ate" (examples: "convey", "advance", "demonstrate"). Monosyllabic verbs ("give"), verbs with germanic prefixes[5] ("overcharge", "afford"), and denominal derivations ("catapult", "telephone") have a negative value for the feature.

---

[5] "announce" and "assign" were categorized as latinate although it is not clear whether the linguistically naive speaker would recognize their non-germanic origin.

feature	examples	
	positive	negative
latinate	contribute	give
simultaneous	give	fine
accompanied	throw	begrudge
specified direction	lower	(most verbs)
manner	bounce	move
speaking	babble	speak
ballistic	throw	(most verbs)
communication	email	(most verbs)
worthy	award	(most verbs)
needed	supply	(most verbs)
transfer	give	begrudge

TABLE 16 Morphosemantic features and example verbs.

"latinate" is the only morphological feature, all others are semantic.

simultaneous This feature applies to verbs for which the initiation of transfer and the transfer itself are simultaneous. For example, the transfer can take months to be completed after initiation for "ship", but is immediate for "give". The feature is negative for verbs that specify no transfer or a transfer from beneficiary or maleficiary to agent ("charge").

accompanied This feature formalizes the concept of "accompanied motion" (Levin 1993:136) used by Levin and Pinker to differentiate the "throw" class (ditransitive possible) from the "carry" class (ditransitive not possible). The agent doesn't accompany the thing thrown, but she does accompany whatever she is carrying. If the object of the transfer is abstract as for "speak" or "begrudge", the value of the feature is negative.

specified direction This feature characterizes a small class of verbs that specify a direction of physical motion: "lower", "raise", "drop", "hoist", and "lift".

manner If we were to characterize every distinctive chunk of a verb's meaning as manner, then all verbs would specify manner. So the meaning of the verb has to be divided into what one could call basic meaning elements and special meaning elements. The problem is that this division is to some extent arbitrary. For example, we can put the complete meaning of "tell" into the background part, which would mean that it does not specify manner. Or we can take the meaning "to transfer a message" as background. In this case, "tell" specifies the manner of transfer: speaking. (cf. (Naigles 1991:73) for a detailed discussion of the problems of the feature "manner")

The solution to this problem is to define manner as contrastive manner. If there is a large class of verbs with similar meanings in the language and if they contrast by a relatively small part of their meaning, the other parts being constant, then it is plausible to assume that the presence of this small part is cognitively salient and available for grammatical categorization such as subcategorization. The following classes of verbs satisfy the conditions of sufficient size and semantic variation in only one limited part of their meaning, and will therefore be categorized as specifying manner:

- verbs of manner of motion: "bounce", "float"
- verbs of direction of motion: "drop", "raise"
- verbs of manner of causation of accompanied motion: "carry", "pull", "push"
- verbs of manner of causation of unaccompanied (ballistic) motion: "kick", "throw"
- verbs of manner of speaking: "babble", "groan"
- manner of communication: "mention", "confess", "remark"

speaking Verbs like "babble" that describe the manner of speaking are specified for this feature.

ballistic The feature characterizes verbs like "throw" that are about ballistic motion.

communication Verbs of means of communication like "email" are specified for this feature.

worthy Verbs with this feature describe a transfer to someone who is worthy of what she gets, for example "award", "bestow".

needed Similarly, some verbs describe a transfer to someone who needs what is being given to her: "supply", "provide".

transfer This feature specifies whether the verb is about a (possible) transfer or not. It distinguishes verbs like "give" that are only true of transfer situations and verbs like "bequeath" that imply that transfer will take place in the future (positive value for "transfer") from verbs like "begrudge", called "verbs of future not having" by Green (negative value for "transfer").

Example target pattern. Table 17 shows the two possible target patterns for "throw". In contrast to "throw", some verbs occur with only one of them. For example, "pull" is always used with the prepositional frame (pattern 2). Even for these verbs pattern 2 in Table 17 does not

	feature	value
pattern 1	ditransitive	1.0
	prepositional	0.0
pattern 2	ditransitive	0.0
	prepositional	1.0

TABLE 17 The two possible target patterns for "throw".

provide negative evidence, i.e. evidence against the admissibility of the ditransitive, although the ditransitive has a zero value in the pattern. This is because verbs like "throw" that allow the ditransitive are also trained with this pattern.

Example input pattern. Table 18 displays an example input pattern for *kick*. The localist unit for "kick" is on, all other localist units are off. The contextual features selected for this pattern are negative for focus and positive for instantaneous. The four types of possible contextual constellations for focus/instantaneous (negative/positive (as shown in the figure), negative/negative, positive/negative, and positive/positive) are presented in random variation to the net. However, if "instantaneous" is specified as negative, only pattern 2 in Table 17 is presented to the net as the target pattern. This part of the training regime models the fact that "kick" can be used with the ditransitive only if it describes an instantaneous action.

The remaining features in Table 18 are morphosemantic features. Two input units are assigned to each feature. One is on if and only if the feature has a negative value, and the other is on if and only if the feature has a positive value. The value of the features for "kick" is derived from the application of their definitions to the semantics of "kick".

4.3.2   Experimental Results

4.3.2.1   Successful learning

The first important question is whether the model succeeded at learning the verbs in the training set. Since children acquire subcategorization successfully, learning the training set is the minimal requirement for an adequate model.

Table 19 looks at the subcategorization selection that was learned by the network. For each class, it shows how many verbs are in the class, how many were learned correctly, how many were not learned, and both largest and average error for the verbs in the class. It is apparent from the table that all verbs are learned correctly.

Most classes are not completely homogeneous. The *majority type*

input type	feature	value
localist	"throw"	1.0
	(all other verbs)	0.0
context	+ focus	0.0
	− focus	1.0
	+ instantaneous	1.0
	− instantaneous	0.0
morphosemantics	+ simultaneous	0.0
	− simultaneous	1.0
	+ manner	1.0
	− manner	0.0
	+ latinate	0.0
	− latinate	0.0
	+ accompanied	0.0
	− accompanied	1.0
	+ worthy	0.0
	− worthy	0.0
	+ needed	0.0
	− needed	0.0
	+ speaking	0.0
	− speaking	0.0
	+ specified direction	0.0
	− specified direction	0.0
	+ transfer	1.0
	− transfer	0.0
	+ ballistic	1.0
	− ballistic	0.0
	+ communication	0.0
	− communication	0.0

TABLE 18 Example input pattern for "kick".

class	label	example	majority type learned?	# members	learned	not learned	largest error	average error
9.4	putting with a specified direction	lower	yes	5	5	0	0.02	0.01
11.1	"send" verbs	send	yes	13	13	0	0.02	0.00
11.2	"slide" verbs	slide	yes	6	6	0	0.05	0.01
11.3	bring and take	bring	yes	3	3	0	0.02	0.00
11.4	"carry" verbs	carry	yes	8	8	0	0.02	0.01
13.1	"give" verbs	give	yes	13	13	0	0.01	0.00
13.2	"contribute" verbs	contribute	yes	14	14	0	0.04	0.01
13.3	future having	bequeath	yes	23	23	0	0.04	0.00
13.4.1	fulfilling	furnish	yes	8	8	0	0.03	0.01
17.1	throwing	throw	yes	14	14	0	0.02	0.01
37.1	transfer of a message	preach	yes	19	19	0	0.05	0.01
37.3	manner of speaking	babble	yes	8	8	0	0.02	0.01
37.4	instrument of communication	email	yes	13	13	0	0.01	0.00
37.7	communication of propositions	announce	yes	21	21	0	0.04	0.01
119	future not having	begrudge	yes	11	11	0	0.04	0.02

TABLE 19 Preferred subcategorization frames for verbs after training (10 hidden units per block).

of a class is the morphosemantic profile that is most frequent among the verbs in the class. The column "majority type learned?" indicates that all major types are learned. This information is redundant here since all verbs are correctly learned, but will be helpful in analyzing the generalization capability of the network.

The error for a verb with a particular set of contextual specifications is calculated as follows. Let o_P be the output of the prepositional unit (i.e., the network's preference for this frame), o_D the output for the ditransitive unit, t_P the correct preference for the prepositional frame, and t_D the correct preference for the ditransitive frame. Then the error for this combination of verb and context is the maximum difference between output and target for the two frames:

$$error = \max((o_P - t_P), (o_D - t_D))$$

If the verb in the context in question allows only one frame, then the target preference is 1.0 for that frame and 0.0 for the other frame. If the verb in the context in question allows both frames then the target for each frame is 0.5. (Notice that a target of 0.5 is used for the purpose of evaluation only, the network is never trained with a value of 0.5. The only values used in training are 0.0 and 1.0, corresponding to presence or absence of a subcategorization frame.)

Table 19 shows that all verbs are categorized correctly as exhibiting the dative alternation or allowing only the prepositional frame or only the ditransitive frame. The highest error for any verb is 0.05 which is well below the value of 0.25 for which the subcategorization behavior of the verb would be miscategorized. The following example shows why an error of more than 0.25 would result in miscategorization. If a verb allows both frames (target 0.5 for both frames), and the preferences output by the network are 0.8 and 0.2, then the error is 0.3. This distribution is closer to 1.0/0.0 than to 0.5/0.5, so this output by the subcategorization selector would trick the generator into believing that only the first frame is possible. Since there is no such case in Table 19 (all errors are below 0.25), the network has learned the subcategorization behavior of verbs in the training set correctly.

4.3.2.2 Generalization

Leaving aside training patterns that model errors, perfect performance on the training set can be achieved by simply memorizing all occurrences. The crucial test for the adequacy of the model is whether it generalizes correctly for novel verbs.

Generalization was tested by presenting the morphosemantic, contextual, and localist features of novel verbs (i.e., verbs not seen during

class	label	example	majority type generalized?	# members	generalized	not generalized	largest generalization error	average generalization error
9.4	putting with a specified direction	lower	yes	5	4	1	0.02	0.01
11.1	"send" verbs	send	yes	13	11	2	0.03	0.01
11.2	"slide" verbs	slide	yes	6	4	2	0.14	0.08
11.3	bring and take	bring	no	3	0	3	0.00	0.00
11.4	"carry" verbs	carry	yes	8	8	0	0.09	0.02
13.1	"give" verbs	give	yes	13	13	0	0.06	0.04
13.2	"contribute" verbs	contribute	yes	14	10	4	0.16	0.09
13.3	future having	bequeath	yes	23	16	7	0.15	0.03
13.4.1	fulfilling	furnish	no	8	4	4	0.15	0.04
17.1	throwing	throw	yes	14	14	0	0.02	0.01
37.1	transfer of a message	preach	yes	19	16	3	0.16	0.06
37.3	manner of speaking	babble	yes	8	8	0	0.03	0.01
37.4	instrument of communication	email	yes	13	13	0	0.04	0.02
37.7	communication of propositions	announce	yes	21	20	1	0.09	0.01
119	future not having	begrudge	no	11	4	7	0.10	0.04

TABLE 20 Generalization of subcategorization selection for novel verbs (10 hidden units per block).

training) to the network. The idiosyncratic information about a novel verb (as represented in the verb's localist features) is meaningless for the network, since it has never seen it. Adding this localist information would have meant to add additional randomly initialized localist units which would have not changed the network's behavior. Since a simpler network without these additional units has the same behavior, only two input types will be presented for a novel verb: its morphosemantics and its contextual features. All localist input units are set to zero, indicating to the network that this is a verb that it has not seen in training. Notice that what is novel about the new verbs is their localist encoding. See at the end of this section on page 153 for a discussion.

Table 20 evaluates generalization for novel verbs. For each class, it shows whether the majority type was generalized correctly, the total number of verbs that were generalized correctly and not generalized correctly, and largest and average errors. For the computation of largest and average error, only verbs that were generalized correctly are taken into account.

I will refer to the new verbs using the names of verbs in the training set that have the same morphosemantic features. For example, one of the new verbs has the same morphosemantic features as "drop". I will therefore refer to it as the *morphosemantic equivalent* of "drop". (Are there verbs with morphosemantic feature combinations that didn't occur in the training set? See discussion at the end of this section on page 153.)

A discussion of all verbs that were not generalized correctly follows. In each case, an explanation is given why a novel verb that shared all characteristics with a verb in the training set, except for idiosyncratic information, was treated differently from the verb in the training set. We will see that what appears to be an error is actually what the network should do to model subcategorization behavior correctly.

9.4. drop. The verb "drop" is the only verb in this class that involves ballistic motion. This caused interference from class 17.1 (verbs of throwing) and the model gave equal preference in instantaneous contexts to the two frames for the morphosemantic equivalent of "drop".

11.1. dispatch, shift. The error for "dispatch" is due to interference from the "send" class 11.1. "dispatch" differs in the feature "latinate" from it, but there is no class with fewer feature differences. Therefore, the morphosemantic equivalent of "dispatch" is analogized to "send". The morphosemantic grid of "shift" differs in only one feature from "give" (the feature "simultaneous") and is therefore assimilated to the large group of verbs of giving which allow the dative construction in contrast to "shift".

11.2. bounce, move. The case of "bounce" is similar to "drop". The verb "bounce" is also ballistic, and again there was interference from verbs of throwing. For non-instantaneous contexts, only the prepositional frame was chosen in analogy to non-instantaneous contexts of "throw", "kick" etc. The verb "move" differs only in "simultaneous" from "give" and is therefore assimilated to the verbs of giving (cf. "shift" above).

11.3. bring, take, get. The morphosemantics of "bring" and "take" are indistinguishable from the "carry" class, therefore only the prepositional construction is selected for their morphosemantic equivalents, not the dative construction. Like "shift" and "move", "get" was assimilated to the verbs of giving since it differs only in "simultaneous" from "give".

13.2. forfeit, extend, refer, refund. The verbs "extend" and "refund" (which allow both constructions) have the same morphosemantics as the other verbs of class 13.2 that do not allow the dative construction. Therefore, the model predicts their equivalents to have the same property. "forfeit" doesn't satisfy the criteria for the feature "latinate". Therefore its equivalent is not treated as a member of 13.2. (which only contains latinate verbs except for "forfeit"), but as a member of the "germanic" class 13.1. which allows both constructions. "refer" is most similar to the "send" class which allows the dative construction in contrast to "refer".

13.3. Verbs of future having. Equivalents of the seven latinate verbs in this class that allow the dative alternation (e.g., "accord", "assign", "prescribe") were generalized in analogy to the non-dativizable "contribute" class (13.2.), the dominant class with the feature latinate.[6]

13.4.1. credit, trust, furnish, present. "credit" and "trust" differ from class 13.1 ("give" verbs) only in the feature "worthy", "furnish" only in the feature "needy". The features "worthy" and "needy" in themselves do not reliably indicate that the dative construction is not possible (e.g., "award" also describes a transfer to someone who is worthy of the thing transferred). Therefore, the model analogized "credit" and "trust" to class 13.1. As a latinate verb, "present" is most similar to "contribute" verbs (class 13.2). Therefore, the model excluded the possibility of the da-

---

[6]The verb "prescribe" is dativizable according to Boguraev and Briscoe (1989:257). Their example is "She prescribed him some pills."

tive construction for its morphosemantic equivalent (in contrast to "present" which does allow the dative construction).

37.1. ask, pose, recommend. "ask" and "pose" have the same features as other verbs of transfer of a message, but they allow only one frame: "ask" only the dative construction, "pose" only the prepositional construction. Their morphosemantic equivalents are treated as verbs of message-transfer and both frames are given equal preference. "recommend" allows the dative construction in contrast to other latinate verbs with the same morphosemantic grid. ("administer" etc.)

37.7. say. Other verbs of communication of propositions are latinate and specify the manner in which the proposition is communicated. Neither is the case for "say". This makes its morphosemantic grid indistinguishable from the "give" class and its equivalent is predicted to allow both frames.

119. begrudge, charge, fine, envy, guarantee, save, spare. These verbs are not contextually conditioned (subcategorization behavior independent of context), but have the same features as the contextually conditioned verbs such as "allow" and "deny". Their equivalents are predicted to be similar to "allow" and "deny" in that they are compatible with the prepositional frame if the beneficiary or maleficiary is focussed.

These generalization results and errors will be taken up again in the discussion section. Before presenting the remaining results of the simulation, I would like to address a question that the experimental setup may have raised in the reader's mind: Does the model test all types of generalization that people make for subcategorization? The novel patterns presented to the network only differ in localist features from patterns in the training set, not in morphosemantic features. Since each morphosemantic feature can have three possible values (positive, negative, unspecified), there are $3^{11} = 177,147$ theoretically possible morphosemantic patterns. Only 26 occur in the training set and hence in the test set. What about the $177,147 - 26$ theoretically possible novel combinations of morphosemantic values that are not attested in the training set?

First of all, posing the question this way vastly overstates the number of actually possible morphosemantic patterns since there are many constraints that a pattern must satisfy. To illustrate this point, I ran a random number generator and constructed five random morphosemantic patterns. Four were not well-formed, either because one of the features had an inadmissible value (specified direction and communication had the value negative, instead of being either positive or unspecified) or because two feature values were incompatible ("+ accompanied" was incompatible with both "- simultaneous" and "+ speaking"). The fifth pattern was: "+ latinate", "- needed", "+ speaking", "+ communication". This pattern would encode a latinate verb of speaking and communication that describes the transfer of an object (presumably some information) that the recipient does not want to receive. (If the recipient had a positive or neutral attitude with respect to receiving the information, then the encoding would have "0 needed" or "+ needed".) A verb coming close to this description could be "to expatiate", but it is not clear whether "- needed" is part of its semantics or just a pragmatic inference that is made in many of its uses. This example shows that finding an existing verb with a novel morphosemantic pattern is hard if not impossible. One could instead create new verbs (verbs that are not part of the English language) according to the specifications of new morphosemantic patterns, but then expensive psychological experiments would be necessary to determine which subcategorization frames human subjects would choose for such verbs.

An easy way out would be to set several groups of verbs aside in the initial training phase, and then test the model on these groups. This would guarantee a set of verbs, truly novel to the network, for which we would know the correct subcategorization behavior. However, this is not a situation occurring in human subcategorization learning. Instances of all types of subcategorization behavior are experienced by language learners during acquisition. (Subcategorization is one of the last parts of grammar that is learned by children. So even the more learned latinate verbs are encountered by children before acquisition of subcategorization is completed.)

For these reasons, I think that the experimental setup as it was described here is adequate for subcategorization learning. This means that subcategorization is a relatively simple problem from the point of view of machine learning. It would be more challenging to devise an architecture that could correctly infer subcategorization behavior for novel morphosemantic patterns. But this does not seem to happen in English, so I will follow LRT and not address the question of generalization across morphosemantic patterns. It turns out that despite its apparent simplicity there is still a considerable amount of complexity present in the acquisition experiments described here as will become clear in the discussion section later in this chapter.

4.3.2.3 Overgeneralization

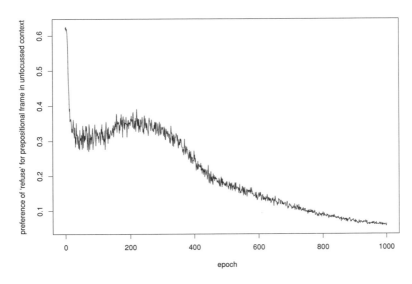

FIGURE 16 Overgeneralization for "refuse".

While the model was trained, overgeneralization occurred initially for the verb "refuse" in unfocussed contexts. Although "refuse" cannot be used with the prepositional frame in unfocussed contexts and the model thus did not see any such instances, the preference for the "to + NP" frame ranges from 0.3 to 0.4 in the first 300 epochs of training (Figure 16). The network recovers from the overgeneralization in later training and eventually gives close to zero preference to the prepositional frame when the maleficiary of "refuse" is not focussed. The implication of this result for the network as a model for language acquisition will be discussed in the discussion section of this chapter.

4.3.2.4 Sensitivity to Network Architecture

One parameter of the architecture in Figure 15 was chosen arbitrarily: The number of hidden units in each hidden unit block. If the simulations described in this section depend on a particular setting of this parameter, then little could be concluded from the experiments. For this reason, three additional experiments with different settings for the parameter were run in addition to the original setup. Tables 21 – 26 show learning results and generalization errors for networks with 20, 30 and 40 units per hidden unit block. The networks were trained in exactly the same way as the 10-unit network.

As far as learning the verbs in the training set is concerned, there is virtually no difference between the networks, except for variations in the error. (Tables 19, 21, 23, 25)

As for generalization, the same verbs are generalized in all four networks. However, the error increases slowly with the number of hidden units. For example, the average error is 0.18 for class 13.2 with 40 hidden units, but only 0.09 with 10 hidden units. The reason for this increase is that the more "capacity" the model has, the more idiosyncrasies can be learned by dedicating hidden units to specific verbs. Such hidden units will only respond to the verb in question, and can thus not be used in generalization. If a large number of hidden units were added to the hidden-unit blocks, generalization would eventually deteriorate. On the other hand, if the number of hidden units is too small, then the network would not be able to learn the training set, because of a lack of capacity of the learning model.

These considerations suggest that extreme values for the number of hidden units per hidden-unit block would lead to different results in the simulations. However, the experiments on different hidden unit block sizes in Tables 21 – 26 demonstrate that the results are robust over a fairly broad range of sizes for the hidden unit blocks.

4.4 Discussion

The goal of this chapter is to provide an adequate model of subcategorization learning. This section discusses to what extent the connectionist model on the one hand and Lexical Rule Theory on the other achieve this goal. There are six properties that characterize children's subcategorization learning, including the three premises of Baker's paradox:

- successful learning
- error robustness
- limited predictability (first premise of the paradox)
- lack of negative evidence (second premise of the paradox)
- productivity (= generalization, third premise of the paradox)
- overgeneralization

The first part of the section examines whether these properties are accurately modeled in the two accounts. The second part of the section looks at the three problems of ambiguity, transition and innateness:

- Do the models account for learning in the presence of ambiguity?

class	label	example	majority type learned?	# members	learned	not learned	largest error	average error
9.4	putting with a specified direction	lower	yes	5	5	0	0.02	0.01
11.1	"send" verbs	send	yes	13	13	0	0.02	0.00
11.2	"slide" verbs	slide	yes	6	6	0	0.05	0.01
11.3	bring and take	bring	yes	3	3	0	0.02	0.01
11.4	"carry" verbs	carry	yes	8	8	0	0.02	0.01
13.1	"give" verbs	give	yes	13	13	0	0.00	0.00
13.2	"contribute" verbs	contribute	yes	14	14	0	0.03	0.01
13.3	future having	bequeath	yes	23	23	0	0.04	0.00
13.4.1	fulfilling	furnish	yes	8	8	0	0.02	0.01
17.1	throwing	throw	yes	14	14	0	0.02	0.01
37.1	transfer of a message	preach	yes	19	19	0	0.05	0.01
37.3	manner of speaking	babble	yes	8	8	0	0.02	0.01
37.4	instrument of communication	email	yes	13	13	0	0.01	0.00
37.7	communication of propositions	announce	yes	21	21	0	0.03	0.01
119	future not having	begrudge	yes	11	11	0	0.04	0.02

TABLE 21 Preferred subcategorization frames for verbs after training (20 hidden units per block).

class	label	example	majority type generalized?	# members	generalized	not generalized	largest generalization error	average generalization error
9.4	putting with a specified direction	lower	yes	5	4	1	0.01	0.01
11.1	"send" verbs	send	yes	13	11	2	0.03	0.01
11.2	"slide" verbs	slide	yes	6	4	2	0.14	0.11
11.3	bring and take	bring	no	3	0	3	0.00	0.00
11.4	"carry" verbs	carry	yes	8	8	0	0.09	0.03
13.1	"give" verbs	give	yes	13	13	0	0.06	0.05
13.2	"contribute" verbs	contribute	yes	14	10	4	0.19	0.16
13.3	future having	bequeath	yes	23	16	7	0.15	0.04
13.4.1	fulfilling	furnish	no	8	4	4	0.15	0.06
17.1	throwing	throw	yes	14	14	0	0.02	0.01
37.1	transfer of a message	preach	yes	19	16	3	0.19	0.09
37.3	manner of speaking	babble	yes	8	8	0	0.03	0.02
37.4	instrument of communication	email	yes	13	13	0	0.05	0.03
37.7	communication of propositions	announce	yes	21	20	1	0.09	0.02
119	future not having	begrudge	no	11	4	7	0.15	0.06

TABLE 22 Generalization of subcategorization selection for novel verbs (20 hidden units per block).

class	label	example	majority type learned?	# members	learned	not learned	largest error	average error
9.4	putting with a specified direction	lower	yes	5	5	0	0.02	0.01
11.1	"send" verbs	send	yes	13	13	0	0.02	0.00
11.2	"slide" verbs	slide	yes	6	6	0	0.03	0.01
11.3	bring and take	bring	yes	3	3	0	0.02	0.01
11.4	"carry" verbs	carry	yes	8	8	0	0.02	0.01
13.1	"give" verbs	give	yes	13	13	0	0.00	0.00
13.2	"contribute" verbs	contribute	yes	14	14	0	0.02	0.01
13.3	future having	bequeath	yes	23	23	0	0.03	0.00
13.4.1	fulfilling	furnish	yes	8	8	0	0.02	0.01
17.1	throwing	throw	yes	14	14	0	0.02	0.01
37.1	transfer of a message	preach	yes	19	19	0	0.04	0.01
37.3	manner of speaking	babble	yes	8	8	0	0.02	0.01
37.4	instrument of communication	email	yes	13	13	0	0.00	0.00
37.7	communication of propositions	announce	yes	21	21	0	0.02	0.01
119	future not having	begrudge	yes	11	11	0	0.04	0.01

TABLE 23 Preferred subcategorization frames for verbs after training (30 hidden units per block).

class	label	example	majority type generalized?	# members	generalized	not generalized	largest generalization error	average generalization error
9.4	putting with a specified direction	lower	yes	5	4	1	0.01	0.01
11.1	"send" verbs	send	yes	13	11	2	0.03	0.01
11.2	"slide" verbs	slide	yes	6	4	2	0.12	0.08
11.3	bring and take	bring	no	3	0	3	0.00	0.00
11.4	"carry" verbs	carry	yes	8	8	0	0.10	0.04
13.1	"give" verbs	give	yes	13	13	0	0.03	0.02
13.2	"contribute" verbs	contribute	yes	14	10	4	0.20	0.16
13.3	future having	bequeath	yes	23	16	7	0.10	0.02
13.4.1	fulfilling	furnish	no	8	4	4	0.10	0.05
17.1	throwing	throw	yes	14	14	0	0.02	0.01
37.1	transfer of a message	preach	yes	19	16	3	0.20	0.08
37.3	manner of speaking	babble	yes	8	8	0	0.02	0.02
37.4	instrument of communication	email	yes	13	13	0	0.03	0.02
37.7	communication of propositions	announce	yes	21	20	1	0.10	0.03
119	future not having	begrudge	no	11	4	7	0.16	0.06

TABLE 24 Generalization of subcategorization selection for novel verbs (30 hidden units per block).

class	label	example	majority type learned?	# members	learned	not learned	largest error	average error
9.4	putting with a specified direction	lower	yes	5	5	0	0.02	0.01
11.1	"send" verbs	send	yes	13	13	0	0.02	0.01
11.2	"slide" verbs	slide	yes	6	6	0	0.04	0.01
11.3	bring and take	bring	yes	3	3	0	0.02	0.01
11.4	"carry" verbs	carry	yes	8	8	0	0.02	0.01
13.1	"give" verbs	give	yes	13	13	0	0.01	0.00
13.2	"contribute" verbs	contribute	yes	14	14	0	0.02	0.01
13.3	future having	bequeath	yes	23	23	0	0.04	0.00
13.4.1	fulfilling	furnish	yes	8	8	0	0.02	0.01
17.1	throwing	throw	yes	14	14	0	0.02	0.01
37.1	transfer of a message	preach	yes	19	19	0	0.04	0.01
37.3	manner of speaking	babble	yes	8	8	0	0.02	0.01
37.4	instrument of communication	email	yes	13	13	0	0.01	0.00
37.7	communication of propositions	announce	yes	21	21	0	0.02	0.01
119	future not having	begrudge	yes	11	11	0	0.04	0.02

TABLE 25 Preferred subcategorization frames for verbs after training (40 hidden units per block).

class	label	example	majority type generalized?	# members	generalized	not generalized	largest generalization error	average generalization error
9.4	putting with a specified direction	lower	yes	5	4	1	0.01	0.01
11.1	"send" verbs	send	yes	13	11	2	0.04	0.02
11.2	"slide" verbs	slide	yes	6	4	2	0.17	0.15
11.3	bring and take	bring	no	3	0	3	0.00	0.00
11.4	"carry" verbs	carry	yes	8	8	0	0.13	0.06
13.1	"give" verbs	give	yes	13	13	0	0.05	0.04
13.2	"contribute" verbs	contribute	yes	14	10	4	0.22	0.18
13.3	future having	bequeath	yes	23	16	7	0.12	0.03
13.4.1	fulfilling	furnish	no	8	4	4	0.14	0.07
17.1	throwing	throw	yes	14	14	0	0.02	0.01
37.1	transfer of a message	preach	yes	19	16	3	0.22	0.10
37.3	manner of speaking	babble	yes	8	8	0	0.03	0.03
37.4	instrument of communication	email	yes	13	13	0	0.07	0.04
37.7	communication of propositions	announce	yes	21	20	1	0.13	0.04
119	future not having	begrudge	no	11	4	7	0.12	0.05

TABLE 26 Generalization of subcategorization selection for novel verbs (40 hidden units per block).

- Do the models account for the transition from a rule-less to a rule-governed state?

- Do the models demonstrate the need for innate language-specific knowledge for successful learning?

The section concludes with a discussion of limitations of the models and related work.

4.4.1 Successful Learning

Both models succeed in learning subcategorization frames attested in the input, but in quite different ways. One element of LRT is *conservatism*, i.e. the tendency to prefer frames that are attested, regardless of the semantic characteristics of the verb (Pinker 1989:318). Since the "rule module" of LRT does not have access to idiosyncratic information, verbs and their frames must also be stored in memory although I have not found an explicit statement of this in LC. Successful learning of attested subcategorization frames is thus guaranteed because they are stored in memory.

In the connectionist network, *exceptions* are also stored in memory, which is realized here by the connections between the localist unit of the exception verb and the rest of the network. For example, the exception verb "drop" is the only ballistic verb that is not dativizable (in contrast to the "throw" class). It is the localist part of the representation of "drop" that guarantees non-dativizability. If the localist unit of "drop" is switched off, the verb is analogized to other ballistic verbs and both frames are predicted to be possible (cf. description of network behavior for "drop" on page 151).

The network's representation is different for *regular verbs,* i.e. members of a large class of verbs with similar morphosemantics and identical subcategorization behavior. In Table 20, regular verbs are those whose morphosemantic grid corresponds to the majority type of large, homogeneous classes (those whose majority type is successfully generalized, e.g., "send" verbs, "give" verbs, "contribute" verbs). Regular verbs are stored in the hidden unit layer by means of distributed class representations. The morphosemantics of a class of regular verbs produces a unique pattern of hidden unit activations. This pattern is then propagated to the output layer and in turn produces the appropriate preferences for the class (manifested as activations of the output units). Table 20 shows that the localist units do not influence the choice of subcategorization frames for regular verbs. The subcategorization behavior of the major types in the table does not change if the localist units are switched off ("yes" entries for regular classes in the column "majority type generalized?").

Plunkett and Marchman (1993) describe the same kind of behavior in article about their past tense model (their model is a connectionist simulation in the tradition of Rumelhart and McClelland's (1986) past tense model):

> [T]he transition from rote learning to system building emerges from the capacity of connectionist networks to *simultaneously*:
>
> 1. *Memorize* individual patterns and their transformations when the number of pattern types is sufficiently small.
> 2. *Generalize* on the basis of regularities observed in the input when the number of patterns (types) is sufficiently large. (page 25)

So although both models learn attested frames successfully, they employ different methods. LRT seems to require that all instances are stored in memory. The connectionist model stores only exceptions in memory and represents regular instances by distributed class representations. This difference will turn out to be crucial for error robustness, exception handling and overgeneralization.

4.4.2 Robustness

One phenomenon a model of subcategorization learning needs to account for is learning in the presence of errors. Although subcategorization errors are not frequent, they do occur. Gropen et al. give an extensive list of examples they observed in natural writing and speech (page 251). Two of these examples are repeated in (24).

(24) a. I'll suggest her that she come over.
      b. We'll credit you back the full purchase price.

Misconstruals of a verb's meaning are another source of erroneous input in training. For example, the child may watch a situation in which Mary walks over to Peter and gives him a book. This situation could later be referred to by sentence (25). If the child thinks at this point in learning that "give" means "carry", then (25) would be a misleading training instance since it suggests that verbs of carrying allow the dative construction. Such cases are called "misconceptions about the meanings of particular verbs" in LC (page 292).

(25) Mary has given Peter the book.

Unfortunately, there is no mechanism in LRT to handle errors. This applies both to the memory module and the rule module. No provision is made to keep the child from keeping errors in memory and using them as correct subcategorization frames. The rule module relies on similarity: if the lexicosemantic representation of verb A is similar to that of verb B, and if B was used with the prepositional construction, then A will also be used with this construction. Nothing in LRT prevents the child from basing such generalizations on errors. It has to be concluded that LRT does not account for learning in the presence of errors.

The connectionist model is trained with errors in the input. Recall that 1% of the input patterns are randomly selected and corrupted. If the correct pattern specifies that the dative construction occurred, then the pattern is changed to specify the prepositional construction and vice versa. This corruption of training patterns does not change the outcome of learning because gradient descent, the learning mechanism at the heart of neural network training, is sensitive to frequency. Introducing errors amounts to changing the error surface, so that the "correct" minimum of the error surface is displaced. This may misdirect the search for the correct model parameters temporarily, but the small overall proportion of bad patterns (one percent) does not have a lasting effect on training. Thus the connectionist model is able to learn in the presence of errors due to its quantitative nature.

4.4.3 Exceptions and arbitrariness

Pinker's (1989) and Gropen et al.'s (1989) solution to Baker's paradox is to weaken the premise of arbitrariness:

> The third way out of the paradox involves weakening the assumption of arbitrariness. According to this hypothesis, the learner makes use of a productive rule, but one that is constrained to operate only on certain subclasses of verbs, delineated by some independent criteria, so that the dativizability of a verb in the language can be predicted in advance (Gropen et al. 1989:205).

According to Pinker and Gropen et al., this subclass-specific regularity enables children to learn narrow-range classes. However, there remains a large number of verbs that are exceptions. The question arises how these verbs are learned in LRT.

In their discussion of exceptions, Gropen et al. distinguish positive and negative exceptions. *Positive exceptions* are said to be unproblematic:

> (Positive exceptions [...] are more benign, because they could be learned through positive evidence, as long as they are not so numerous that they cause the child to abandon the constraint altogether.) (Gropen et al. 1989:239)

Apparently, LRT relies on the implicitly stated memorization of attested subcategorization frames here.

Negative exceptions are said to be a problem only for a naive theory of semantic determination of subcategorization ("the prospective-possession constraint on the double-object dative"). The more intricate classification into narrow-range classes is claimed to solve the problem. But it is simply not true that there are no exceptions to the narrow-rule classification. Oehrle writes in his 1975 review of Green (1974), whose classification is the basis for Lexical Rule Theory:

> In fact, a significant number of verbs fall into one (or more) of G's classes, yet do not manifest the syntactic properties which she would require of them. In my speech, these include "transfer," "convey," "get (to)," "provide (for)," "divulge," "display," "reveal," "invent," "devise," "create," "produce," "deliver," "obtain," "purchase," "return," "voice," "turn over (to)," "procure," and "select." As far as I can tell, G's classification would include these verbs. Thus they are all counter-examples both to her analysis of the dative alternation and, more importantly, to her more general thesis that semantic properties determine syntactic properties.

Boguraev and Briscoe (1989) also find a substantial amount of arbitrariness:

> None of the four approaches above appears to offer a very convincing way to predicting which verb senses will undergo the dative alternation. Therefore, we conclude this section by noting that, at least for the moment, the "arbitrary" approach to subcategorization [...] seems more accurate. (page 116)

Gropen et al. acknowledge this problem in passing:

> First, how can the morphophonological constraint on the dative be psychologically real but at the same time be so ridden with exceptions? [...] The answer is that the constraint, when properly formulated, so as to apply to some semantic subclasses but not others, may not have exceptions after all. (page 248)

No attempt is made to check the claim that a properly formulated constraint would have no exceptions. Gropen et al. do not come back to the problem of exceptions after this remark. Thus the problem of negative exceptions is not addressed.

Positive exceptions (narrow rules do not license the dative for a verb although it is grammatical) are also a serious problem for LRT since they cause incorrect generalizations. Suppose positive exception A (compatible with the dative) has a close neighbor B (not compatible with the dative) according to the similarity metric. Then B would be analogized to A, wrongly predicting that B can appear in the dative construction.

As shown in Table 19, the connectionist model does not make incorrect generalizations for plausibly productive verb classes (the majority type of larger, more homogeneous classes is correctly generalized, e.g., the "send", "give", and "contribute" classes). Neither do positive exceptions give rise to bad subcategorization frames for close neighbors (e.g., "extend" is a positive exception for the "contribute" class: double-object bad for the class, good for "extend"), nor is there any negative exception for which bad subcategorization frames are predicted (e.g., "shift" is a negative exception for the "send" class: double-object good for the class, bad for "shift").

The explanation lies in the different representations for exceptions and regular verbs discussed above. The correct subcategorization frames for exceptions are "memorized" in the connections between localist units and the rest of the network. Knowledge about the correct subcategorization frames for regular verbs resides in the hidden unit layer and is not influenced by the activation of any of the localist units (see page 163). Since exceptions and regular verbs are separated, they cannot interfere with each other's subcategorization behavior in a negative way. Exceptions therefore do not pose a problem for generalization in the connectionist model.

Is it really important to account for exceptions or should one be content with an account of how subcategorization regularities are learned? I think exceptions are a much-overlooked topic in linguistics, as pointed out by Sally Rice:

> During the 1970s, in a classic critique of generative theory, Maurice Gross (1979) analyzed two types of embedded infinitival clause structures in French and wondered how a so-called universal rule, in this case Raising, could be maintained for three verbs at the expense of over 600 exceptions. In linguistics, minor constructions (like the Raising case in French) are routinely "inflated by formalization." The volume of abstract discussion is often way out of proportion to the arbitrary selection of data. After analyzing over 12,000 lexical items in French, Gross and his colleagues found that no two lexical items had the same syntactic properties. (Rice 1993:3)

Connectionist models can capture generalizations that are not all-or-none since they do not impose an exception-or-perfect-rule dichotomy on linguistic phenomena. I have devoted more space to exceptions than is customary because I am convinced that much explanatory adequacy could be gained by a satisfactory treatment of partial regularity.

4.4.4 Negative Evidence

The second premise of Baker's paradox is that children do not have access to negative evidence. Recent research (Hirsh-Patek et al., 1984; Demetras et al., 1986; Penner, 1987; Bohannon and Stanowicz, 1988) has shown that there is in fact some negative evidence. Even though parents rarely correct their children, they react differently to grammatical and ungrammatical sentences. Marcus (1993) summarizes the literature as follows:

> Some discourse patterns, such as expansions [...], are claimed to be elicited more often by ungrammatical speech than by grammatical speech. Other discourse patterns such as exact repetitions [...] are claimed to be elicited more often by grammatical speech than by ungrammatical speech. (1993:56)

After a careful study of this type of negative evidence, Marcus concludes that it is not powerful enough to solve the negative evidence problem in and of itself. I will call this kind of negative evidence *explicit negative evidence*. If Marcus is right, then explicit negative evidence is too unreliable to be helpful.

Neither LRT nor the connectionist model depend on explicit negative evidence. Recall that the connectionist network is trained with only one frame at a time. This constraint models the fact that for a given situation only one of the frames, dative or prepositional, occurs. For those verbs that do not exhibit the dative alternation, only one of the two frames will occur in training. But this constellation does not provide any negative information. For example, the training patterns for a dative-only verb do not imply that the prepositional construction is ungrammatical. This is because alternating verbs are trained with the same pattern, but in their case the prepositional construction *is* possible. The training regime therefore guarantees that only positive evidence is available during training. Thus both models respect the lack of explicit negative evidence in children's learning.

There is however a second kind of negative evidence, which I will call *implicit negative evidence*. Consider the class of verbs of manner of speaking. These verbs are never used in the ditransitive construction. If a collection of uses of these verbs is available for analysis, then the ungrammaticality of the dative construction is immediately apparent. For example, the probability of event A_{200} of seeing 200 consecutive uses of members of an alternating class with the prepositional frame and no use of the ditransitive frame is virtually zero:

$$P(A_{200}) = \binom{n}{n} p^n (1-p)^{n-n} = \binom{200}{200} * 0.5^{200} = 6.2 * 10^{-61}$$

For verbs with non-equiprobable frames, $P(A_{200})$ would still be small, although somewhat larger. So if there are enough instances of a class and one of the two constructions is never used, then the ungrammaticality of one of the frames can be safely inferred.[7]

These considerations show that if such a "global" analysis is admissible, implicit negative evidence, i.e. the absence of a certain construction from the input, is a powerful source of information for learning.

The question is whether "global" evidence of this sort can be used by children. In its most naive form, the analysis would need access to all past occurrences of verbs and their subcategorization frames. Such an intensive use of memory for acquisition seems doubtful, but there may be a variant of global learning that uses fewer memorized instances while still being effective.

Lexical Rule Theory's algorithm for forming generalizations is not stated clearly enough to decide whether global information, in whatever form, is used. The fact that it relies on memorization for the acquisition of positive examples (see comments above) makes it seem likely that some form of global learning is used.

Still, LRT may have an implementation that processes subcategorization instances one by one without having to look at dozens or hundreds of instances at a time. In this case, LRT would not depend on either explicit or implicit negative evidence.

The connectionist model does not use any global information about the distribution of subcategorization frames, so it has no access to implicit negative evidence. This is because it is strictly trained pattern by pattern. In other words, the next state of the model in training only depends on the current input-output pattern and the current parameters of the model. Neural networks can also be trained in "batch-mode" in which a large number of input-output patterns simultaneously determines the next state of the model. Since it is not clear whether global information is a feature of human subcategorization learning, I have

---

[7]Even with some noise in the input the odds in favor of an alternating verb would still be vast. For example, the probability of seeing at least 198 prepositional frames in 200 occurrences (and up to two ditransitive frames, due to error) are:

$$P(A_{198}) + P(A_{199}) + P(A_{200}) \approx P(A_{198}) = \binom{200}{198} 0.5^{200} \approx 5.0 * 10^{-56}$$

chosen a strictly local learning algorithm for the experiment presented here.

In summary, both models respect the constraint on child language acquisition that no or very little explicit negative information is available. LRT may use some implicit negative information instead. The connectionist model uses none.

4.4.5 Generalization

The third premise of Baker's paradox is that children use subcategorization productively, i.e., that they generalize from attested subcategorization frames to novel ones. Productivity in LRT occurs for clusters of morphosemantically similar verbs, the narrow-range classes:

> [T]he only verbs that would be allowed to undergo a lexical rule freely are those verbs that have actually been heard to undergo that alternation, or verbs that are semantically similar to them. A narrow conflation class would simply be the set of verbs that are similar to a verb heard to alternate. (Gropen et al. 1989:246)
>
> The empirical prediction is that children, especially older children, should spontaneously and freely generalize new argument structures to newly acquired verbs when the grammatically relevant parts of their semantic representations are similar to verbs that already alternate in their vocabulary. (Pinker 1989:348)

As pointed out in section 4.2.2.2, the difficulty with this account lies in the definition of similarity. Various proposals are entertained and rejected: identical lexicosemantic representations, a difference in at most n features (for an undetermined n), a difference in at most one less important feature etc. In her review of Pinker (1989), Naigles criticizes the imprecise definition of what constitutes semantic similarity (or equivalently, when two verbs are in the same narrow-range class) (1991:71–73). Is a single feature difference significant in some cases and not significant in others? If so, how would the child learn such distinctions? She concludes:

> All of the above-mentioned procedures and biases must surely play a role, yet nowhere in Pinker's presentation is there a demonstration of how the various procedures operate, singly or in concert, in order to yield this (or any other) deceptively simple yet absolutely critical component (for Pinker's theory) of verb representation. (1991:77)

In contrast, the parameters of the connectionist model define a precise measure of similarity. Crucially, the morphosemantic and the localist input units jointly determine similarity. As a result, the network may categorize two verbs with identical morphosemantic representations to be dissimilar if one of the verbs is an exception verb. This is what happened for the verbs in section 4.3.2.2 whose subcategorization preferences differed from their morphosemantic equivalents (verbs with identical morphosemantic features). In these cases, the verb's morphosemantics is often identical to a class of verbs with different subcategorization behavior. In the other cases, the verb's morphosemantics is part of a small cluster of exception verbs. Such a small cluster does not have the critical mass to give rise to hidden unit representations capturing its particular profile.

Table 27 looks at all exception verbs, i.e. all verbs that were not generalized by the network (see section 4.3.2.2). For each verb, it lists its possible frames, its closest regular neighbor (where proximity is measured by the number of different features), the possible frames of the neighbor, and feature mismatches between exception verb and regular verb if any. The majority of the exception verbs has the same morphosemantics as a larger verb class with different subcategorization behavior.

For example, "begrudge," which is only used in the ditransitive construction, has the same morphosemantics as "cost", but "cost" can be used with the prepositional construction in focussed contexts.[8]

For a novel verb, the significance of its idiosyncrasies for subcategorization cannot be known. The subcategorization selector needs to rely on morphosemantics. If there are two verbs that are morphosemantically identical, but differ in subcategorization, then a choice must somehow be made. Table 27 shows that the connectionist network bases generalizations on relatively large clusters of verbs rather than on small clusters or individual verbs. This is the reason that the verbs in the table are not generalized.

Similar considerations apply to those exception verbs which differ in one or two features from their closest regular neighbor. For example, "trust" differs from "give" in that the beneficiary is worthy of receiving

---

[8]This categorization for "cost" was chosen because of the following usages found in the New York *Times*:

Preliminary estimates suggested that this provision could cost $5 billion to the government over five years [. . .] (NYT-10-27-90)

"It means if they insist on putting that thing here, the commission is going to have to make a good-faith effort at identifying and notifying all 6,000 or so of us," said John Pike, a 42-year-old attorney. "That means slowing the hell out of the process and costing million of dollars to the state." (NYT-06-04-90)

No uses of "begrudge" with the prepositional construction were found in the same corpus. However, such uses do seem to occur (Tom Wasow, personal communication). In the light of this evidence, it might have been better to classify "begrudge" and "cost" as exhibiting the same subcategorization behavior.

exception	frames	close regular	frames	different features
drop	prep	throw	$ditr_i$, prep	physical direction
dispatch	prep	send	ditr, prep	latinate, simultaneous
refer	(same as "dispatch")			
shift	prep	give	ditr, prep	accompanied
move	(same as "shift")			
get	(same as "shift")			
bring	ditr, prep	carry	prep	manner
take	(same as "bring")			
bounce	ditr, prep	throw	$ditr_i$, prep	(none)
forfeit	prep	give	ditr, prep	(none)
extend	ditr, prep	contribute	prep	(none)
refund	(same as "extend")			
accord	ditr, prep	contribute	prep	(none)
advance	(same as "accord")			
allocate	(same as "accord")			
allot	(same as "accord")			
assign	(same as "accord")			
concede	(same as "accord")			
prescribe	(same as "accord")			
credit	prep	give	ditr, prep	worthy
trust	(same as "credit")			
furnish	prep	give	ditr, prep	needed
present	ditr, prep	contribute	prep	worthy
recommend	ditr, prep	contribute	prep	(none)
ask	ditr	give	ditr, prep	(none)
pose	prep	give	ditr, prep	(none)
say	(same as "pose")			
begrudge	ditr	cost	ditr, prep	(none)
save	(same as "begrudge")			
charge	ditr	give	ditr, prep	simultaneous
fine	(same as "charge")			
envy	ditr	give	ditr, prep	transfer
guarantee	ditr, prep	deny	ditr, $prep_f$	(none)

TABLE 27 Exception verbs and their closest regular neighbor in semantic space. "$ditr_i$" stands for ditransitive constructions in instantaneous contexts only, "$prep_f$" for prepositional constructions in focussed contexts only.

what is transferred. The model predicts that this small cluster does not generalize to novel verbs. In other words, if the verb "gream" were to be created with the same meaning as "trust something to someone", then it would analogize to "give", not to "trust" and allow the ditransitive construction.

The exact conditions of generalizations depend on the architecture of the connectionist model. For example, the fewer hidden units there are, the more small clusters will be analogized to large clusters. However, it was demonstrated that the basic results on learning and generalization of the model are valid for a broad range of sizes of the hidden-unit blocks.

In summary, LRT and connectionist account differ in two important aspects of generalization:

- LRT does not account for constellations in which morphosemantically identical verbs manifest different subcategorizations. The connectionist model generalizes the subcategorization behavior of the majority of types with this morphosemantic profile. That is, the overall distribution of verbs determines subcategorization behavior.

- Depending on the definition of similarity in LRT, even small clusters of verbs (only one verb in the extreme case) can give rise to generalization. For example, the verbs "credit" and "trust" have unique morphosemantics. In LRT, the single feature "worthy" (which differentiates them from "give") may cause a novel verb that describes transfer to someone worthy of it to disallow the dative construction. In contrast, the connectionist model integrates two different kinds of information in determining generalization: a) the similarity of the novel verb's morphosemantics with any of the possible prototype verbs, and b) the size of the cluster of the prototype verb as well as its "naturalness." A cluster is more natural if the effect of its features on subcategorization behavior is similar to other clusters. So even if there is a difference of two or more features between a novel verb v and possible prototype p_1 and no feature difference between v and possible prototype p_2, p_1 is the basis for generalization if p_1 is part of a large cluster and p_2 is morphosemantically unique or part of a small cluster.

The first difference is a fundamental problem for LRT: The model's generalization behavior should not be compromised by isolated exceptions. As for the second difference, one should be able to test the predictions of the two models empirically. Unfortunately, the results would depend too much on the representations of individual verbs. With a different choice of representational features, a cluster of three could become a cluster of five which would be more likely to be generalized in both models. One would therefore need to run psychological experiments to establish an empirically reliable feature representation (cf. the triad experiments by Fisher et al. (1991)). Unfortunately, such an experiment is beyond the scope of this book.

4.4.6 Overgeneralization

As shown by Mazurkewich and White (1984), overgeneralization occurs during the acquisition of subcategorization. That is, children produce subcategorization frames that are incorrect, presumably because the initial analysis of the occurring subcategorization frames strongly suggests generalizations that are in fact ungrammatical. Overgeneralization can be observed both in production and comprehension. It is relatively rare in production: Gropen et al. find only 22 overgeneralizations in 86332 child utterances (1989:219).

It seems to have a stronger effect on comprehension. Mazurkewich and White (1984) find that children at ages nine, twelve and sixteen accept double-object constructions violating the morphophonological constraint in 46.7%, 33%, and 11% of all cases, respectively. In the early stages of learning, children seem to be too permissive because they have overgeneralized dativizability.

If overgeneralizations occur early in acquisition, children need to unlearn them later to gain complete command of subcategorization. How do LRT and the connectionist model account for occurrence and unlearning of overgeneralization?

Pinker (1989) proposes the following solution. There are two types of overgeneralizations:

(26) a. **Adult error.** The verb is in the broad-range class, but not in one of the narrow-range classes.

 b. **Semantic error.** The verb is located in the wrong part of the semantic space, a part that licenses the subcategorization frame in question. The real semantics of the verb would not license it.

The second error is specific to language acquisition, having to do with initially incomplete understanding of the semantics of a new word.

Errors of the first type should be similar to adults' errors. But this prediction is not borne out by the errors that children actually make:

> At first glance the minimalist theory would seem implausible, as many of the overgeneralizations children make have an unmistakably childlike sound to them and would surely never be found among the

kinds of innovative or unconventional usages shown by adults [...]
But this reservation is inconclusive.
(Pinker 1989:293)

Several important factors that differentiate adults' and children's speech
are cited as evidence (e.g., lexical gaps). But the fact remains that the
internal mechanism for subcategorization changes between the state of
overgeneralization and the state of correct production. If the narrow-
range class that prevents an overgeneralization from being uttered in the
later stage does not operate in the earlier stage, there must be a learning
mechanism that changes it at some point between the two phases in
development. At some point, the child has to learn how to differentiate
between subcategorization frames that are odd-sounding and should be
avoided (although licensed by a broad-range rule) and subcategorization
frames that are perfect (because they are licensed by a narrow-range
rule). Unfortunately, this important part of Lexical Rule Theory is not
provided in LC.

Naigles comes to the same conclusion in her review of LC:

No theory-external evidence is offered for either the existence of this
level [narrow range classes HS], or for any of the precise NR subclass
characterizations. [...]
Thus, there is currently no evidence for the existence of NR sub-
classes or rules in children, nor for Pinker's claim that it is the acquisition of these NR rules that puts the brakes on child overgeneralizations. (Naigles 1991:73)

The connectionist model exhibits overgeneralization and recovery
from it in a natural way because its learning algorithm is backpropagation. Backpropagation is an implementation of gradient descent. In
gradient descent, parameters are modified so that the largest sources
of error are accounted for first. As a result, the main generalizations
are learned in the first phase, since acquiring them covers most cases
and decreases the error most rapidly. Idiosyncrasies, for which the main
generalizations make wrong predictions, are then learned in the second
phase of learning. An example was given in Figure 16.

Figure 17 reveals that there are actually more than two phases in
learning. The figure shows the overall error (summed over all verbs) in
each iteration. In the first twenty iterations or so, the error decreases
from 600 to 500. The network simply learns to average all values occurring as targets and thereby reduces the initial error. No subcategorization frames are predicted correctly at this point. For about 300
iterations, the stochastic learning algorithm remains on a plateau. Finally, it finds a set of major generalizations and the error is reduced to

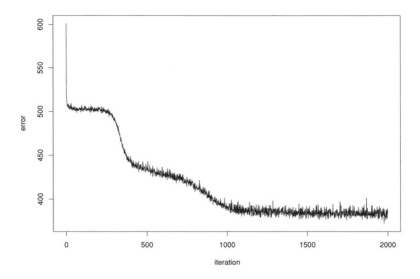

FIGURE 17 How the connectionist network learns major and minor generalization.

about 440. Now frames for all verbs that are part of the major classes ("throw", "give", "contribute") are selected correctly. Between iterations 350 and 1000 the error declines gradually. Here minor classes and exceptions are learned. After iteration 1000, it takes several thousand additional iterations to learn contextually conditioned subcategorization frames such as the focussed prepositional construction for "deny".

In each phase, the learning algorithm concentrates on verb groups that are responsible for most of the error at that point. Since minor verb groups or individual verbs are neglected, they are generalized incorrectly, giving rise to overgeneralization. Overgeneralization is unlearned because each type of verb, be it part of a regular class, a subregularity, or the exceptions, has its phase as finer and finer distinctions are learned. Thus no additional assumptions are necessary to account for overgeneralization in this framework. The phenomenon is naturally explained by the properties of gradient descent learning as it is implemented by backpropagation.

This account of the recovery from overgeneralization bears some resemblance with the account based on the principles of contrast and conventionality proposed by Clark (1987, 1993). She writes about recovery in the case of past tense learning:

The length of time children take to resolve such problems [recovery from overgeneralization HS] is in part a direct consequence of the difficulty they face in identifying violations of contrast. Violations only become apparent where children conclude that two forms have the *same* meaning. They then have to make a choice; they cannot retain both. The choice is determined by conventionality: the conventional, adult form wins. ... (Clark 1993:104)

In the case of subcategorization, this account is directly applicable to verbs for which the two subcategorization frames license different pragmatic implications, for example instantaneity for "throw" and focus for "refuse". Semantic-pragmatic variants of a verb like "refuse" (in this case focusses and unfocussed) will be represented the same way at the hidden unit level in the initial training phase. This would correspond to the phase where the child believes that both variants of "refuse" can be used with the prepositional construction. After major generalizations have been learned, the only way the error can be reduced further is to find the crucial distinction focussed vs. unfocussed and to realize that only the focussed variant allows the prepositional construction (more on about how exactly this happens in the next section, 4.4.7). This would correspond to the point in learning when the child eliminates one of the two variants, the unfocussed one, and retains the other, the conventional, focussed one.

The connectionist network thus presents a precise model of how the existence of competing forms can be established and how the conventional one can be retained and the unconventional one eliminated.

4.4.7 Ambiguity

As discussed in section 4.2, the problem of ambiguity is not addressed in Lexical Rule Theory. Contextual features like instantaneity influence subcategorization only for a few verb classes such as the "throw" class. Hence, the child needs to learn what the underlying representation of a verb for determining subcategorization is: only its basic morphosemantics or its morphosemantics plus a representation of context. This type of ambiguity is similar to part-of-speech and word-sense ambiguity in that one of several possible underlying representations of the same surface form must be selected.

Could one extend LRT to account for acquisition in the presence of ambiguity? A fundamental assumption in LRT is that verbs have a unique lexicosemantic representation which determines subcategorization. Contextually conditioned subcategorization requires different underlying representations in each context. Crucially, the contextual features influence only some verbs. In order to discriminate contextually conditioned verbs from other verbs, the child has to learn conjunctions of a contextual feature and one or more morphosemantic features. For example, the feature "instantaneous" plays a role for the subcategorization of the ballistic class ("throw" etc.), but is not relevant for the "give" class. It is much harder to acquire dependence that is conditioned on context ("ditransitive ok if instantaneous action AND verb of throwing") than simple, uncontextualized dependence ("ditransitive not ok if physical direction specified"). As far as I can see there is no straightforward modification of the LRT learning mechanisms that would accommodate contextual dependence. This is a serious limitation of the theory.

As shown in Table 20, the connectionist network succeeds at learning contextualized dependence. For example, in instantaneous contexts of "throw", equal preference is given to prepositional and ditransitive constructions. In non-instantaneous contexts, the network gives a preference of 1.0 to the prepositional construction. So the model acquired the correct behavior of verbs with contextualized subcategorization. What is more, this group of verbs is also generalized correctly. So if a new verb of throwing is presented to the network, its subcategorization behavior is correctly predicted to allow the ditransitive construction only in instantaneous contexts.

The kind of neural network used here, a multi-layer perceptron, can learn contextualized dependence because its hidden units can be trained to become feature detectors. Suppose that at a given point in training there already is a feature detector i for "instantaneity" (in the hidden unit block for context) and a feature detector t for "verb of throwing" (in the hidden unit layer for morphosemantics). Suppose further that there is a hidden unit h in the second layer that indicates better than the other hidden units that both i and t are on. h may be a bad indicator, but there must be one hidden unit that is a better indicator than the others.[9] Then backpropagation will strengthen h's connections to i and t more than the other units' connections to i and t. If this process is repeated for many iterations, then h will eventually become an excellent feature detector for the presence of both instantaneity and a verb of throwing.[10]

---

[9]With probability 1, random initialization guarantees that there is such a unit. It is virtually impossible that two units will behave exactly the same way if their weights are randomly selected. With non-random initialization, this crucial initial condition would not be satisfied, and learning of conjunctive feature detectors would fail in many cases.

[10]The feature detectors i and t are formed along the same lines. The process is not really sequential as described here, but the three detectors develop simultaneously.

This is what in fact happened in the model described here. The third hidden unit (in the second layer) specialized in detecting the conjunction "instantaneity and throwing" — or rather its negation. If a verb of throwing is presented, then hidden unit 3 is off (activation 0.01) if and only if the action is instantaneous. It is on otherwise (activation 0.63).

No such process of incremental strengthening of a feature detector for instantaneity will occur for other classes such as the "lower" class. Since in their case such a feature detector would not contribute to error reduction, connections for a potential feature detector "physical direction specified and instantaneous action" are not strengthened. The hidden unit that would have grown into a detector of this feature will serve another purpose instead.

This example demonstrates how the connectionist model learns to choose among all possible feature conjunctions those that do useful work for prediction. This process eliminates many possible underlying representations for a given verb so that some verbs will end up with a contextual representation, some will end up with a non-contextual representation. Thus the connectionist model solves the ambiguity problem for subcategorization by forming problem-specific representations.

4.4.8   Innateness

Both models discussed here rely on innate knowledge. The morphosemantic feature representations could not be induced by a learning machine that didn't know anything about physical laws and social interaction. For example, finding out that transfer from one person to another is an important concept (as opposed to any movement of an object) presupposes that the concept of a person is in place. From the hard-wired brain circuitry for face recognition to the special sensitivity of the ear to the frequency range of human voices, there are many innate features of humans that facilitate acquiring the concept of personhood.

Similarly, both methods rely on innate mechanisms. The connectionist model uses feedback learning, one of the learning methods employed by humans and animals. LRT relies on general capacities like forming similarity judgments or making generalizations.

However, there is an important difference between the two models. LRT uses some specifically syntactic innate knowledge whereas the connectionist model uses none. There are two types of syntactic innate knowledge in LRT:

- innate knowledge about which features are syntactically relevant and which are not[11]

---

[11] The point that the neural network does not depend on a correct preselection of

- innate knowledge about linking rules

As was pointed out in Section 4.2.2.1, positing linking rules as innate is problematic since some languages violate them. It is not clear what it means for a constraint on linking to be innate if it is easy to override.

The first type of innate knowledge (constraints on features) is used to enable the LRT learning mechanism to build narrow-range class definitions. If there were dozens of extraneous features like: "the thing transferred is blue" or "the beneficiary's birthday is today" in addition to the morphosemantic ones, then none of the various criteria that are mentioned in LC (difference of at most one feature, at most one important feature, two features etc.) would work.

It is unclear whether there is a universal set of syntactically relevant categories. For example, honorifics and evidentials are categories that are syntactically relevant in a few languages but not in most (Trask, 1993). Is it really plausible to claim that such specialized categories are part of our genetic heritage and specified to be available for syntactic categorization?

Naigles (1991) provides another argument against an innate delimitation of what affects grammatical categorization. She points out that in her midwestern dialect "lower" dativizes in contrast to other "physical direction specified" verbs ("raise", "hoist") which don't (page 70). She suggests that upward vs. downward might differentiate the two verbs. This is another feature for which it seems implausible that our genes specify that it is potentially syntactically relevant. Put differently, if upward vs. downward is plausible, then why not blue vs. red and any other conceivable feature?

The connectionist model provides an existence proof that no syntactic innate knowledge is necessary to learn subcategorization.[12] No

---

the right features for subcategorization selection could have been made more forcefully by adding several morphosemantic features to the simulation with no impact on subcategorization. Just as the localist features do not give rise to generalizations, this type of information which cannot be exploited to predicty regularity would have been ignored by the network. In fact, for several classes of verbs there are morphosemantic features that are ignored because they are not important for generalizations for this group. For example, the feature latinate is not helpful in forming generalizations for the verbs of not having ("refuse", "cost", "deny" etc.). In the same way, morphosemantic features not relevant for any group would be ignored for all groups.

[12]The feature "latinate" is language-specific, even if not syntax-specific. I am confident that if the constituent parts of the feature (syllable structure, stress etc.) were directly presented, the model would perform at the same level of accuracy and generalization. Note that I am only claiming that the representation of syntactic properties of words is not structured by innate constraints. I think it is plausible that the representation of phonological and prosodic properties of words is indeed partially determined by innate constraints.

linking rules are provided and no restrictions on the type of feature that can be used are imposed. Notice that the connectionist model is faced with literally hundreds of features that are definitely not in the class of potentially syntactically relevant ones: the localist units that are assigned to individual verbs. This abundance of non-grammatical features does not confuse it. Of course, after the completion of learning the knowledge present in the weights of the network is highly specific to language. But when the randomly generalized network begins the task of acquisition, it does not know anything about language.

It could still be that, although subcategorization is learnable without syntactic innate knowledge in principle, it cannot be learned by humans without some help beyond general cognitive biases. But the existence of a successful model lacking syntactic innate knowledge seriously undermines the arguments for the need of such knowledge for the acquisition of subcategorization.

4.4.9 Transition

Even though LRT relies partially on syntax-specific innate knowledge to learn subcategorization, an important part of the theory is not claimed to be innate: narrow-range classes. Consequently, even if LRT is right and some broad characterization of the dative alternation is present at birth, both theories must explain how children learn the narrower generalizations (captured in LRT by narrow-range classes) without recourse to innateness. The process of learning is a progression from a state without any knowledge of narrow-range classes (the child at birth) to the final state in which the adult speaker masters subcategorization. Since class definitions correspond to rules of classification and vice versa, this process can be viewed as a transition from a rule-less to a rule-governed state.

I repeat here from section 4.2.2.2 the most explicit specification I have been able to find in LC of how this transition comes about in LRT:

> Upon noticing that a pair of individual verbs are morphologically and semantically related in a way captured by a nonaffixing broad-range rule, the learner would create a rule whose semantic operations mapped the narrow conflation class specification for one onto the narrow conflation class specification of the other. In other words, the generalization that the learner would make would be: if verb X alternates, other verbs with the same grammatically relevant semantic structure alternate, too. (Pinker 1989:274)

This account of the transition process is revised later because of the problems with generalization discussed above: identity of lexicosemantic representations is neither a necessary nor a sufficient condition for identical subcategorization behavior. Despite this acknowledgment (that identity of lexicosemantic grids cannot be the basis of narrow-range class formation) no alternative is provided.

Is it possible to extend LRT to account for the transition? The problem for LRT is that quantitative factors play a role in class formation. Suppose two languages have a large number of verbs with a particular morphosemantic profile p. Suppose further that in the first language one verb undergoes the dative alternation and all other verbs can only be constructed with prepositional indirect objects; and that in the second language one verb allows only the prepositional construction and all other verbs undergo the dative alternation. Novel verbs with morphosemantic profile p would have different subcategorization behavior in the two languages because they would be analogized in accordance with the regular verbs rather than the single exception. In the first language, a novel verb with profile p would be restricted to the prepositional construction, whereas it would undergo the dative alternation in the second language.

This example demonstrates that quantitative factors cannot be ignored in the transition from rule to non-rule. Since LRT has no capability for quantitative reasoning, it does not solve the transition problem.

The connectionist network solves the transition problem as shown, for example, in Figure 17. In the beginning of training, there is no knowledge about subcategorization in the network (very high error), at the end of training subcategorization has been acquired correctly (small error, no categorization errors as shown in Table 19). The reason for the successful transition from non-rule to rule in connectionism is simple: A gradual accumulation of small quantitative changes can eventually become a qualitative change. One example was given in section 4.4.7. A randomly initialized hidden unit can evolve into a discrete detector for a symbolic feature ("instantaneous action AND verb of throwing") by gradual strengthening of weights. Another example is the recovery from overgeneralization. Figure 16 shows how the initial network essentially produces random output for "refuse" in the first epochs, but then gradually evolves into a sharp classifier, giving a preference of close to 1.00 to the correct frame and close to 0.00 to the incorrect frame.

Plunkett and Marchman (1993) have also discussed the transition problem, in the context of connectionist models for past tense acquisition. They ask which factors trigger the transition "from rote learning to system building," i.e. from memorizing input examples to creating a system of generalizations that will handle novel linguistic material correctly. Their primary goal is

... to determine whether gradual *quantitative* and *structural* changes in the verb vocabulary can lead to *qualitative* shifts in the manner in which a network organizes the mapping relationship between verb stems and their past tense forms.[13] (page 28)

They conclude from their experiments:

The comparison of performance in networks using various initial vocabulary conditions [...] suggests that the trigger for the transition from rote learning to system building in these networks is associated with the *quantity* of verbs in the training set which undergo systematic mapping processes. With respect to this vocabulary, the prime instigator of generalization (and hence internal reorganization in the network) was the number of *regular verbs* included in the initial vocabulary. [...]

These results are additional evidence that neural networks can solve the transition problem.

A different perspective on the transition problem is provided by Harris: She shows that connectionist networks can represent systematicities of varying degrees of regularities: from exceptionless rules to small subregularities to exceptions. On this view, the transition from non-rule to rule consists simply of moving a systematicity from its initial point on the "weak subregularity" part of the continuum to the other end of the cline where exceptionless rules are located. (Harris, 1994)

In summary, LRT does not explain how the formation of subcategorization classes is triggered. In contrast, the problem of transition doesn't arise in connectionism because a unified framework for rules, analogy, and exceptions is provided. A rule emerges if no evidence to the contrary (or very little) is present in training, so that the regularity gets ever stronger in training to the point of exhibiting rule-like behavior.

One of the virtues of a rule-based account lies in the fact that many regularities are most elegantly described by rules. An example are the verbs of manner of speaking ("babble" etc.). There doesn't seem to be an exception to the rule "if a verb specifies manner of speaking, then the ditransitive construction is ungrammatical." So the best static description of adult subcategorization competence may be Lexical Rule Theory. But it is a poor account of how the child attains this competence.

---

[13]Plunkett and Marchman (1993) also model the increasing size of the vocabulary over time ("structural changes in verb vocabulary"). This is a complexity in acquisition that neither model discussed here addresses.

4.4.10 Limitations of the Connectionist Model

In addition to correct acquisition and overgeneralization, Lexical Rule Theory aims to model systematic differences in meaning between the dative and prepositional constructions. Example (7), here repeated as (27), demonstrates that for some verbs, the dative construction implies successful transfer, whereas the prepositional construction has no such implication.

(27) a. He taught me English.
     b. He taught English to me.

However, as pointed out by Goldberg (1992:45), such pragmatic differences between the two frames do not hold for many other verbs of transfer. She cites "send" as an example:

(28) a. She sent me flowers.
     b. She sent flowers to me.

If the differences are not systematic, but idiosyncrasies of individual verbs, then an adequate model must explain why some verbs' pragmatics depend on subcategorization and others don't, a task that LRT does not address. Still, the fact that pragmatic changes are not accommodated in the connectionist model in its current form is a possible limitation.

Another limitation of the model concerns token frequencies. The same token frequency was assumed for all verbs in the simulation. This is clearly inadequate since some verbs are much more frequent than others. Research on the past tense has shown that there is a strong correlation between token frequency and irregularity (Marcus et al., 1992). A large proportion of irregular verbs are frequent. And the more irregular a verb is, the more frequent it often is. The most irregular form "went" is the past tense of one of the most frequent English verbs. I suspect that similar correlations hold in the case of subcategorization. On average, regular verb types are probably less frequent than exceptions.

Token frequencies could also be problematic for the model if they are higher than those that children naturally encounter during acquisition. Some of the medium and low frequency verbs treated here are rare so that they probably will not be encountered more than a thousand times as is the case in the simulation. However, this argument assumes a straightforward relationship between the number of times a verb is uttered in the child's environment and the number of times it can be used for training. Such a relationship does not necessarily hold. For example, the child could remember any given occurrence several times, so that the number of training instances could be larger than the number of perceived utterances of a particular verb.

Finally, the most serious limitation of the model in the context of this book is that it does not address the problem of gradience in verb subcategorization. It was assumed that for each verb in a particular context there are three possibilities: only the double-object construction is good, only the prepositional construction is good, or both constructions are good. But many combinations of verbs and subcategorization frames are intermediate in grammatical acceptability. Sentence (29a) is a case in point. Many speakers find it marginal, but it is not as bad as (29b).

(29) a. ? Newt Gingrich, the Republican whip, ceded them some points. (NYT-10-22-90)
     b. * Newt Gingrich contributed them part of his book advance.

I haven't addressed gradient subcategorization because a categorization of verbs into a multitude of categories (0.1-ditransitive + 1.0-prepositional, 0.5-ditransitive + 0.0-prepositional, 1.0-ditransitive + 1.0-prepositional etc.) would be much harder than a categorization into three different categories (prep, ditr, prep + ditr). Also, the latter categorization is available from dictionaries and (Levin, 1993), but there is no data base for gradient subcategorization. For these reasons, I have not attempted to model gradience in the simulation although I find the problem extremely interesting.[14]

4.4.11 Other Related Work

Brent (1993), Manning (1993) and several more recent papers address the question of how particular subcategorization frames can be recognized. They simply collect all possible subcategorization for a given verb and are not concerned with generalization. The representation of the output in my model assumes that subcategorization frames in the input can be recognized (possibly with a certain error rate, as modeled by the incorrect subcategorization frames in training). Brent and Manning's computational models constitute linguistic modules which could interact with the subcategorization selector, providing the categorization that is necessary for the output patterns.

Another body of related work is the literature on syntactic bootstrapping (Fisher et al., 1991). Syntactic bootstrapping is the hypothesis that subcategorization frames are one of the cues (or even the main cue) used by children to acquire the meaning of verbs. For example, a child hearing "She faxed him the proposal" can infer that "to fax" is a verb of transfer, which may be the first step in building up a complete lexical entry for the verb. The question of syntactic bootstrapping seems or-

---

[14]Pinker also seems to be sympathetic to graded subcategorization judgments. (Pinker 1989:280)

thogonal to the question of selecting subcategorization frames for a verb when its meaning is known, which has been our focus here.

Resnik's work on selectional restrictions may help in accounting for how the input features of the subcategorization selector are acquired (Resnik, 1993). Selectional constraints address the question: "Is argument A appropriate for verb V?", whereas subcategorization selection asks: "Given that verb V has argument A, what are the syntactic possibilities for expressing it?" The semantic similarity metric proposed by Resnik may be important in accounting for the acquisition of the semantic features that the connectionist model is based on, a question I have not addressed here.

4.5   Conclusion

This chapter compares the explanatory adequacy of Lexical Rule Theory and a connectionist model for the acquisition of verb subcategorization. An adequate theory must model several properties of learning, including the three (possibly weakened) premises of Baker's paradox: successful acquisition, erroneous input, exceptions in the input, (limited) arbitrariness, lack of negative evidence, productivity, and overgeneralization.

It was found that both models account for successful acquisition of verbs that occur during training and for learning without negative evidence. The connectionist model exhibits additional desirable properties that LRT lacks: learning in the presence of errors and exceptions, generalization and overgeneralization.

LRT does not address two other problems: learning of ambiguity, i.e., determining the correct underlying representation of verbs for subcategorization decisions; and transition from a rule-less to a rule-governed state. Both problems are solved by the quantitative nature of connectionist learning, in which small changes can accumulate to the point of making a qualitative difference.

Finally, the two models have access to the same learning information: observations of verbs being used with one subcategorization frame or the other. In addition, LRT relies on syntax-specific innate knowledge. Although no such knowledge is available to the connectionist model, it learns subcategorization perfectly. This success provides an existence proof for the possibility of acquiring subcategorization using only general cognitive capacities and thus undermines the poverty-of-stimulus argument for subcategorization.

5

A Look Back

In this book, I have investigated the notion of ambiguity, presented models of acquisition in the presence of ambiguity and algorithms for ambiguity resolution. The two principal lessons from the study concern the nature of linguistic representations and innateness.

The mechanisms of the acquisition models crucially rely on gradient representations. Neither unsupervised classification for syntactic and semantic learning nor connectionist gradient descent would be possible with purely discrete representations. The disambiguation algorithms proposed have a similar critical need for gradience. In most cases, there are no yes-no criteria for deciding whether one reading is better than another. Gradient representations make it possible to rank readings and select the best one. This shows that gradient representations or a combination of discrete and gradient representations are indispensable to representing linguistic objects.

The study presented here is also relevant for innateness. The computational models are examples of systems that learn categories and properties that have been claimed to be unlearnable without syntax-specific innate knowledge. This means that the argument of the poverty of the stimulus has been seriously undermined for syntactic categorization and subcategorization. Syntax-specific innate knowledge could still be necessary for other phenomena such as island constraints. But given its dispensability for the three areas examined here, the burden of proof is on those who postulate innate knowledge. I hope that the success of TAG SPACE, WORD SPACE, and the connectionist model will make it harder to justify nativism without a thorough investigation of general cognitive learning.

I have argued in this book that ambiguity is pervasive in natural language and that an account of how it can be learned is important both for computational and theoretical linguistics. My hope is that the models presented here are a start that can be developed fruitfully. I am convinced that ambiguity, if understood properly as inherent in the nature of language, will lead to a fresh look at language that will allow us to examine many linguistic problems in a new light.

A

Mathematical Methods

A.1 Singular Value Decomposition

This section introduces the technique of singular value decomposition (SVD). SVD is applied in the induction of TAG SPACE and WORD SPACE for two reasons: a) It generalizes the distributional and associational information extracted from corpora. b) It creates compact representations. Let me first work through an example that demonstrates generalization and compactness. A formal description of SVD and a discussion of related work follows.

A.1.1 An Example

This example concerns head-modifier relationships, for example adjectives that modify nouns. One way to build a record of such relationships is a distributional matrix such as the one in Figure 18.

	...	government	...	minister	...
...					
foreign		2		210	
...					
communist		75		0	
...					

FIGURE 18 A matrix recording head-modifier relations.

Element $a_{i,j}$ in this matrix records how often word w_i occurred at most 3 words to the left of w_j in the corpus. This can be seen as a crude approximation of the frequency of head-modifier relationships in cases where the order of head and modifier is fixed. In the hypothetical example in Figure 18, "foreign" occurred 210 times at most 3 words to the left of "minister" and "communist" occurred 75 times at most 3 words to the left of "government".

189

The role of SVD is to transform distributional matrices in order to bring out generalizations in distributional patterns that the original matrix does not show due to natural randomness in sampling from a corpus. For example, "read" and "write" take similar arguments. But in a particular data sample, the agents used with "read" may be different from the agents used with "write". This is the kind of fluctuation that occurs in natural samples. However, if there are other verbs like "publish" and "author" that share arguments with both "read" and "write", then it is possible to infer the similarity of "read" and "write" from this fact. This inference is the work that SVD can do in certain circumstances.

The following experiment demonstrates both generalization and compactness. A 5000-by-5000 matrix analogous to the one in Figure 18 was collected from a large text corpus (the Oxford Hector Pilot corpus). The 5000 rows and columns correspond to 5000 high-frequency words (the same for rows and columns). We can think of the rows and columns of the matrix as vectors in a multi-dimensional space, with each of the 5,000 selected words corresponding to one dimension. The SVD finds an approximation of the row and column vectors in a low-dimensional space. SVD decomposes a matrix C, the collocation matrix in Figure 18 in our case, into three matrices T_0, S_0, and D_0 such that:

$$C = T_0 S_0 D_0'$$

S_0 is a diagonal matrix that contains the singular values of C in descending order. The ith singular value can be interpreted as indicating the strength of the ith principal component of C. By restricting the $n \times n$ matrices T_0, S_0, and D_0 to their first $m < n$ columns (= principal components) one obtains the matrices T, S, and D. Their product $\hat{C}$ is the best least square approximation of C by a matrix of rank m (i.e. one representable as a product of the $n \times m$ and $m \times n$ matrices T_s and D_s'):

$$\hat{C} = TSD' = [TS^{\frac{1}{2}}][S^{\frac{1}{2}}D'] =: T_s D_s'$$

The major axes of variation found by the SVD all have the same weight in the matrices T and D. By multiplying them by $S^{\frac{1}{2}}$ they are rescaled so that their different importance is accurately reflected.

We can compute comparisons between rows and comparisons between columns. With the cosine of the angle between two rows/columns as a measure for their closeness, we get a measure of their relatedness. In the original matrix, the cosine between two rows is a measure of how many right neighbors two words have in common. Similarly, the cosine between two columns is a measure of how many left neighbors they have in common. The truncated space is a good approximation in that the angle between rows (or columns) in the reduced space is as close as possible to the angle between rows in the unreduced space.[1]

Recall the case of "write" and "read": two words may not share any left neighbors although their left contexts are very similar intuitively. As another example, consider the nouns "government" and "party". Their left contexts often contain adjectives designating party affiliation to specify the political party in question. But in this case there is less overlap than expected since governments are rarely communist in our corpus, but the communist parties of Eastern and Southern Europe are a frequent topic of discussion. We want a measure of context similarity that will abstract away from such idiosyncrasies of the corpus.

The vectors produced by the dimensionality reduction can capture generalizations such as "occurring with a political adjective to its left." Each direction in the original 5000-dimensional space corresponds to a set of left neighbors that a particular word may take. If a particular set occurs frequently, then this direction will be preserved in the process of dimensionality reduction. If a set is rare, then it will be projected onto a direction corresponding to a frequent set, roughly the direction that it is most similar to (i.e. the angle between the two directions is as small as possible).

In our example, one of the frequent sets of left neighbors is the set of political adjectives. So one of the directions in the reduced space will correspond to this set. The adjective "communist" is a political adjective that occurs with many political nouns like "party" and "leader". But "communist" did not occur with words like "mp" and "spokesman" in the British National corpus. This is an infrequent idiosyncrasy, so the direction in the original space that corresponds to "political adjective without 'communist' " will be assimilated to the direction "political adjective". As a result the difference in frequency between "conservative mp" and "communist mp" disappears.

This effect can be demonstrated by comparing actual and virtual cooccurrence counts that can be inferred from the original and the reduced space. The frequency of the syntagma "v w" can be computed in the original space as the inner product of the right context vector of word v and the left context vector of word w. (This corresponds to the multiplication of the matrices T_0, S_0, and D_0.) In the reduced space, the "generalized" right context vector of v is multiplied with the "gener-

---

[1]More precisely, SVD preserves euclidean distance, not correlation. But since we work with normalized vectors here, euclidean distance and correlation are closely related since $(|\vec{a} - \vec{b}|)^2 = \sum (a_i - b_i)^2 = \sum a_i^2 - 2\sum a_i b_i + \sum b_i^2 = 1 - 2corr(\vec{a}, \vec{b}) + 1 = 2(1 - corr(\vec{a}, \vec{b}))$.

alized" left context vector of w. (This corresponds to the multiplication of the matrices T_s and D_s.)

	# cooccurrences in corpus	reconstructed count	Δ
"mp"	5	105	100
"spokesman"	2	81	79
"mps"	2	70	68
"government"	42	97	55
"group"	9	45	36

TABLE 28 Words with a high increase in reconstructed cooccurrence counts.

Table 28 lists the five right neighbors of "communist" with the highest increase in generalized cooccurrence count. The table gives the number of times that each of the five words occurred to the right of "communist" in the corpus (this is the count from the cooccurrence matrix $C = T_0 S_0 D_0'$), the generalized number of cooccurrences in the low-rank approximation of the high-dimensional space (this is the count from matrix $\hat{C} = T_s D_s'$) and the difference. In each case, the increase seems justified: MPs, spokesmen, governments and groups can all plausibly be communist from a linguistic point of view, although they rarely if ever are in Britain due to the insignificance of its communist party.

This example demonstrates the generalization property of SVD. Compactness is achieved because the reduced space has a much smaller number of dimensions. In the experiment just described the reduced space had 100 dimensions. So the left and right context vectors of a word can be represented as 100-dimensional vectors instead of 5000-dimensional vectors. Unless most of the 5000-dimensional vectors are extremely sparse, using the 100-dimensional vectors will result in considerably more compact representations.

All singular value decompositions reported in this book are computed using Michael Berry's SVDPACK routines (Berry, 1992).

A.1.2 Formal Description

Golub and van Loan define Singular Value Decomposition as follows.

Singular Value Decomposition. If A is a real m-by-n matrix then there exist orthogonal matrices

$$U = [u_1, \ldots, u_m] \in \mathcal{R}^{m \times m}$$

and

$$V = [v_1, \ldots, v_n] \in \mathcal{R}^{n \times n}$$

such that
$$U^T A V = diag(\sigma_1, \ldots, \sigma_p) \in \mathcal{R}^{mxn}$$
($p = \min\{m, n\}$), where $\sigma_1 \geq \sigma_2 \geq \ldots \geq \sigma_p \geq 0$.

Equivalently, the singular value decomposition can be defined by the following equation which can simply be derived from the one just given by multiplying with U on the right and V^T on the left. (If U and V are not orthonormal, i.e. if not $UU^T = I$ and $VV^T = I$, then additional multiplications by diagonal matrices are necessary to complete the transformation.)

$$(*) A = U diag(\sigma_1, \ldots, \sigma_p) V^T$$

Singular Value Decomposition is closely related to principal component analysis. The squares of the singular values are the eigenvalues of the matrix AA^T and the matrix U contains the eigenvectors as the following derivation shows:

$$A = USV^T$$
$$AA^T = USV^T(USV^T)^T$$
$$AA^T = USV^T VS^T U^T$$
$$AA^T = US^2 U^T$$
$$AA^T U = US^2$$

So the dimensionality reduction performed by SVD can also be thought of as an identification of the major axes of variation in a way that is very similar to principal component analysis.

The assertion that SVD finds the most important axes of variation can be made more precise (Berry 1992:14):

Eckart and Young. Let the SVD of A be given by $[(*)]$ with $r = rank(A) \leq p = \min(m, n)$ and define

$$A_k = \sum_{i=1}^{k} u_i \sigma_i v_i^T \text{ with } k < r,$$

then

$$\min_{r(B)=k} ||A - B||_F^2 = ||A - A_k||_F^2 = \sigma_{k+1}^2 + \ldots + \sigma_p^2.$$

This theorem states that if the three matrices U, S, and V are restricted to their first k columns and multiplied, then the result A_k of the multiplication is the best least square approximation of A that has at most rank k. In other words, of all matrices that can be represented in a k-dimensional space, A_k differs least from A according to the least-square measure (the sum of the squares of all element-wise differences). This is the crucial property for generalization as explained in the above example: The idiosyncratic bits of vectors in the high-dimensional space (like a lacking "communist" with MP) will be assimilated to larger groups of vectors. SVD chooses the most cautious projection possible and preserves the overall similarity structure of the original space as much as possible.

A.1.3 Related Work

The work on SVD in this book owes a great deal to Latent Semantic Indexing, an Information Retrieval technique that originated at Bell-CoRe (Deerwester et al., 1990). In LSI, document-by-word matrices are processed by SVD instead of word-by-word matrices. This technique addresses the synonymy problem in document retrieval. A query about "cosmonauts" will not retrieve any documents about "astronauts" in a system based on word-matching. Loosely speaking, the dimensionality reduction computed by a SVD on the document-by-word matrix collapses synonyms onto the same underlying dimension. Therefore, SVD-based representations of the query about cosmonauts will successfully retrieve documents about astronauts.

As far as the use of SVD is concerned, the novelty of the work presented in this book is the way word vectors are used and the definition of the underlying matrix. The main use of word vectors here is to cluster them (or the context vectors they give rise to) to arrive at various unsupervised classifications. The underlying matrix is a word-by-word matrix and defined in two different ways, associationally (neighbors in a context) and distributionally (adjacent neighbors). In contrast, only word-by-document matrices are processed by SVD in LSI and word vectors are not used independently. The goal in LSI-based work is to improve document representations.

The difference between associational word-by-word matrices and word-by-document matrices is actually not as great as it may appear at first. Suppose that A is a word-by-document matrix with the following decomposition:

$$A = USV^T$$

Then $C = AA^T$ is a word-by-word matrix that records in entry c_{ij} how often words i and j cooccur with each other in the same documents as is immediately apparent from the definition of matrix multiplication. From the last section, we know that C has the following decomposition:

$$C = AA^T = US^2U^T$$

So SVD produces the same reduced word vectors from word-by-word matrices and word-by-document matrices. The only difference is that the higher dimensions are more strongly weighted for the word-by-word matrices (squared values rather than simple values from S).

Let me conclude with a short discussion of factor analysis, a technique closely related to LSI which has been used by Biber (1993) for language analysis. Factor analysis is also a principal component analysis, but it is applied to identify orthogonal *factors* in the transformed space rather than for dimensionality reduction. Each of the dimensions in the transformed space is interpreted as capturing a particular hidden variable in the data. For example, in a factor analysis of collocations of "certain" Biber finds that collocations with high values on Factor 1 correspond to uses in the meaning "particular" for concrete objects and high values on Factor 2 to the same meaning for abstract objects. Collocations with high values on Factor 3 correspond to the meaning that expresses certainty.

One could apply the same technique to SVD-based vector representations by trying to interpret the dimensions of the reduced space. However, I have not been able to find good interpretations of the dimensions of reduced SVD-spaces. Apparently, meaningful generalizations can only be made about patterns of values that involve all dimensions. This is precisely what the clustering techniques I have used do. They define classes by centroids which have non-zero values on all dimensions.

A.2 Unsupervised Classification

This section explains Buckshot, the group-average clustering method that is used for unsupervised classification in TAG SPACE and WORD SPACE, and derives an algorithm for implementing it efficiently.

A clustering algorithm searches for a partitioning of vectors in a multi-dimensional space such that each region of the partitioning is well separated from other regions and that points within a region are relatively close to each other.

colors	beautiful blue colour colours flowers green light orange paper piece pink red sky sun white yellow
inanimate nouns	conversation coup phrase smile stories
people	american anyone billy brothers doctor genius girl man men players reading star stars student writer young

TABLE 29 Three clusters of words modified by "brilliant".

Let me give an example before I present a formal definition of clustering. The head-modifier relations from Section A.1.1 can again serve as an illustration. For the experiment, all nouns that are modified by "brilliant" in the Hector Pilot Corpus were collected. For each word, its SVD-reduced left context vector was extracted from the matrix in Figure 18, that is, a vector recording which modifiers occurred to the left of the word in the corpus. These left context vectors were then clustered into three coherent groups using the Buckshot clustering algorithm to be described presently.

Table 29 shows three clusters of words that are modified by "brilliant" in the Oxford Hector Pilot Corpus. As can be seen from the table, the clusters correspond well to the intuitive categories of entities that can be modified by "brilliant": "color", "inanimate object" and "people". Since the context vectors of color terms are more similar to each other than to context vectors from other groups they were put into one group. The clusters "inanimate objects" and "people" were likewise recognized as separate groups.

A.2.1 Group-Average Agglomerative Clustering

All the clustering experiments reported in this book were performed using Buckshot, which is based on one of the heuristic clustering algorithms that are commonly used in Information Retrieval. Some early experiments with alternative algorithms and systems like AutoClass (Cheeseman et al., 1988) and the EM algorithm (Dempster et al., 1977) did not yield qualitatively different results, but clustering usually was on an order of magnitude faster with Buckshot.

Three of the clustering algorithms that are discussed by van Rijsbergen (1979) are single-link, complete-link, and average-link clustering. They start out with each element being assigned to its own cluster. Clusters are then merged until the desired number of clusters is reached. At each step, the two closest clusters are merged. The three different algorithms differ in their definition of cluster distance. Single-link defines cluster similarity as the maximum of the similarities between any pair of points in the two clusters. For complete link, the minimum pairwise similarity is defined as the similarity between the clusters and for average link, cluster similarity is the average pairwise similarity (Jain and Dubes, 1988).

Single-link clustering can lead to elongated clusters (for example, long parallel lines). Complete-link clustering is strongly affected by outliers. Average-link clustering is a compromise between the two extremes, which generally avoids both problems.

A direct implementation of average-link clustering has complexity $O(n^2)$ where n is the number of elements to be clustered (see below). The key idea for achieving a more efficient computation in Buckshot is to choose a random sample of size $\sqrt{n}$. If this sample is clustered with a $O(n^2)$ algorithm, overall time complexity is $O(n)$. (see also van Rijsbergen (1979:59) for a similar idea)

This algorithm is described by Cutting et al. (1992) for the similarity measure cosine. The assumption is that all vectors have unit length.

Instead, I substitute Euclidean distance as a measure of document relatedness here, since it can be applied to both normalized and unnormalized vectors.

A.2.2 Formal Description

Let Γ be a vector group, then the average distance between any two vectors in Γ is defined to be:[2]

$$D(\Gamma) = \frac{1}{2} \frac{1}{|\Gamma|(|\Gamma| - 1)} \sum_{\vec{v} \in \Gamma} \sum_{\vec{w} \in \Gamma} d(\vec{v}, \vec{w})$$

Let G be a set of disjoint vector groups. The basic interaction of group average agglomerative clustering finds the two different clusters Γ' and Δ' which minimize $D(\Gamma \cup \Delta)$. A new, smaller, partition G' is then constructed by merging Γ' with Δ'.

$$G' = (G - \{\Gamma', \Delta'\}) \cup \{\Gamma' \cup \Delta'\}$$

The inner minimization can be done in linear time if Euclidean distance is employed as a distance measure.

$$d(\vec{v}, \vec{w}) = (\vec{v} - \vec{w})^2$$

In order to compute the average distance of a candidate pair in constant time, two values have to be precomputed for each vector group: The sum of its members $\hat{p}(\Gamma)$ and the sum of the inner squares of its members $\hat{Q}(\Gamma)$.

$$\hat{p}(\Gamma) = \sum_{\vec{v} \in \Gamma} \vec{v}$$

$$\hat{Q}(\Gamma) = \sum_{\vec{v} \in \Gamma} \vec{v}^2$$

The sum of the distances between any two vectors $\hat{D}$ can be computed from $\hat{p}$ and $\hat{Q}$ as follows.

$$\hat{D}(\Gamma) = |\Gamma|(|\Gamma| - 1)D(\Gamma) = \frac{1}{2} \sum_{\vec{v} \in \Gamma} \sum_{\vec{w} \in \Gamma} d(\vec{v}, \vec{w})$$

$$\hat{D}(\Gamma) = \frac{1}{2} \sum_{\vec{v} \in \Gamma} \sum_{\vec{w} \in \Gamma} (\vec{v} - \vec{w})^2$$

---

[2]See Cutting et al. (1992) for a similar derivation of cosine-based group-average agglomerative clustering.

$$\hat{D}(\Gamma) = \frac{1}{2} \sum_{\vec{v} \in \Gamma} \sum_{\vec{w} \in \Gamma} (\vec{v}^2 - 2\vec{v}\vec{w} + \vec{w}^2)$$

$$\hat{D}(\Gamma) = \frac{1}{2} \sum_{\vec{w} \in \Gamma} \sum_{\vec{v} \in \Gamma} \vec{v}^2 - \sum_{\vec{v} \in \Gamma} \sum_{\vec{w} \in \Gamma} \vec{v}\vec{w} + \frac{1}{2} \sum_{\vec{v} \in \Gamma} \sum_{\vec{w} \in \Gamma} \vec{w}^2$$

$$\hat{D}(\Gamma) = \frac{|\Gamma|}{2} \sum_{\vec{v} \in \Gamma} \vec{v}^2 - (\sum_{\vec{v} \in \Gamma} \vec{v})(\sum_{\vec{w} \in \Gamma} \vec{w}) + \frac{|\Gamma|}{2} \sum_{\vec{w} \in \Gamma} \vec{w}^2$$

$$\hat{D}(\Gamma) = \frac{|\Gamma|}{2} \hat{Q}(\Gamma) - \hat{p}(\Gamma)\hat{p}(\Gamma) + \frac{|\Gamma|}{2} \hat{Q}(\Gamma)$$

$$\hat{D}(\Gamma) = |\Gamma|\hat{Q}(\Gamma) - \hat{p}^2(\Gamma)$$

$$D(\Gamma) = \frac{|\Gamma|\hat{Q}(\Gamma) - \hat{p}^2(\Gamma)}{|\Gamma|(|\Gamma| - 1)}$$

Therefore, if $\hat{p}$ and $\hat{Q}$ are known for two groups Γ and Δ, then the average distance of their union can be computed in constant time as follows:

$$D(\Gamma \cup \Delta) = \frac{(|\Gamma| + |\Delta|)[\hat{Q}(\Gamma) + \hat{Q}(\Delta)] - [\hat{p}(\Gamma) + \hat{p}(\Delta)]^2}{(|\Gamma| + |\Delta|)(|\Gamma| + |\Delta| - 1)}$$

Given this result, group-average agglomerative clustering has complexity $O(n^2)$ since initially all pairwise distances have to be computed. The following step that performs $k \leq n$ mergers (each in constant time) has linear complexity, so that overall complexity is quadratic.

References

Abney, S. 1991. Parsing by chunks. In R. C. Berwick, S. P. Abney, and C. Tenny, eds., *Principle-Based Parsing*, pages 257–278. Dordrecht; Boston: Kluwer Academic Publishers.

Agarwal, R. and L. Boggess. 1992. A simple but useful approach to conjunct identification. In *Proceedings of ACL 30*, pages 15–21. Morristown NJ: Association of Computational Linguistics.

Alshawi, H. and D. Carter. 1994. Training and scaling preference functions for disambiguation. *Computational Linguistics* 20:635–648.

Atkins, B. T. S. 1993. The contribution of lexicography. In M. Bates and R. M. Weischedel, eds., *Challenges in natural language processing*, pages 37–75. Cambridge: Cambridge University Press.

Baker, C. L. 1979. Syntactic theory and the projection problem. *Linguistic Inquiry* 10:533–581.

Benson, M., E. Benson, and R. Ilson. 1993. *The BBI combinatory dictionary of English*. Amsterdam; Philadelphia: John Benjamins Publishing Company.

Berry, M. W. 1992. Large-scale sparse singular value computations. *The International Journal of Supercomputer Applications* 6:13–49.

Biber, D. 1993. Co-occurrence patterns among collocations: A tool for corpus-based lexical knowledge acquisition. *Computational Linguistics* 19:531–538.

Boguraev, B. and T. Briscoe. 1989. *Computational Lexicography for Natural Language Processing*. London; New York: Longman.

Bohannon, J. and L. Stanowicz. 1988. The issue of negative evidence: Adult responses to children's language errors. *Developmental Psychology* 24:684–689.

Bolinger, D. L. 1961. *Generality, gradience, and the all-or-none*. 's-Gravenhage: Mouton & Co.

Braine, M. D. S. 1987. What is learned in acquiring word classes – A step toward an acquisition theory. In B. MacWhinney, ed., *Mechanisms of Language Acquisition*, pages 65–87. Hillsdale NJ: Lawrence Erlbaum Associates.

Bréal, M. 1899. *Essai de sémantique science des significations*. Paris: Librairie Hachette. 2. ed. rev.

Brent, M. R. 1993. From grammar to lexicon: Unsupervised learning of lexical syntax. *Computational Linguistics* 19:243–262.

Brill, E. 1993a. Automatic grammar induction and parsing free text: A transformation-based approach. In *Proceedings of ACL 31*, pages 259–265. Morristown NJ: Association of Computational Linguistics.

———. 1993b. *A Corpus-Based Approach to Language Learning*. Ph.D. thesis, University of Pennsylvania.

Brill, E., D. Magerman, M. Marcus, and B. Santorini. 1990. Deducing linguistic structure from the statistics of large corpora. In *Proceedings of the DARPA Speech and Natural Language Workshop*, pages 275–282. San Mateo CA: Morgan Kaufmann.

Brill, E. and M. Marcus. 1992. Tagging an unfamiliar text with minimal human supervision. In R. Goldman, P. Norvig, E. Charniak, and B. Gale, eds., *Working Notes of the AAAI Fall Symposium on Probabilistic Approaches to Natural Language*, pages 10–16. Menlo Park CA: AAAI Press.

Brown, P. F., S. A. Della Pietra, V. J. Della Pietra, and R. L. Mercer. 1991. Word-sense disambiguation using statistical methods. In *Proceedings of ACL 29*, pages 264–270. Morristown NJ: Association of Computational Linguistics.

Charniak, E. 1993. *Statistical language learning*. Cambridge MA: The MIT Press.

Charniak, E., G. Carroll, J. Adcock, A. Cassandra, Y. Gotoh, J. Katz, M. Littman, and J. McCann. 1994. Taggers for parsers. Tech. rep., Brown University.

Charniak, E., C. Hendrickson, N. Jacobson, and M. Perkowitz. 1993. Equations for part-of-speech tagging. In *Proceedings of the Eleventh National Conference on Artificial Intelligence*, pages 784–789. Menlo Park CA: AAAI Press.

Cheeseman, P., J. Kelly, M. Self, J. Stutz, W. Taylor, and D. Freeman. 1988. AutoClass: A Bayesian classification system. In *Proceedings of the Fifth International Conference on Machine Learning*, pages 54–64. San Francisco CA: Morgan Kaufmann.

Chen, S. F. 1995. Bayesian grammar induction for language modeling. In *Proceedings of ACL 33*, pages 228–235. San Francisco CA: Morgan Kaufmann.

Chierchia, G. and S. McConnell-Ginet. 1991. *Meaning and Grammar*. Cambridge MA: The MIT Press.

Chomsky, N. 1957. *Syntactic Structures*. The Hague: Mouton.

———. 1961. On generative grammar. *Word* 17:230–239.

———. 1964. *Current Issues in Linguistic Theory*. The Hague: Mouton & Co. Second Printing (1966).

———. 1986. *Knowledge of Language*. New York: Prager.

Church, K. W. 1989. A stochastic parts program and noun phrase parser for unrestricted text. In *Proceedings of ANLP*, pages 136–143. Morristown NJ: Association of Computational Linguistics.

Clark, E. V. 1987. The principle of contrast: A constraint on language acquisition. In B. MacWhinney, ed., *Mechanisms of language acquisition*, pages 1–33. Hillsdale NJ: Lawrence Erlbaum Associates.

———. 1993. *The Lexicon in Acquisition*. Cambridge: Cambridge University Press.

Cottrell, G. W. 1989a. *A Connectionist Approach to Word Sense Disambiguation*. London: Pitman.

———. 1989b. Toward connectionist semantics. In Y. Wilks, ed., *Theoretical Issues in Natural Language Processing*, pages 64–72. Hillsdale NJ: Lawrence Erlbaum Associates.

Crangle, C. and P. Suppes. 1994. *Language and Learning for Robots*, vol. 41 of *CSLI Lecture Notes*. Stanford CA: CSLI Publications.

Cruse, D. A. 1982. On lexical ambiguity. *Nottingham Linguistic Circular* 11:65–80. Cited in Geeraerts (1993).

Cutting, D., J. Kupiec, J. Pedersen, and P. Sibun. 1991. A practical part-of-speech tagger. In *The 3rd Conference on Applied Natural Language Processing*, pages 133–140. Trento, Italy.

Cutting, D. R., J. O. Pedersen, D. Karger, and J. W. Tukey. 1992. Scatter/gather: A cluster-based approach to browsing large document collections. In *Proceedings of SIGIR '92*, pages 318–329. New York: Association of Computing Machinery.

Dagan, I. and A. Itai. 1994. Word sense disambiguation using a second language monolingual corpus. *Computational Linguistics* 20:563–596.

Dagan, I., A. Itai, and U. Schwall. 1991. Two languages are more informative than one. In *Proceedings of ACL 29*, pages 130–137. Morristown NJ: Association of Computational Linguistics.

Deerwester, S., S. T. Dumais, G. W. Furnas, T. K. Landauer, and R. Harshman. 1990. Indexing by latent semantic analysis. *Journal of the American Society for Information Science* 41:391–407.

Demetras, M. J., K. N. Post, and C. E. Snow. 1986. Feedback to first language learners: The role of repetitions and clarification questions. *Journal of Child Language* 13:275–292.

Dempster, A., N. Laird, and D. Rubin. 1977. Maximum likelihood from incomplete data via the EM algorithm. *J. Royal Statistical Society Series B* 39:1–38.

Duda, R. O. and P. E. Hart. 1973. *Pattern classification and scene analysis*. New York: Wiley.

Elman, J. L. 1990. Finding structure in time. *Cognitive Science* 14:179–211.

———. 1991. Incremental learning, or the importance of starting small. Tech. rep., Center for Research on Language, University of California at San Diego.

Finch, S. and N. Chater. 1992. Bootstrapping syntactic categories using statistical methods. In W. Daelemans and D. Powers, eds., *Background and*

Experiments in Machine Learning of Natural Language, pages 229–235. Tilburg University: Institute for Language Technology and AI.

———. 1994. Distributional bootstrapping: From word class to proto-sentence. In *Proceedings of the Sixteenth Annual Conference of the Cognitive Science Society*, pages 301–306. Hillsdale NJ: Lawrence Erlbaum.

Finch, S. P. 1993. *Finding Structure in Language*. Ph.D. thesis, University of Edinburgh.

Fisher, C., H. Gleitman, and L. R. Gleitman. 1991. On the semantic content of subcategorization frames. *Cognitive Psychology* 23:331–392.

Fodor, J. A. 1975. *The language of thought*. Cambridge MA: Harvard University Press.

Gale, W., K. W. Church, and D. Yarowsky. 1992a. Estimating upper and lower bounds on the performance of word-sense disambiguation programs. In *Proceedings of ACL 30*, pages 249–256. Morristown NJ: Association of Computational Linguistics.

———. 1992b. A method for disambiguating word senses in a large corpus. Tech. rep., AT&T Bell Laboratories, Murray Hill NJ.

———. 1992c. Work on statistical methods for word sense disambiguation. In R. Goldman, P. Norvig, E. Charniak, and B. Gale, eds., *Working Notes of the AAAI Fall Symposium on Probabilistic Approaches to Natural Language*, pages 54–60. Menlo Park CA: AAAI Press.

Gallant, S. I. 1991. A practical approach for representing context and for performing word sense disambiguation using neural networks. *Neural Computation* 3:293–309.

Geeraerts, D. 1989. Introduction: Prospects and problems of prototype theory. *Linguistics* 27:587–612.

———. 1993. Vagueness's puzzles, polysemy's vagaries. *Cognitive Linguistics* 4:223–272.

Goldberg, A. E. 1992. The inherent semantics of argument structure: The case of the English ditransitive construction. *Cognitive Linguistics* 3:37–74.

Golub, G. H. and C. F. van Loan. 1989. *Matrix Computations*. Baltimore; London: The Johns Hopkins University Press.

Green, G. M. 1974. *Semantics and Syntactic Regularity*. Bloomington; London: Indiana University Press.

Gropen, J., S. Pinker, M. Hollander, R. Goldberg, and R. Wilson. 1989. The learnability and acquisition of the dative alternation in English. *Language* 65:203–257.

Gross, M. 1979. On the failure of generative grammar. *Language* 55:859–885.

Guthrie, J. A., L. Guthrie, Y. Wilks, and H. Aidinejad. 1991. Subject-dependent co-occurrence and word sense disambiguation. In *Proceedings of ACL 29*, pages 146–152. Morristown NJ: Association of Computational Linguistics.

Harris, C. L. 1994. Back-propagation representations for the rule-analogy continuum. In K. J. Holyoak and J. A. Barnden, eds., *Analogical Connections*, pages 282–326. Norwood NJ: Ablex.

Harris, Z. S. 1951. *Structural Linguistics*. Chicago: The University of Chicago Press.

Hearst, M. A. 1991. Noun homograph disambiguation using local context in large text corpora. In *Seventh Annual Conference of the UW Centre for the New OED and Text Research*, pages 1–22. England: Oxford.

———. 1994. *Context and Structure in Automated Full-Text Information Access*. Ph.D. thesis, University of California at Berkeley.

Hindle, D. and M. Rooth. 1991. Structural ambiguity and lexical relations. In *Proceedings of ACL 29*, pages 229–236. Morristown NJ: Association of Computational Linguistics.

Hirsh-Patek, K., R. Treiman, and M. Schneiderman. 1984. Brown and Hanlon revisited: Mothers' sensitivity to ungrammatical forms. *Journal of Child Language* 11:81–88.

Hirst, G. 1987. *Semantic Interpretation and the Resolution of Ambiguity*. Cambridge: Cambridge University Press.

Hopper, P. J. and E. C. Traugott. 1993. *Grammaticalization*. Cambridge: Cambridge University Press.

Hornby, A. S. 1974. *Oxford Advanced Learner's Dictionary of Current English*. Oxford: Oxford University Press. Third Edition.

Hudson, S. B. and M. Tanenhaus. 1984. Ambiguity resolution in the absence of contextual bias. In *Proc. of the Sixth Annual Conference of the Cognitive Science Society*, pages 188–192. Boulder CO.

Jain, A. K. and R. C. Dubes. 1988. *Algorithms for Clustering Data*. Englewood Cliffs NJ: Prentice Hall.

Jelinek, F. 1985. Robust part-of-speech tagging using a hidden Markov model. Tech. rep., IBM, T.J. Watson Research Center.

Joos, M. 1950. Description of language design. *The Journal of the Acoustical Society of America* 22:701–708.

Kaplan, R. M. and J. Bresnan. 1982. Lexical-functional grammar: A formal system for grammatical representation. In J. Bresnan, ed., *The mental representation of grammatical relations*, pages 173–281. Cambridge MA: The MIT Press.

Kay, M. 1984. Functional unification grammar: a formalism for machine translation. In *Proceedings of COLING 84*, pages 75–78. Amsterdam: North-Holland.

———. 1986. Parsing in functional unification grammar. In B. J. Grosz, K. Sparck-Jones, and B. L. Webber, eds., *Readings in Natural Language Processing*, pages 35–70. Los Altos CA: Morgan Kaufmann.

Kelly, E. and P. Stone. 1975. *Computer Recognition of English Word Senses*. Amsterdam: North-Holland.

Kilgarriff, A. 1993. Dictionary word sense distinctions: An enquiry into their nature. *Computers and the Humanities* 26:365–387.

Kiss, G. R. 1973. Grammatical word classes: A learning process and its simulation. *The Psychology of Learning and Motivation* 7:1–41.

Kneser, R. and H. Ney. 1993. Forming word classes by statistical clustering for statistical language modelling. In R. Köhler and B. B. Rieger, eds., *Contributions to Quantitative Linguistics*, pages 221–226. Dordrecht, The Netherlands: Kluwer Academic Publishers.

Krovetz, R. and W. B. Croft. 1989. Word sense disambiguation using machine-readable dictionaries. In *Proceedings of SIGIR '89*, pages 127–136. New York: Association of Computing Machinery.

Kullback, S. 1959. *Information Theory and Statistics*. New York: Wiley.

Kupiec, J. 1992. Robust part-of-speech tagging using a hidden Markov model. *Computer Speech and Language* 6:225–242.

Labov, W. 1972. The boundaries of words and their meanings. In C.-J. N. Bailey and R. W. Shuy, eds., *New ways of analyzing variation in English*, pages 340–373. Washington DC: Georgetown University Press.

Lakoff, G. 1970. A note on vagueness and ambiguity. *Linguistic Inquiry* 1:357–359.

———. 1987. *Women, Fire, and Dangerous Things*. Chicago: The University of Chicago Press.

Langacker, R. W. 1987. *Foundations of Cognitive Grammar*, vol. 1. Stanford CA: Stanford University Press.

———. 1988. A usage-based model. In B. Rudzka-Ostyn, ed., *Topics in Cognitive Linguistics*, pages 4–48. Amsterdam; Philadelphia: John Benjamins Publishing Company.

Leacock, C., G. Towell, and E. Voorhees. 1993. Corpus-based statistical sense resolution. In *Proceedings of the ARPA Workshop on Human Language Technology*. San Mateo CA: Morgan Kaufman.

Lenat, D. B. and R. V. Guha. 1989. *Building Large Knowledge-Based Systems*. Reading MA: Addison-Wesley.

Lesk, M. 1986. Automatic sense disambiguation: How to tell a pine cone from an ice cream cone. In *Proceedings of the 1986 SIGDOC Conference*, pages 24–26. New York: Association for Computing Machinery.

Levin, B. 1993. *English Verb Classes and Alternations*. Chicago: The University of Chicago Press.

Lightfoot, D. 1991. *How to Set Parameters: Arguments from Language Change*. Cambridge MA: The MIT Press.

Ling, C. X. 1994. Learning the past tense of english verbs: The symbolic pattern associator vs. connectionist models. *Journal of Artificial Intelligence Research* 1:209–229.

Lyons, J. 1969. *Introduction to theoretical linguistics*. Cambridge: Cambridge University Press.

Magerman, D. D. 1994. *Natural language parsing as statistical pattern recognition*. Ph.D. thesis, Stanford University.

Manning, C. D. 1993. Automatic acquisition of a large subcategorization dictionary from corpora. In *Proceedings of the ACL 31*, pages 235–242. Morristown NJ: Association of Computational Linguistics.

Maratsos, M. P. and M. A. Chalkley. 1980. The internal language of children's syntax: The ontogenesis and representation of syntactic categories. In K. E. Nelson, ed., *Children's language*, vol. 2, pages 127–214. New York: Gardner Press.

Marcus, G. F. 1993. Negative evidence in language acquisition. *Cognition* 46:53–85.

Marcus, G. F., S. Pinker, M. Ullman, M. Hollander, T. J. Rosen, and F. Xu. 1992. *Overregularization in Language Acquisition*, vol. 57:4 of *Monographs of the Society for Research in Child Development*. Chicago: The University of Chicago Press.

Marcus, M. P., B. Santorini, and M. A. Marcinkiewicz. 1993. Building a large annotated corpus of English: The Penn Treebank. *Computational Linguistics* 19:313–330.

deMarcken, C. G. 1990. Parsing the LOB corpus. In *Proceedings of the ACL 28*, pages 243–259. Morristown NJ: Association of Computational Linguistics.

Mazurkewich, I. and L. White. 1984. The acquisition of the dative alternation: Unlearning overgeneralizations. *Cognition* 16:261–283.

McClelland, J. L., M. S. John, and R. Taraban. 1989. Sentence comprehension: A parallel distributed processing approach. *Language and cognitive processes* 4:287–335.

McRoy, S. W. 1992. Using multiple knowledge sources for word sense disambiguation. *Computational Linguistics* 18:1–30.

Miller, G. A. and W. G. Charles. 1991. Contextual correlates of semantic similarity. *Language and Cognitive Processes* 6:1–28.

Morgan, J. and E. Newport. 1981. The role of constituent structure in the induction of an artificial language. *Journal of Verbal Learning and Verbal Behaviour* 20:67–85.

Morton, H. C. 1994. *The story of Webster's third: Philip Gove's controversial dictionary*. Cambridge: Cambridge University Press.

Naigles, L. 1991. Review of learnability and cognition: The acquisition of argument structure. *Language and Speech* 34:63–79.

Oehrle, R. T. 1975. Review of Georgia M. Green: Semantics and syntactic regularity. *Language* 53:198–208.

———. 1976. *The Grammatical Analysis of the English Dative Alternation*. Ph.D. thesis, Massachusetts Institute of Technology.

Penner, S. 1987. Parental responses to grammatical and ungrammatical child utterances. *Child Development* 58:376–384.

Pinker, S. 1979. Formal models of language learning. *Cognition* 1:217–283.

————. 1984. *Language Learnability and Language Development*. Cambridge MA: Harvard University Press.

————. 1989. *Learnability and Cognition*. Cambridge MA: The MIT Press.

Plunkett, K. and V. Marchman. 1993. From rote learning to system building: Acquiring verb morphology in children and connectionist nets. *Cognition* 48:21–69.

Pollard, C. J. and I. A. Sag. 1995. *Head-Driven Phrase Structure Grammar*. Stanford CA: CSLI Publications.

Prince, A. and P. Smolensky. 1997. *Optimality Theory: Constraint Interaction in Generative Grammar*. Cambrige MA: The MIT Press. To appear.

Pullum, G. K. 1996. Learnability, hyperlearning, and the poverty of the stimulus. In *Proceedings of the 22nd Annual Meeting of the Berkeley Linguistics Society*. Berkeley CA: Berkeley Linguistics Society.

Quine, W. V. O. 1960. *Word and Object*. Cambridge MA: The MIT Press.

Regier, T. 1992. *The Acquisition of Lexical Semantics for Spatial Terms: A Connectionist Model of Perceptual Categorization*. Ph.D. thesis, University of California at Berkeley.

Resnik, P. S. 1993. *Selection and Information: A Class-Based Approach to Lexical Relationships*. Ph.D. thesis, University of Pennsylvania.

Rice, S. 1993. (Quasi-)Systematicity and (Non-)Compositionality in language. Position Paper presented at the Fifteenth Annual Meeting of the Cognitive Science Society.

van Rijsbergen, C. J. 1979. *Information Retrieval*. London: Butterworths. Second Edition.

Robertson, S. and K. Sparck Jones. 1976. Relevance weighting of search terms. *Journal of the American Society for Information Science* 27:129–146.

Roget, P. M. 1946. *Roget's International Thesaurus*. New York: Thomas Y. Crowell Company.

Ross, H. 1987. Islands and syntactic prototypes. In *Papers from the 23rd Annual Regional Meeting*, pages 309–320. Chicago: Chicago Linguistic Society.

Ross, J. R. 1972. The category squish: Endstation Hauptwort. In *Papers from the Eighth Regional Meeting*, pages 316–328. Chicago: Chicago Linguistic Society.

————. 1973a. Clausematiness. In E. L. Keenan, ed., *Formal Semantics of Natural Language*. Cambridge: Cambridge University Press.

————. 1973b. A fake NP squish. In C.-J. N. Bailey, ed., *New ways of analyzing variation in English*. Washington: Georgetown University Press.

————. 1973c. Nouniness. In O. Fujimura, ed., *Three dimensions of linguistic theory*, pages 137–257. Tokyo: The Tokyo English Corporation.

————. 1974. There, there, (there, (there, (there,...))). In *Papers from the Tenth Regional Meeting*, pages 569–587. Chicago: Chicago Linguistic Society.

——. 1985. *Infinite Syntax*. Norwood NJ: Ablex.

Rumelhart, D. E., R. Durbin, R. Golden, and Y. Chauvin. 1995. Backpropagation: The basic theory. In Y. Chauvin and D. E. Rumelhart, eds., *Backpropagation: Theory, Architectures, and Applications*, pages 1–34. Hillsdale NJ: Lawrence Erlbaum.

Rumelhart, D. E., G. E. Hinton, and R. J. Williams. 1986. Learning internal representations by error propagation. In D. E. Rumelhart, J. L. McClelland, and the PDP Research Group, eds., *Parallel Distributed Processing. Explorations in the Microstructure of Cognition. Volume 1: Foundations*, pages 318–362. Cambridge MA: The MIT Press.

Rumelhart, D. E. and J. L. McClelland. 1986. On learning the past tenses of English verbs. In J. L. McClelland, D. E. Rumelhart, and the PDP Research Group, eds., *Parallel Distributed Processing. Explorations in the Microstructure of Cognition. Volume 2: Psychological and Biological Models*, pages 216–271. Cambridge MA: The MIT Press.

Salton, G. and C. Buckley. 1990. Improving retrieval performance by relevance feedback. *Journal of the American Society for Information Science* 41:288–297.

de Saussure, F. 1962. *Cours de linguistique générale*. Paris: Payot.

Schachter, P. 1985. Parts-of-speech systems. In T. Shopen, ed., *Language typology and syntactic description: Clause structure*, vol. 1, pages 3–61. Cambridge: Cambridge University Press.

Schäufele, S. 1995. X^0-fronting in vedic sanskrit and binding theory. *Linguistics* In revision.

Schütze, H. 1992. Context space. In R. Goldman, P. Norvig, E. Charniak, and B. Gale, eds., *Working Notes of the AAAI Fall Symposium on Probabilistic Approaches to Natural Language*, pages 113–120. Menlo Park CA: AAAI Press.

——. 1993. Part-of-speech induction from scratch. In *Proceedings of ACL 31*, pages 251–258. Morristown NJ: Association of Computational Linguistics.

——. 1995. *Ambiguity in Language Learning – Computational and Cognitive Models*. Ph.D. thesis, Stanford University.

Seidenberg, M. S., M. K. Tanenhaus, J. M. Leiman, and M. Bienkowski. 1982. Automatic access of the meanings of ambiguous words in context: Some limitations of knowledge-based processing. *Cognitive Psychology* 14:489–537. Cited in Hudson and Tanenhaus (1984).

Siskind, J. M. 1994. Lexical acquisition in the presence of noise and homonymy. In *Proceedings of AAAI-94*, pages 760–766. Menlo Park CA: AAAI Press.

——. 1995. A computational study of lexical acquisition. *Cognition* Submitted for publication.

Steedman, M. 1991. Structure and intonation. *Language* 67:260–296.

Stolcke, A. 1994. *Bayesian Learning of Probabilistic Language Models*. Ph.D. thesis, University of California at Berkeley.

Suppes, P., M. Böttner, and L. Liang. 1991. Comprehension grammars generated from machine learning of natural languages. In Dekker and Stokhof, eds., *Proceedings of the Eighth Amsterdam Colloquium*, pages 93–112. University of Amsterdam: Institute for Logic, Language and Computation.

Suppes, P., L. Liang, and M. Böttner. 1992. Complexity issues in robotic machine learning of natural language. In V. Naroditsky, ed., *Modeling Complex Phenomena*, pages 102–127. New York: Springer Verlag.

Swinney, D. A. 1979. Lexical access during sentence comprehension: (Re)-Consideration of context effects. *Journal of Verbal Learning and Verbal Behavior* 18:645–659.

Tabor, W. 1994. *Syntactic Innovation: A Connectionist Model*. Ph.D. thesis, Stanford University.

Tanenhaus, M. K., J. M. Leiman, and M. S. Seidenberg. 1979. Evidence for multiple stages in the processing of ambiguous words in syntactic contexts. *Journal of Verbal Learning and Verbal Behavior* 18:427–440.

Trask, R. L. 1993. *A dictionary of grammatical terms in linguistics*. London; New York: Routledge.

Tuggy, D. 1993. Ambiguity, polysemy, and vagueness. *Cognitive Linguistics* 4:273–290.

Wasow, T. 1981. Comments on the paper by Baker. In C. L. Baker and J. J. McCarthy, eds., *The logical problem of language acquisition*, pages 325–329. Cambridge MA: The MIT Press.

Wierzbicka, A. 1986. The semantics of 'internal dative' in English. *Quaderni di semantica* 7:121–165.

Wilks, Y. A., D. C. Fass, C. ming Guo, J. E. McDonald, T. Plate, and B. M. Slator. 1990. Providing machine tractable dictionary tools. *Journal of Computers and Translation* 2.

Wong, S. K. M. and Y. Y. Yao. 1992. An information-theoretic measure of term specificity. *Journal of the American Society for Information Science* 43:54–61.

Yarowsky, D. 1992. Word-sense disambiguation using statistical models of Roget's categories trained on large corpora. In *Proceedings of Coling-92*, pages 454–460. Association of Computational Linguistics.

Zipf, G. K. 1949. *Human Behavior and the Principle of Least Effort*. Cambridge MA: Addison-Wesley Press.

Zwicky, A. M. and J. M. Sadock. 1975. Ambiguity tests and how to fail them. In J. P. Kimball, ed., *Syntax and Semantics 4*, pages 1–36. New York: Academic Press.

Name Index

Subject Index